SOUTHERN ROCKERS

THE ROOTS AND LEGACY OF SOUTHERN ROCK

Marley Brant

SOUTHERN ROCKERS

THE ROOTS AND LEGACY OF SOUTHERN ROCK

Marley Brant

Marley Brant, a resident of West Cobb, Georgia, is a former producer and artist development executive who has worked with a wide variety of rock and country stars. She is also a versatile writer whose three previous books have dealt with legendary outlaws.

First published in 1999 in New York by Billboard Books,

an imprint of Watson-Guptill Publications,

a division of BPI Communications,

1515 Broadway, New York, NY 10036

Library of Congress Cataloging in Publication Data

The CIP data for this title is on file with the Library of Congress.

Manufactured in the United States

2 3 4 5 6 7 8 9/07 06 05 04 03 02 01 00 99

Senior Editor: Bob Nirkind

Editor: Liz Harvey

Production Manager: Ellen Greene

Designer: Tony Farenga

DEDICATION

*F*or my brother Willie, whose love of the music planted the passion for it within my own heart and soul and opened my life to innumerable rock and roll experiences; and for Kathie, who has been a supportive and enthusiastic student of the music and the biz. Rock on, Brother and Sister.

And for Berry, Ronnie, Toy, and Tommy. Rock and roll will never die.

This book is dedicated to Dean Kilpatrick, "Godfather of the Road," and Duane Allman, "King of the Guitar World." We miss you guys. We're doing it without you, but far less than what we would be doing with you. We still have the music; we still have the memories.

ACKNOWLEDGMENTS

W hat a ride the creation of this book has been. Little did I know that when I started this project it would be met with such enthusiastic interest and support by the Southern Rock community. So many musicians and industry insiders helped bring this history together that I can freely say that this book wouldn't have been possible without their involvement. I also have to say that there were many people I wished to involve but, due to deadline, I ran out of time and couldn't interview. Their omission doesn't in any way reflect their lack of importance to the subject or to the genre, but is rather a demonstration of the restrictions word count and time can sometimes cost.

A tremendous thank you, however, to those musicians who took the time to share their insights and memories with me: Gregg Allman, Buddy Buie, Duane Betts, Jeff Carlisi, Mike Causey, Danny Chauncey, Charlie Daniels, Doug Gray, Jimmy Hall, Warren Haynes, Charlie Hargrett, Paul Hornsby, Ed King, Al Kooper, Waylon Kreiger, Dru Lombar, George McCorkle, Jim Dandy Mangrum, Rickey Medlocke, Wayne Moss, Berry Oakley, Billy Powell, Alec Puro, Artimus Pyle, Hughie Thomasson, Leon Wilkeson, Allen Woody, Donnie Van Zant, and Johnny Van Zant.

A huge thanks to the people who might have been behind the scenes but who also made a tremendous contribution to Southern Rock and its rockers: Abbie Caldwell, Harriett Kilpatrick, Judy Van Zant Jenness, Rodney Mills, Phil Walden, and Jerry Wexler.

A big thanks to those who "make it all happen": Kirk Anderson, Marsha Beamish, Paula Donner and Carolyn Killian of Capricorn Records, EJ Devokaitis, Julia Hepfer, Susan Stewart, Susan Sullivan, Paula Szeigis; and to Rowland Archer, Gloria Boyce, Charlie Faubion, the Georgia Music Hall of Fame, Pat Halverson, Kerri Hampton, Joseph Johnson, Don Kunstel, Pam Lewis, Lisa Love, Laura Martin, Lana Mazarelli, Mary Mills, and Michael B. Smith.

Thanks for the use of their photographs to Abbie Caldwell, Jeff Carlisi, Mike Causey, Charlie Hargrett, Paul Hornsby, Dru Lombar, George McCorkle, Judy Van Zant Jenness, Bob Johnson, Marta Martin, Rodney and Mary Mills, Wayne Moss, Michael B. Smith, and Kirk West.

Thanks to Jesus, for allowing me a voice and for the opportunity to know and work with such special people.

I appreciate the support of Billboard Books, which stepped in when the rest of the publishing world seemed to think this subject was too regional (!), and my editor, the erudite Bob Nirkind. Thanks to Liz Harvey for her professional and helpful contributions.

I also appreciate the perseverance of my agent, Shelley Lewis, a woman whose connections and encouraging personality helped "get it done," and to the folks at DHS Literary.

The reportings and musings of the rock press were always helpful, and they're owed a thanks for always keeping us "edacated" and informed. Thanks to my brother, Willie Olmstead, for helping me get started on this project and for always being there to bounce ideas around. Thanks also to Mary Lou Layne, who transcribed hours of interviews. She hung in there even when we thought they were completed, only to hear "Just one more."

I am always thankful for the love and support of my family: my husband, Dave Bruegger; son Tim Bruegger; mom, Gladys Olmstead; Kathie Montgomery; John, Nanette, and William Olmstead; Carol Saenz Olmstead; John, Ralph, Rosie, and Lara Saenz; and the Averys, Barringtons, Brueggers, Olmsteads, Scklores, and Walls. Thanks also to all my friends for the encouraging words—you know who you are. I sure do. And thanks, Janel Wiles—my wild and crazy rock and roll days never prepared me for the life-saving experience of carpooling!

Most of all, thanks to the musicians who brought us this thing called Southern Rock: The Allman Brothers Band, Duane and Gregg Allman, A.P.B., The Atlanta Rhythm Section, Barefoot Jerry, Blackfoot, Toy Caldwell, Charlie Daniels, Gov't Mule, Grinderswitch, Hour Glass, Lynyrd Skynyrd, The Marshall Tucker Band, The Outlaws, Stillwater, .38 Special, Ronnie Van Zant, and Wet Willie. The past has been musically extraordinary, and the future promises more of the same. I'll keep listening as long as you keep rocking. Millennium be damned . . . Southern Rock is timeless.

CONTENTS

Gregg Allman, ca. 1975. Credit: Kirk West.

PREFACE

In Their Own Words

ON SOUTHERN ROCK

"It was The Allman Brothers Band, which is kind of a blues band. Lynyrd Skynyrd, which is a pure rock band. Marshall Tucker Band, which was kind of a country sort of a band. And us, which were lost out in the ozone somewhere. I think basically where the cohesiveness came was that most of the people that were involved in it all came from the same type background. About the same type financial background, the same type of educational background and social background. We had a close camaraderie with each other."

Charlie Daniels

"I don't know who came up with that [term]. Some journalist somewhere, I think. Somebody in the record business or somebody in the retail business. Somebody that worked at Tower Records or something just gave us a slot.

"But it wasn't any of us."

Gregg Allman, The Allman Brothers Band

"We got labeled that, being as we're from the South. Maybe Southern bands or Southern Rock bands have a reputation for being rowdy, too. In those early days we had a very big reputation for being a real rowdy band. But it could be the lyrics. It just seems to me like there's more truth in the lyrics of Southern music. That's one of things that made Skynyrd famous, to me . . . truth, real life stories like 'Three Steps' and 'That Smell.' To me the lyrics are more down to earth, and they're more genuine than a lot of stuff, you know?"

Billy Powell, Lynyrd Skynyrd

"Obviously the influences were the blues. But for a new generation and a different twist on the music, they kind of redefined these stories. They were stories from the South, and there was an intrigue. Whether you lived in New England or whether you lived on the West Coast, or wherever, you heard these stories about swamps and snakes and gators and drinking. It was almost like reading a Zane Gray novel. Wow, what a cool place this is or what a strange place this is. You don't want to go down there. These stories have been told a million times, but they all of a sudden came into the mainstream of rock music and people heard 'em on the radio."

Jeff Carlisi, .38 Special

"I've always felt that we just played really good rock and roll music, and we just happened to live in the South. I think a lot of us felt that way. That's a label that was stuck on us. We didn't put it on ourselves."

Hughie Thomasson, The Outlaws/Lynyrd Skynyrd

"Originally when that term was used it made all the sense in the world because all the bands that you'd heard of and that had made it were either from the North like in New York, specifically, or out in California. Any Southern bands that made it, they always made 'em move from down this way up to New York or out West. It's like they were ashamed of being from the South. I think Duane Allman actually was just like, 'No. We're not going to do that shit.' He just, once again, stuck by his guns, and it resulted in making a whole new genre, basically."

Allen Woody, The Allman Brothers Band/Gov't Mule

"We obviously got put in the Southern Rock frame, but we've always sort of looked at ourselves as just being an American rock and roll band."

Donnie Van Zant, .38 Special

"It's like saying that because you're from the South you sound a certain way, which in some cases is true. But it's like saying that everyone from Seattle sounds the same, and that's definitely not true because [Jimi] Hendrix is from Seattle and so is Kurt Cobain."

Warren Haynes, The Allman Brothers Band/Gov't Mule

"I feel that some people have more of a stereotypical image of it. Of the Confederate flag waving, cowboy hat wearing, more redneck kind of bands, of having that image. But overall, I'm proud of it, today, the term. And I'm proud to be associated with it. The emphasis is on good songs. If you look at what it is to grow up in the South, the family values, the spiritual side . . . the Bible Belt is part of our heritage, interracial interaction, the black culture, the love of the land . . . all those things make it what it was and what it still is."

Jimmy Hall, Wet Willie

"I don't care if somebody wants to say I'm Southern Rock. I'm proud of that.
"But to me there's only two kinds of music. And that's good and bad, honest and fabricated."

Dru Lombar, Grinderswitch

"I care for these people, and I respect them. They are strange kids and yet they look on me with love. There's a closeness I feel to these young people."

Jimmy Carter, fan and former President of the United States

ON THE ALLMAN BROTHERS BAND

"You had the twin guitars, which seemed like some magical communication between two musicians. You had the twin drums. And you had the fact that these players were grounded in the blues in a much more significant, intimate, and real way than the British bands, who did a pretty good job of it."

Jerry Wexler, producer/Atlantic Records executive

"The Allman Brothers Live at the Fillmore East . . . that's like the Southern Rock primer. Gregg [Allman] is really the Godfather of the Southern Rock thing. A song like 'Midnight Rider' is the epitome of the Southern Rock anthem."

Danny Chauncey, .38 Special

"I think they're one of [the greatest], if not the greatest, American rock bands. There are probably very few people who don't recognize the Allmans when they hear a song kicked off. I don't think Gregg's [Allman] ever really been given his due. He's always been a fabulous singer. And a wonderful keyboard player. He has his own unique style. Also, these incredible songs. He is one of my favorite songwriters."

Phil Walden, Capricorn Records

"The Allman Brothers showed us that it would work and it was worth pursuing, you know, putting your head on the chopping block."

Leon Wilkeson, Lynyrd Skynyrd

"I must have listened to the Fillmore East album a thousand times. There're probably more people playing with Dickey's [Betts] influence now then there were ten years ago. There are very few people who made that kind of impact on slide guitar [as did Duane Allman]."

Warren Haynes, The Allman Brothers Band/Gov't Mule

"[Duane] was so sweet in his playing, it was almost like singing. It was almost like he was a vocalist on the guitar. He made that guitar sing and made it talk. I just thought he was the greatest."

Rickey Medlocke, Blackfoot/Lynyrd Skynyrd

"[Gregg Allman's] one of these guys who's one of the blackest white guys walking. He has an unbelievably unique talent that is so special that it will live forever. That voice is one in a million. When he was twenty, he had a voice like a forty-five-year-old black man. It exudes passion. It ached, and it moaned, and you'd feel the blues when he sang."

Jimmy Hall, Wet Willie

"The great instrumentals and the spirit of the whole twin guitar thing that [Dickey Betts] and Duane [Allman] did together. They were really plowing some ground with that. I think Berry Oakley's playing had as much to do with the live sound and the studio . . . the sonic things that you would hear. Everything that you would hear with your ears, I think he had as much or more to do with that than any other single person in the band. [Duane] didn't seek fame—he just wanted to play. Duane passed away right as they were getting huge. He saw it on the horizon, but he didn't really get how big it would become. George Harrison started playing slide after that Fillmore album came out. Now why was that? Well, he started seeing Duane. Eric [Clapton] was playing more slide, and where did he get it? He got it from Duane. Duane is probably single-handedly responsible for most of the guys in England, later, that played any slide. [Gregg] was responsible for writing some of the very finest flagship tunes they ever had, and just the whole voice, man. That voice. He's as good a singer as God ever poured into flesh."

Allen Woody, The Allman Brothers Band/Gov't Mule

"I remember seeing Duane play at a place called The Electric Zoo, St. Petersburg, Florida, when they were called The Allman Joys. I'd never seen anybody play a slide before. When they started playing, and he started playing slide guitar, my mouth hit the floor and stayed there 'cause I'd never seen or even heard of anything like this before. I was just flabbergasted. I became an instant fan right then, for life."

Hughie Thomasson, Outlaws/Lynyrd Skynyrd

"What I remember about The Allman Brothers is right there in Jacksonville, Florida. They used to come down to a place called The Forest Inn on a Sunday afternoon or something like that. They would actually just bring their trucks right up there, unload the equipment, set it right outside, and just start jamming. They would get out there and jam for three or four hours. They didn't charge a penny.

"And when you say [Warren Haynes's] name, you're talking about one of the best singers around and a great guitar player."

Donnie Van Zant, .38 Special

ON THE ATLANTA RHYTHM SECTION

"We used to go see them all the time, playing the same clubs that we played back in Atlanta, years and years and years ago, before we made it. If Atlanta Rhythm Section and Skynyrd were playing, you know, boy, everybody flocked to those shows."

Billy Powell, Lynyrd Skynyrd

"They knew how to make the studio work for them instead of against them, which is a real thing to figure out, I gotta tell you. Those songs that they had. They had a whole string of radio hits because they were carefully written and they were accessible to people. They were good; they made you want to sing them."

Allen Woody, The Allman Brothers Band/Gov't Mule

ON BLACKFOOT

"Rickey Medlocke: Mr. Showman. Great guitar player; great, great singer. Just one of the best showmen that's around. He can get an audience going."

Donnie Van Zant, .38 Special

ON THE CHARLIE DANIELS BAND

"He [Charlie Daniels] was just there for everybody. He's just an open, honest, genuine kind of man. When you're a smaller band coming up, man, and you got guys like that . . . they're our mentors instead of our tormentors, you know?"

Dru Lombar, Grinderswitch

"We still love Charlie and all those guys. Their keyboard player, Tas De Gregorio . . . his [real] name is Joel . . . but the name Tas is after the Tazmanian Devil. I named my second son after him. My second son's name is Joel Powell. His full name is Billy Joel Powell."

Billy Powell, Lynyrd Skynyrd

ON GRINDERSWITCH

"Working with Dru Lombar was always a pleasurable experience."

Leon Wilkeson, Lynyrd Skynyrd

"I can't begin to tell you how many dates we did together . . . lots and lots of 'em. Good people. Joe Dan Petty and Dru Lombar and all those guys, they're nice folks and very talented people."

Charlie Daniels

ON LYNYRD SKYNYRD

"Skynyrd had a bunch of different sides earlier on. They had that jug band thing. They had a deep blues thing. They had the dobro thing and everything going on in their early records. I think they were very influenced by The Allman Brothers, but they took it to a different place. They were absolutely musically at their peak when the plane went down 'cause they were really rockin', man. They were playing so good it's not even funny."

Allen Woody, The Allman Brothers Band/Gov't Mule

"It's just a basic thing, you know, telling a story where the common person can understand it. You know, you don't have to be a damn brain to understand it. I think music is emotion. If you can hit someone in the heart with it. It even says that in the 'Brick Yard Road' song. It says, 'Brother do you realize what you've done, touched the hearts of everyone?' I'll tell you, if I could switch places with [Ronnie Van Zant], I'd do it in a second. Anytime you could be on this earth and touch people like he did. . . ."

Johnny Van Zant, Lynyrd Skynyrd

"I knew they were headed for big things from the first album. There was a sound there that was radio friendly. There was a big, fat, chunky guitar sound going on. It worked live; it really worked live. And there was good songwriting all the way through."

Jimmy Hall, Wet Willie

"'Freebird' . . . that soaring solo that every kid in the world tries to emulate."

Artimus Pyle, Lynyrd Skynyrd

"[Ronnie] just said it the way the working man would say it. It was a blue collar town here, and he just offered truth there. He was real, you know? There was no fakiness to him whatsoever. What you see is what you got."

Donnie Van Zant, .38 Special

"I'll always remember [Allen Collins] as one of the best guitar players there was."

Billy Powell, Lynyrd Skynyrd

"Ed King's another great guitar player. I thought he got one of the best guitar sounds that I'd ever heard. [Gary Rossington's] got a style that is so unique. Nobody else plays like him. He's very original, and it stayed that way, which is hard to do. If you're there because of the money, or the superstar status, or any of that stuff, that meant nothing to Ronnie. It was about the music."

Hughie Thomasson, The Outlaws/Lynyrd Skynyrd

"[Ronnie is] almost like the James Dean of rock and roll, I guess. He was just such a genuine person, and he wasn't afraid of anybody. He wouldn't let anybody push him around. He's one of the most generous people I've ever met in my life. He was a great storyteller, and he was just real humble and real nice and real fun to be around when he was straight. When he drank a lot, you know, then it's look out."

Billy Powell, Lynyrd Skynyrd

"One of the biggest memories that stands out in my head is standing out in the studio when Ronnie was singing vocals for [First and Last]. Ronnie would look over at me—he was having a hard time with some different songs—and he would say, 'Am I sharp? Am I flat? Am I sharp? Am I flat?' I'd go, 'Ronnie, you're dead on man, it's great.' I just remember in my head seeing him standing at the microphone. I loved that guy so much, man. That boy [Steve Gaines] never really had a chance to really let people know what he could do. There was a talented writer, very talented guitar player and, from what I understand, just a hell of a nice guy overall, you know? I just really respected that in him."

Rickey Medlocke, Blackfoot/Lynyrd Skynyrd

"[Ronnie] was the mastermind. He was a genius. I've always felt that Allen is like Duane Allman . . . has never been recognized as much as he should for his talent. He was just kind of taken for granted. I like the way Paul Rodgers puts it in a song. '. . . if you listen to the wind, you can still hear him play.'"

Leon Wilkeson, Lynyrd Skynyrd

ON THE MARSHALL TUCKER BAND

"We just toured for long periods of time together. We'd come out and do our show and then I'd come out and sit in with them on their show, play fiddle with them. A lot of times we'd end the night up with almost everybody on stage. It was some wonderful experiences. [Toy Caldwell] was a good young'un. He was generous, just a personable, good friend. And highly, highly talented. I don't think the importance of his contribution has been anywhere close to realized. I think it's maybe up to future generations to do that, but I think it will be."

Charlie Daniels

"They were like a Southern Grateful Dead. They took it way out there."

Allen Woody, The Allman Brothers Band/Gov't Mule

"They're a unique sound. Part country, part rock and roll, part jazz, the blues, the horns, just a different sound. First time I heard them, I thought this could only come out of the South, organically grown."

Jimmy Hall, Wet Willie

"I just remember Toy Caldwell riding in the back of .38 Special's bus. He was the biggest jokester I've ever seen. Just a fun guy to hang around. He was telling us stories about him in a studio with Carlos Santana, and Carlos Santana burning incense. He thought that was weird. He couldn't get past the incense."

Donnie Van Zant, .38 Special

"We used to go four wheeling together. [George McCorkle] had a great big Toyota Land Cruiser that he put a V8 engine in, and I had Jeeps. We'd all get up on the back part of those mountains up there around Spartanburg. You talk about the Wild Bunch. . . ."

Artimus Pyle, Lynyrd Skynyrd

"[Toy's] life was cut short and along with that the music went with it. I really love him and miss him, to tell you the truth. I think the whole music industry does. I know the bands do."

Hughie Thomasson, The Outlaws/Lynyrd Skynyrd

ON .38 SPECIAL

".38 Special was kind of the new generation. Ronnie [Van Zant] was proud of his little brother [Donnie], you know."

Charlie Daniels

".38's done wonderful. There's no competition. Hell, I hope .38 sells millions and millions of records. That's my brother's band. I hope they sell a million, eight and I hope we sell a million . . . nine."

Johnny Van Zant, Lynyrd Skynyrd

ON WET WILLIE

"My memories of Wet Willie come from being in college. Every time you'd go to a keg party someone would be playing 'Keep On Smilin.'"

Danny Chauncey, .38 Special

"Jimmy Hall to me is probably one of the best kept secrets out of the South. What a frontman, what a singer, what a player."

Dru Lombar, Grinderswitch

"I think [Jimmy Hall] must've listened to the [Rolling] Stones a lot because to me he had that Mick Jagger sound to him. Except [Jimmy's] a better singer."

Donnie Van Zant, .38 Special

"Jimmy Hall is one of the greatest talents around."

Charlie Daniels

"Just the talent that Jimmy Hall had is enough to propel most bands. Then you look past that, and everybody in that band was a really good player. I think they were underrated, extremely underrated."

Allen Woody, The Allman Brothers Band/Gov't Mule

INTRODUCTION

They've captured the imaginations of millions of diehard rock and roll fans with their charismatic, hard-driving musical rebellion. Their names continue to loom large not only as rock legends, but as active participants in the evolution and growth of popular music: The Allman Brothers Band, Lynyrd Skynyrd, The Marshall Tucker Band, The Charlie Daniels Band, Wet Willie, The Outlaws, .38 Special, Grinderswitch, Blackfoot. . . .

Duane Allman, Ronnie Van Zant, Gregg Allman, and Toy Caldwell, along with the other extraordinary musicians who constitute their bands, represent an evolution from rural roots to international legends. Their names are spoken in revered tones by those who have any appreciation at all for the American musical genre called "Southern Rock."

As independent as the Confederate states they come from, these bands quickly forged an alliance to rock the music world off its feet with soulful, primal rhythm anthems to hard living and problematic romance. The bands possess a Dixie lock on the market for good time, no holds barred celebrations of both stoic independence and bar hopping camaraderie. Over the years their music has infiltrated our souls with beautiful melodies of gentle Southern landscapes and mysterious ladies who can break the hearts of country boys with just a backward glance. The bands offer songs of political and social relevance and exalt the glories of America, as well as sing of the hard times of their daddies and the importance of love and family. The bands

Charlie Daniels (fourth from left) and The Charlie Daniels Band, 1998. Credit: Dean Tubb/Charlie Daniels.

offer these heartfelt glimpses into their psyches with a style so unique that we are compelled not only to listen to them, but also to surrender to whatever emotion they're trying to evoke.

Backed by some of the foremost guitarists and songwriters of their generation, these bands have placed an indelible mark on the history of rock and roll. Though plagued by devastating personal tragedies, personnel changes due to the untimely departure of seminal founding members, the disenchantment of record companies, and the public's fickle flirtations with such musical trends as disco, techno-pop, and new wave, they continue to record and tour. Today's high numbers of baby boomers and teenagers alike at the concerts of the bands who introduced it make a crystalline statement that Southern Rock is alive, well, and, most definitely, here to stay.

Yet what exactly is Southern Rock, other than a nebulous term applied to rock and rollers from the South? Was it a phrase developed by Capricorn Records as a marketing tool or by a group of rock journalists that felt the need to subclassify it? When you ask Phil Walden, founder of Capricorn, he says he doesn't know what it means. "It's not a term I'm particularly crazy about," he claims. "I can recall in that '70s era, reading reviews where they called [Capricorn act] Martin Mull a Southern Rocker. I thought, 'My God, how is that?' Anything that we touched was 'Southern Rock.' I don't care what it was. I guess if I'd recorded Pavarotti he would have been called 'Southern Rock.' We had buttons made that said 'Support Southern Music,' not Southern *Rock* music. It has always been my thesis that all original American music originated in these sunny Southern states. I view the South as the motherlode of all of this wonderful music."

The acts themselves aren't any more comfortable with the label than Walden. They, too, feel it is limiting and not representative of their contribution to rock music. "We tried to form our own sound and tried to be really different from everybody else," says Blackfoot/Lynyrd Skynyrd guitarist Rickey Medlocke. "Evidently there was great talent that came out of the South and was viewed as talent. They should've viewed it as being really talented bands instead of being redneck bands."

Because of the tag, many people feel that these important contributors to the development of rock and roll have been minimized in rock's history. More than one of the artists I spoke to complained that when histories of rock and roll appear on television the bands who have been classified as "Southern Rock" receive insignificant mention. These artists don't like to be saddled with the term, yet the "Southern Rockers" I examine do have a substantial sameness within the roots of their music that could only stem out of their collective Southern experiences.

The bands included here have their feet firmly planted in the soil of black rhythm and blues (R&B): America's music. Their influences include soul, jazz, and gospel. Almost to a man, they told me how the music of B.B. King, King Curtis, Taj Mahal, Son House, and other black artists affected their early musical lives. The music of Southern Rock combines various genres of music, but most of all it is a music celebrating these much respected early influences.

Jerry Wexler, of Atlantic Records, has given the subject much thought. He should know: after all, he was the one who thought to tap the resources of the musical South through his association with Stax, Muscle Shoals, and, later, Capricorn Records. "The Southern Rock bands were saturated in blues because they didn't have to learn their blues by buying a Barbecue Bob record at a second-hand counter on Fleet Street," says Wexler. "They lived the life. They were the low end of America's agrarian society, just like the blacks were. They were some poor boys. They did the same things that the blacks did. It was the same black mud that squished between their toes. They knew how to take a shotgun apart and how to tree a raccoon. They knew how to run with the dogs. They knew how to fix a carburetor on a tractor. Their religion was very close to the blacks' religion. They heard the exultation, the frenzy of black church, directly in church, not off records. They eventually related."

"Willie Morris was the editor of the *Atlantic Monthly* for several years," remembers Wexler. "He came from Yazoo City, Mississippi. He came up to New York and wrote some great books. He was in a taxicab on his way in from JFK in New York with another Southern friend of his. [There were some] tough, lowbrow New York taxicab drivers. And this guy [the driver] was going on and on about the 'fuckin' niggers' and this and that. And Willie Morris leaned over and tapped him on the shoulder. And he said, 'I'll thank you not to use that language. You're talkin' about my kin.' That was very telling. His was a strange juxtaposition. The South with the hooded sheets and the burning crosses and the lynchings and the burned bodies, at the same time, was a South of an intimacy that Northerners, no matter how liberal they might be, could never get close to. And certainly Englishmen couldn't get close to understanding. That's what made the Southern Rock. They came from the same matrix as the black players that they loved."

Who might be considered Southern Rockers? For this book I've included the principals of this ambiguous domain, yet I'll likely be called on the carpet more for who I haven't included, than for who I have. My brother, Willie, a serious student of rock and roll, insists that this study wouldn't be complete without the inclusion of Black Oak Arkansas. Yet Jim Dandy Mangrum, the band's frontman, claims, "I was born in Benton Harbor, Michigan. I was conceived down here [the South], and I was dropped up there, so I'm both and I'm neither. I'm not claimed by either one." Most of the musicians who have been labeled Southern Rock seem to agree. While they acknowledge that Black Oak had an impact on rock music, especially in the early 1970s, they don't believe the true spirit of the Southern Rock genre was reflected in either their music or their stage presentations.

The Dixie Dregs had more jazz appeal than rock. "They were a great band, but they were so technical and so over everybody's head that a lot of people didn't get it," says Gov't Mule's Allen Woody. Amazing Rhythm Aces and Elvin Bishop were Southerners, but does their music really fit into the category of Southern Rock?

And where does Molly Hatchet fit into all of this? Is Hatchet one of the grand-father acts of Southern Rock, or is the band part of the legacy? Since the band was conceived in Jacksonville during the late 1970s, it would seem to fit my definition of Southern Rock. But at the same time, since the band began its recording career in 1977, the year of the Lynyrd Skynyrd airplane crash, many of the musicians involved in this book failed to see Hatchet as anything more than weak contenders to the Lynyrd Skynyrd crown. The musicians were all very good, and their music has garnered a large following of fans. Still, even Molly Hatchet itself claimed that it wasn't a "Southern band," but rather a "rock and roll band." I'll leave it at that.

"When you talk about Southern rock," says .38 Special's Danny Chauncey. "It's not a geographical thing [but] more like a time and a place." *Southern Rockers* is an examination of that time and that place. I've chosen to include the artists who most define the term for the majority of us and offer an apology if I've failed to include any bands or individuals who might have been on the fringe of the movement either by musical definition or regional association.

From the Capricorn music explosion in Macon, Georgia, to the club scene in Jacksonville, Florida, the artists involved in Southern Rock were a community of musicians. Their roots were in the blues of their region, their common experiences, their appreciation of music. Their roots were in the Southern Rock family.

The community in Macon was unlike anything the musical South had ever seen. "On just about any given night you could go to one of two or three clubs and there would probably be various members from different bands jamming together or playing together," remembers Phil Walden. "There was a good healthy exchange of music between the bands. If there was any competition, it was quite friendly. I just generally found everybody to be real supportive of the other acts on the label."

In Jacksonville, although less communal and more competitive, the Southern Rock scene was much the same. "Man, you had Skynyrd working as One Percent, I had a band, The Allman Brothers were hanging around as The Second Coming [and Hour Glass], The Bitter Ind with Scot Boyer, Butch Trucks, Dave Brown, who went on with Boz Scaggs. . . ." recalls Grinderswitch's Dru Lombar. ".38 Special were little kids watching all the older guys do their stuff. Same with Hatchet. Rickey Medlocke . . . all the guys. You know what I'm saying? I mean, it's just a bunch of us."

The one thing the artists I've interviewed for this book have stressed to me is the Southern Rock community—a commonality of roots and purpose. Oh, and talent. Extreme amounts of talent. The story of Southern Rock is at times a complexity of emotions and at times a rudimentary study of a group of people determined to make their mark in music and on the musical history of their generation.

Southern Rock is one of the most captivating musical genres of our time. Owing its existence to the young men who turned their wild Southern passions into a musical form that excites while it educates and entertains, the longevity of Southern Rock proves that rock and roll spans generations and has truly become the music of America. The down and dirty throb of the bass, virtuoso slide guitars, and the complex primal drumbeat defy the boredom of the nine to five world and propel listeners through the joys and mysteries of Saturday nightlife in Dixie.

Throughout the pages of *Southern Rockers* I hope to present the detailed story of this exciting concoction of modern day musical techniques coupled with age old sorrow, and the individuals and bands who presented it to an unsuspecting yet zealous audience. I examine the roots of the movement, its evolution, and its emergence into the unique prominence it enjoys today. Interwoven into the chronological presentation are the musical biographies of the major bands of the movement, as well as detailed information about other seminal acts that set the context, explore the scene, and develop the historic aspects of the story.

Don't expect to read detailed album reviews. I'll leave that to the rock critics. This is the story behind the recordings, the story of how this group of unique individuals made their innermost dreams come true. This is a story of determination, hard work, and survival.

I let the artists speak for themselves. If the story sometimes seems confusing or contradicts itself, it might be because the passage of time and the memories of those involved have turned folklore into fact and fact into folklore. I've done my best to fact-check and corroborate stories and chronology but because I was dealing with a variety of personalities, I sometimes found it difficult to determine the truth.

During the course of my research, the fact that all isn't currently harmonious within the Southern Rock family has been brought to my attention on occasion. This fact saddens me, as I can't help but like most of the people involved in this music. And it greatly saddens me that several old friends have come to a parting of ways because of a real or perceived greed and/or need for recognition. Many times suits have been filed as a last effort to reclaim monies earned and owed. The passage of time and seminal band members has only served to confuse the issue. I've mentioned various lawsuits when I've felt the filing of such suits to be pertinent to the chronology of the music, but it isn't my desire to turn this study of the *music* into an *Enquirer*-type expose. My heart goes out to certain band members who have felt betrayed and forgotten, as well as to the widows of founding band members as they struggle to retain and have recognized the financial success of their husbands' music. It is important to these women, their children, and their families that the contributions of those who were there in the beginning, but who fail to have an immediate voice in the music, not be forgotten. It became necessary for me to remember that the music business is, indeed, a business. As with any business, the lines of acceptable behavior are defined by the participants and are sometimes ambiguous.

Another glitch in the fun I had assembling this history was the controversy that surrounds the genre in regard to original band versus current band. Many people would have preferred that the band not continue once the founding members were no longer part of the presentation. Others believe that it is the music that should prevail, rather than the personalities. While I have my own opinion on such matters, it isn't up to me to pass judgment.

What I've attempted to provide is the history of each band, past to present. While it will be fairly obvious that I am a fan of Southern Rock music, I've tried to remain one step back. Perhaps I've succeeded, perhaps not. Please keep in mind that I wrote this book primarily for fans of the genre. You won't find dirt and you won't find undue criticism. If you're looking for a straightforward chronological history of Southern Rock, then by all means read on.

Their hopes, their dreams, their experiences, their musical lives. Herewith, *Southern Rockers*, in their own words. . . .

Marley Brant

February, 1999

CHAPTER 1

Dreams

1959-1969

"I say you take six parts blues and one part country, stir it all up, give it to a poor white Southern boy, and you got yourself some rock and roll," claims Gregg Allman. There can be no doubt that Gregg and his brother, Duane, knew how to rock and roll. Maybe the road the two of them traveled to become Southern Rock icons was as uncomplicated as Gregg's analogy, maybe not. The journey was certainly not without its drama, tenacity, and passion. Through circumstance, indisputable talent, and a loyal dedication to their music and creative partners, the brothers established a body of work that remains untouchable. Gregg believes "rock and roll is as basic as blues." The blues is something both he and Duane understood.

Howard Duane Allman was born November 20, 1946, in Nashville. His parents were Geraldine Robbins of Rocky Mount, North Carolina, and her husband, Willis Allman of Dickson County, Tennessee. Duane's brother, Gregory Lenoir, was born in Nashville on December 8, 1947.

Lieutenant Willis Allman was serving as an Army recruiter when both of his sons were born. Willis had experienced military life up close and personal when he and his brother Howard had been present at Normandy on D-Day. Willis's military career was important to him. So was his family. Willis no doubt had big plans for his boys.

On December 26, 1949, Willis and a friend gave a ride to another veteran they'd played pool with earlier in the day. On the ride home, the stranger pulled a gun and demanded the small amount of money the two men had in their pockets. Allman struggled with the gunman and was shot. He died within minutes.

As a single mother, Geraldine Allman needed to supplement the family's income. She decided to become a certified public accountant, and to enroll Duane and Gregg in Castle Heights Military Academy in Lebanon, Tennessee, while she attended college and attempted to reestablish a comfortable home. The boys weren't crazy about their new lifestyle, but they remained in the Academy until their mother obtained her accounting degree. The three of them moved to Daytona Beach, Florida, in 1957.

On Christmas morning 1959, twelve-year-old Gregg Allman received a guitar as his present. Thirteen-year-old Duane was given a Harley 165 motorcycle. Gregg took to the instrument immediately and was soon teaching Duane basic chords. "Wasn't long after I did that that he quit school and just stayed home and played, you know, just all day," Gregg remembers. Duane managed to attend some classes at Seabrook High, although he eventually dropped out of school. He wrecked his motorcycle and quickly traded in the parts for enough money to buy his own guitar. Duane had caught the fever.

Gregg and Duane listened to as much rhythm and blues (R&B) as they could find on the radio. Ray Charles, B.B. King, Taj Mahal, Lightnin' Hopkins, and Son House were some of the musical artists who caught their attention. "When I first started playing guitar in 1960, I was turned on to a man by the name of Jimmy Reed," remembers Gregg. "All of his songs sounded just about alike. So I learned what they call a three chord turnaround, which was a twelve bar blues thing which consists of three chords, your major, your fourth, and your fifth."

Gregg also became acquainted with a local picker named Floyd Miles. "We kind of grew up together, and he pretty much turned me on to black music," says Gregg. "Kind of taught me the right people to listen to." Most of the "right" people were blues artists. It was a new world for Gregg, yet one into which he quickly assimilated.

Both Duane and Gregg had briefly taken piano lessons when they were children. Gregg favored the guitar but realized that there was more than one instrument at his disposal. He picked up a saxophone and joined the Seabrook High freshman band. Although the saxophone was a blues staple, Gregg's main instrument continued to be his guitar.

Gregg's friend Floyd Miles became involved with an R&B group called The House Rockers. The Rockers were very talented and were soon playing local teen dances nearly every weekend. Gregg, and now Duane, recognized the opportunity to learn more about R&B and started to sit in with the band. They played gigs with The House Rockers whenever they had the opportunity.

Geraldine Allman decided to send her younger son back to Castle Heights after Duane dropped out of school in favor of music. Gregg evidently enjoyed the diversion. "I was really into the study," he recalls. "I took one course of anatomy, and it was really, really interesting. I've always liked to take things apart and put 'em back together. The thought of doing it, and doing it to a living thing, something about it really enchanted me." Gregg became so interested in anatomy and the body that he began to consider going to college to become a dental surgeon. Both music, in general, and the blues, in particular, continued to call to Gregg, regardless of his attraction to a medical career. He returned home on summer breaks and played guitar with Duane. It wasn't long before the two brothers joined The House Rockers as bona fide members.

After Gregg graduated from high school, he and Duane formed a band they named The Escorts. Van Harrison played bass, and Maynard Portwood was the drummer. The brothers enlisted the assistance of Lee Hazen, a local musician who had set up a makeshift recording studio in his kitchen. Duane and Gregg recorded a demo, which included such songs as "Oh, Pretty Woman," "Hi-Heel Sneakers,"and "She's A Woman." Duane handled the vocals, while Gregg provided the rhythm guitar.

During Easter week 1965, The Escorts opened a show at a local baseball park for The Beach Boys. The band was well received. The brothers Allman decided to become more seriously involved in the regional music scene. They realized that playing music could become a full-time venture. The name of The Escorts was changed to The Allman Joys. The band played various clubs, such as The Martinique, and soon developed quite a following. Duane and Gregg had grown their hair long and provided an interesting visual image. Girls were drawn to the handsome young brothers who dared to defy convention while establishing their band's position on the Florida music scene.

Although Duane and Gregg were similar in appearance, their temperaments were quite different. Gregg was shy and laid-back, although he was no stranger to applying charm when he felt it was indicated. He was happy to play music, stand back, and see what developed. Duane, on the other hand, was used to being the man of the house. He felt the need to assert himself to ensure that what he felt should happen would be accomplished. Duane's music provided him with an immense physical and emotional outlet, so he quickly immersed himself in it.

Duane lived life to the fullest. There were very few dares he wouldn't accept or things he wouldn't try. Some of his musician friends introduced him to marijuana, and the drug quickly became a component of his new lifestyle. He was one of the first in his community of teenagers to start smoking regularly. In Duane's mind, marijuana provided those who smoked it with the ability to relax enough to make exceptional music. Smoking dope was an interesting addition to his life, but with Duane, above all, it was the music.

The Allman Joys eventually embarked on a tour of the Southeast bar circuit, tossing into the mix whatever fraternity parties they could book. They loaded their sound system and amps into a station wagon and hit the road. The band wanted nothing more than to have their music heard and appreciated. They knew that the only way to accomplish that was by playing to a variety of audiences.

In 1966 The Allman Joys were playing in a Nashville club called The Briarpatch when songwriter John D. Loudermilk and producer Buddy Killen approached them. The two men expressed an interest in recording the band at the studio of hitmaker Owen Bradley. The Allman Joys took Loudermilk and Killen up on their offer and entered the studio to cut Willie Dixon's "Spoonful" and a handful of other tunes. Unfortunately, the session wasn't all that successful, and nothing ever came of it. The Allman Joys continued to tour, even traveling as far north as Greenwich Village. By the end of the year, the band decided that whatever appeal they had was limited and that it would probably be best if they called it quits.

Duane and Gregg wanted to augment their sound with a different lineup. They joined with some friends who had been involved in a musical venture known as The Men-its. The Men-its had exhausted their run at the musical scene about the same time as The Allman Joys. Johnny Sandlin, Paul Hornsby, and Mabron McKinley were happy to join together with the Allman brothers to see what the collaboration might produce.

Hornsby would figure prominently in the musical history of both The Allman Brothers Band and the Southern Rock movement. His father was a fiddle player who introduced him to music while playing square dances. Hornsby started playing guitar when he was fourteen through listening to such artists as Roy Orbison and

Charlie Rich. He started hearing a lot of R&B while attending the University of Alabama and soon was sitting in with some of the foremost blues artists of the day. He began playing in local bands and eventually became involved with The Men-its.

Hornsby remembers his first introduction to Duane and Gregg Allman. "I was playing guitar in a band," he recalls. "Played one weekend in Mobile, Dolphin Island. One of the guys had gone into town a day or two earlier and was in a club and met them, playing in a place called The Stork Club. They came back raving about these guys called The Allman Joys. They said, 'Man, you gotta see these guys. They got hair down to their shoulders. And, by the way, they play great.' There wasn't many long haired people in the South at that time. It was a big oddity. It was kind of striking to see shoulder length, long blond hair. Then I got to hear them play. Seemed like a few weeks later they played in Tuscaloosa, where I was living at the time. And I thought, 'Man, these guys are just. . . .' I mean, they just had some kind of flair, I guess, is the word, about 'em. They played great, they looked great, and they just had some kind of charisma that I hadn't been seeing."

The association between The Allman Joys and The Men-its seemed to click immediately. Gregg was now handling the vocals and had started to develop a strong, bluesy delivery. People were amazed that the voice they heard singing belonged to such a young man. Gregg took his singing seriously but was rather nonchalant when it came to developing "The Voice." "I wanted it, and I went and got it, I guess," he says now.

Soon the nameless band was playing around the Southeast and being accepted as an innovative, exciting entity. The Allman Joys/Men-its association grew in popularity, and their territory expanded. Within a short time they were playing at a club called Peppy A Go Go in St. Louis. During that St. Louis gig they ran into The Nitty Gritty Dirt Band and came to the attention of the band's manager, Bill McEwen. Impressed, he suggested to the band members that if they were interested, he could perhaps help them obtain a record deal. It was the break that the band had been looking for.

The band weighed keeping the name of The Allman Joys, but then thought something new might be better. The Almanac was considered before they decided on the name Hour Glass. "We just had a bull session one day and kicked around a lot of silly, crazy names," remembers Hornsby. "I don't know who came up with the name Hour Glass. We just sort of all voted on it and that was one of the names we

··

could stomach and live with. We thought, 'You know, it's not offensive; it's okay.'
It was better than Strawberry Alarm Clock. But then again, what does Smashing
Pumpkins mean?"

Through McEwen's efforts, Hour Glass was soon on its way to Los Angeles. A
contract with Liberty Records awaited them there. Gregg wasn't all that certain
about relocating to Los Angeles, but Duane and the others thought it was most
definitely worth a shot. Although being in Los Angeles gave Hour Glass exposure to
the recording industry, the experience didn't enfold as the band had planned. The
unique features that had brought the band to McEwen (who was now managing the
band) and Liberty's attention didn't seem to matter much once the band entered the
recording studio. Hour Glass had very little say as to what songs would constitute
their first album. "It was out of our hands," remembers Gregg. "They handed us a
washtub full of demos. Back then they weren't even cassette tapes. They were
acetates, those old things they made on the lathe. They had about six good
plays in 'em."

Hour Glass, 1968-1969. (Standing, left to right)
Johnny Sandlin, Gregg Allman, Paul Hornsby.
(Seated, left to right) Duane Allman, Jesse "Pete" Carr.
Credit: Paul Hornsby Collection.

Dallas Smith was brought in to produce
the record. The dynamic between
Smith and the band was sorely lacking.
"He had just come off of some hits,"
recalls Hornsby. "He was doing like
Jan and Dean. That was his big record.
He didn't have a clue what to do with
us. He could detect an element of blues
tradition, black music influences in our
band, so he started calling us a Motown
band. The first album is just full of horns,
and black girls, chick singers and . . . he's
trying to put The Supremes behind us,
you know?"

The album the band cut contained a
couple of decent songs, including
"Nothing But Tears," "Heartbeat," and
"Cast Off All My Fears," a song written
by Jackson Browne. The mix and

production did nothing to display the band's familiar appeal. Duane's guitar could barely be heard, and he wasn't happy about it. There was no evidence of the innovative sound that made Hour Glass special.

The band was crushed when they heard the final tracks. "It was just done all wrong," says Gregg. "It wasn't done at all like we wanted to do it. It really matters a lot when the producer gets there 'cause suddenly you got a new guy in the band, sitting off to the side giving his input. (The band) needs to tie in with him in a hurry, or get him the hell out of there and get somebody you can work with. 'Cause producers are a dime a dozen, but the good ones are not."

The Liberty recording experience was certainly not all that the band had envisioned it could be. The band wasn't pleased with its debut album. The finished product, *Hour Glass*, was a huge disappointment for all concerned.

Hour Glass had opened for The Doors at Los Angeles's Hullaballoo while they worked on their album. The set went extremely well, and Duane closed it by tossing his Telecaster into the air. Duane's Telecaster was unique, especially with its Stratocaster neck. That guitar was just one of the many things that made Duane Allman different, even in Los Angeles, where everybody had a story to tell and the next big experience yet to live.

Hour Glass was a hit in the Los Angeles clubs, if not on record. "It was a kickin' ass band," remembers Hornsby. "I mean, we just kicked. We opened shows, the biggest audiences that toured California at that time. All the Buffalo Springfields, Moby Grapes, Jefferson Airplane and Grateful Dead, The Doors. I mean, we played with all these groups, and we were the opening act. And man, I know a lot of these people just hated to follow our band. I mean, we were just killin'."

Hour Glass was playing The Whiskey A Go Go regularly. Sometimes their new friends would jump on stage and jam with them. Anybody could turn up: Neil Young, Buddy Miles, Stephen Stills, and Bonnie Bramlett all sat in at one time or another. "We started a little tradition of jam sessions in The Whiskey," says Hornsby. "Whoever the biggest players that happened to be in town, well, they would all come out when they'd find out we were playing there. They'd come and have jam sessions on the weekends. Our sets, our planned, carefully rehearsed sets, got to turning into jam sessions every time we'd play there."

Duane had heard Jeff Beck playing the slide on "Beck's Bolero" and was intrigued. He heard Taj Mahal's guitarist, Jesse Ed Davis, use the slide on an old blues number called "Statesboro Blues" and became hooked. Duane was anxious to learn to employ the technique himself, and he mastered this little-used guitar gimmick very quickly. It was important to Duane that whatever sounds he was able to pull out of his guitar not only be superb, but unique.

One night while the band members were preparing to play at The Whiskey, they discovered that bassist Mabron McKinley had left town. Fortunately, another Men-its guitar player named Pete Carr was visiting the band. Although Carr had never played the instrument, he was instantly recruited as Hour Glass's new bass player. He would remain with the band for the duration.

In spite of the changes, the bands' musical juices were flowing. It might have been remembered as a magical time had not Liberty stepped in and told the band members that too much exposure would only hurt their unseasoned career. The record label also suggested that they curtail their jams. They were told instead to look to the next album. The boys in the band pointed out to the Liberty executives that they'd tried it the record label's way on the first album, with no success. Hour Glass's members felt they should have a shot at putting some of their own compositions and arrangements on the next album. *Power of Love*, while still not a stellar demonstration of the band members' talents, was a better effort than *Hour Glass*.

Duane's intricate work on "Norwegian Wood" and "Down in Texas" allowed him a bit of the showcase that he'd been denied the first time. Gregg's vocals were the selling point of the band as far as producer Dallas Smith was concerned. Gregg's voice was prominently featured in songs like "Power of Love" and "I Still Want Your Love."

Even though some of the problems of the first album weren't as dominant in this new venture, the band members still thought that it was being pushed toward a pop sound that wasn't at all what they envisioned for Hour Glass. "Duane was probably the most outspoken," says Hornsby. "He always let you know what was on his mind. He was having problems with Dallas, and it was almost a fist fight every day we were recording for Liberty. I seen Duane storm out and quit, and fly back to Florida, and come back. Lord knows, it was an ordeal getting those two albums done."

Johnny Sandlin suggested that by recording at Fame Studios in Muscle Shoals, a studio known for its soul, the true essence of Hour Glass might emerge. "We were so frustrated with the record we had just done," says Hornsby. "And our favorite records and our heroes were the Muscle Shoals people and the sound that they were getting up there. We pooled a little bit of our bucks and went up there and rented a studio and had Jimmy Johnson. I think Jimmy was engineer then, I'm not sure. And Eddie Hinton helped us with it. Eddie had been there for a couple of years. We went in there and cut about three or four tunes."

The band recorded a B.B. King medley and a song Gregg had recently written, called "I've Been Gone Too Long." The band felt that at last the record label would see what Hour Glass was about. But the suits at Liberty didn't get it. "We took it back out to Liberty, and they just thought it was atrocious," claims Hornsby. "I mean, we were so proud. We thought, 'Oh boy, this is the Hour Glass, you know? This is the closest thing to what we've been trying to play.' And we went and played it for 'em, and they just thought it was horrible." It seemed there was no way that Liberty and Hour Glass were going to be able to co-exist in a manner through which they would mutually benefit.

The band members wanted to at least play live dates so that they could perform the type of music they loved. "We'd go out, we wouldn't even play the songs off the album," remembers Hornsby. "We'd do our stuff, you know, or old copy stuff, or things that we had turned around and did our own arrangement with. We couldn't get out of California because we didn't have a hit record anywhere. I mean, we were practically stars in California . . . starving stars. We'd play all these big shows and go over great and kick everybody's ass, but we couldn't get out of town."

Finally, Liberty allowed Hour Glass to embark on a very small tour someplace outside of California. "We came East for one little tour and played Cleveland, Birmingham, some Florida dates, and an Atlanta date, I think," recalls Hornsby. The band was happy to return to Florida, where at least they had fans who understood what they were trying to do.

One of the stops Hour Glass made on its mini-tour was Jacksonville's Comic Book Club. Something happened there that was amusing, depending on your perspective, but that also had an interesting significance in the saga of Southern Rock. "We're headlining in this little club, and we're sitting in the dressing room," Hornsby remembers. "Tuning up, waiting to go on. There's an opening band. I heard something very familiar being played. I stuck my head out the door, and there was the opening band, playing one of the songs from our album that we had just finished. We were supposedly out to promote the album—that was our excuse for being back East. And they went from one song, and then they played nearly every song off our new album. The few songs that we actually played off the album they did as good or better than we played it. So, we came on. 'What are we going to do? Hey, how are we going to follow this band?'"

The band was One Percent, the future Lynyrd Skynyrd. Hornsby later called Ronnie Van Zant on the incident. Van Zant looked embarrassed, according to Hornsby. "Man, I gotta tell you, man," said Van Zant. "We worshipped you guys in those days."

Even the tour couldn't revitalize the band. The unfolding story of Hour Glass seemed to be heading toward an undistinguished ending. The thought of returning to Los Angeles and further disappointment made the members of the band cringe. "Duane got to where he couldn't stand L.A.," remembers Hornsby. "His ego was shattered. It was obvious we weren't getting anywhere with Liberty. We can't identify with the record company and can't deal with them. He wanted to come back East where he could be worshipped. We played St. Louis. We had a big, big following in St. Louis.

"From there it went really downhill. Went back to Nashville and we got in a fight with the club owner, and after one night got fired there. Then we went to Mobile to the old Stork Club, where that was one of [The Allman Joys'] strongholds, and they wanted us to play the old copy stuff. They didn't want to hear anything we were playing. They wanted to hear the old stuff The Allman Joys had played. 'Course we didn't know any of that stuff. Oh, it was so depressing. We were so bummed out we played about three really crummy, crummy dates. It wasn't the way Duane had remembered, you know? The good ol' days all of a sudden weren't the good ol' days they had been a couple of years earlier. I think all of that combined took its toll, and we just quit."

When the band returned to Los Angeles, the decision was made to put Hour Glass to rest. Everyone involved was disappointed but couldn't deny one thing. The magic had evaporated somewhere within the smog.

Duane and Gregg headed back to Florida, where they cut some tracks with a band called The 31st of February. An old friend of the brothers named Butch Trucks was in the band. Gregg had written a song with Sandy Alaimo, the manager of the studio where the recording, titled "Melissa," was done. "Melissa" was recorded for the first time during The 31st of February sessions. Duane was delighted to have the opportunity to debut his slide technique during the recording. He knew his playing was special.

Gregg, on the other hand, decided that he would rather be in Los Angeles. He wasn't feeling particularly committed to the music anymore. Hour Glass owed Liberty money, and Liberty agreed that if Gregg would provide them with solo material, the debt would be canceled. Gregg left for California after telling his brother and their friends that he would return soon to Florida. Within a short time, he called from Los Angeles to say that he'd changed his mind.

Duane played a few gigs with The 31st of February. The band sometimes jammed with Berry Oakley and Dickey Betts, two musicians who were involved with a band named The Second Coming. The 31st of February didn't seem to have the fire, though, and eventually broke up. Duane didn't know what he was going to do next, but it was going to have to be something novel to entice him.

One day Duane received a call from Rick Hall of Fame Studio at Muscle Shoals, Alabama. Hall was recording Wilson Pickett and asked Duane if he would like to do some session work on the album. The Muscle Shoals rhythm section had been attracting a lot of attention through its work with Percy Sledge, but Hall but didn't have a strong lead guitar. Hall had heard Duane's Hour Glass recordings and likely the tracks cut at the studio when Hour Glass had laid down the B.B. King medley. Duane was delighted to receive the call and found himself in Alabama in November, 1968.

Duane was honored, but not intimidated, to be working with a talent like Pickett. Duane had been working with the artist only a short time when he suggested to the soul man that he record "Hey Jude." Pickett initially resisted the idea. When Duane let rip with his guitar and Pickett heard what Duane had in mind, the cut was approved.

Pickett was impressed with Duane's ethereal guitar work and started calling him "Skyman." Since Duane's friends back home had been calling him "Dog," because of his shaggy hair, the two names soon became one: "Skydog." Duane didn't care what they called him, as long as he continued to have the opportunity to show them what he could do.

Duane was asked to stay on at the studio once his talent had been discovered by all of the powers that be at Muscle Shoals. He continued to embellish the recordings cut at Fame with his unique guitar work. Duane packed up his few material possessions in Jacksonville and moved to a small cabin on a lake in Alabama. He didn't much care where he was, as long as he was playing some good music. What was happening at Muscle Shoals certainly was that.

The musicians at Fame were delighted with what Duane brought to their sessions. He soon was building quite a body of work. He recorded "The Road of Love" with Clarence Carter, "The Weight" with Aretha Franklin, and "Games People Play" with King Curtis.

Duane wasn't shy about making suggestions. Not only did his reputation as a player rapidly grow, but his counsel and advice were sought as well. He even got a chance to use his slide on some John Hammond tracks. Duane was having a great time.

Duane's work soon came to the attention of Phil Walden, manager of the late Otis Redding. Walden had been around R&B for over a decade and was now working with Jerry Wexler of Atlantic Records. Wexler had employed the studio at Muscle Shoals to record his artist, Percy Sledge. Duane and his guitar came to the attention of Walden and Wexler at about the same time, with a big bang.

Although born in Greenville, South Carolina, Walden had grown up in Macon, Georgia. He entered the music business by booking acts for the local high school and colleges during his undergraduate years at Mercer University. He'd opened an office by his sophomore year and was booking acts throughout the South. After meeting Macon's Otis Redding, Walden and his brother Alan opened a management agency and were soon representing Redding, Sam and Dave, Percy Sledge, Clarence Carter, Arthur Conley, and others. Walden was right by Redding's side when the charismatic soul singer broke through with such hits as "Try A Little Tenderness" and "I've Been Loving You Too Long."

Phil Walden was impressed when he heard a sample of what Duane Allman was doing at Muscle Shoals. Walden was in New York preparing to go to a meeting at

Atlantic, and producer Rick Hall was in the city to play Wexler a recently completed Wilson Pickett session. Hall stopped by Walden's hotel room before the meeting with Wexler and told Walden that he had something that he wanted Walden to hear. Hall played Pickett's "Hey Jude." "My immediate reaction was, 'My God. Who's that guitar player?'" recalls Walden.

Walden recognized that it wasn't Hall's regular session player. Hall informed Walden that it was a "long haired hippie boy that had come from California, and they called him Skyman." Hall had Skyman under contract as a sideman. Walden began to consider something more for the artist he had been impressed by but had yet to meet.

Walden had a session scheduled at Muscle Shoals at that time, with Tom Dowd producing artist Arthur Conley. After hearing about Skyman, he decided to leave immediately for Alabama. "I went to Muscle Shoals," remembers Walden. "As I walked into the studio, I noticed this red haired guitarist that had earphones on and was sort of doodling around with his guitar. I walked over and he looked up and removed his earphones. I extended my hand and he extended his, and I said 'Are you Duane Allman?' And he said, 'Yes, I am.' I said 'I'm Phil Walden.' He knew who I was, and he knew of my reputation in the music business. I said, 'Duane, I'd love to have lunch.' And he said 'Great. What do you have in mind?' I said, 'Well, I'm here to talk to you about the possibility of becoming involved in your management.' Duane said, 'You got it.' I said, 'Wait a minute. We need to talk about it first.' He said, 'No, you got it. It's great. I'm honored that you're interested in me.'"

Atlantic honcho Jerry Wexler wasn't aware of Duane Allman until Duane's involvement with Muscle Shoals. Wexler worked closely with Pickett as his producer and label chief. Occasionally someone else produced Pickett, and it was during Pickett's session with Rick Hall that Wexler also became aware of Allman. When Hall played "Hey Jude" for Wexler, Wexler was excited. Duane's playing stood out. "For me, it made the whole record," recalls Wexler.

From that moment on, Wexler employed Duane Allman on sessions whenever he had the opportunity. Wexler was interested enough in the young guitarist that he decided to purchase Duane's session contract from Rick Hall for $15,000 in order to free Duane to do other things. "Rick thought the heavens had opened," remembers Wexler, "because Duane Allman was a guitar player who didn't write songs and couldn't sing."

But Duane could play, and he was making a lot of new musician friends. One time while visiting Muscle Shoals, Phil Walden had introduced Duane to Jai Johnny Johnson. Johnson was a drummer who had been playing on the road for Percy Sledge and Otis Redding. He was called Jaimoe.

Jaimoe was born Johnny Lee Johnson in Ocean Springs, Mississippi, on July 8, 1944. He grew up in Gulfport, where his love of jazz and drums found him on the road with R&B singer Ted Taylor. Jaimoe was soon backing up Otis Redding, and he played behind a variety of exciting acts, such as Percy Sledge, Patti LaBelle and The Bluebells, and Sam and Dave. Jaimoe left Redding to take a gig with Sledge and soon after was working for Joe Tex. Walden associate Twiggs Lyndon called Jaimoe to become involved in a recording studio venture he was starting up in Macon, Georgia, but after Jaimoe arrived in Macon he realized that the venture wasn't quite off the ground. He joined up with Bob O'Dea and formed the duo Bob and Jai. Phil Walden eventually connected him with Johnny Jenkins, and he was soon on the road with Jenkins's band.

Jaimoe started to hear talk of Duane Allman and some preliminary plans by Walden and his associates to put the young guitar wizard to work for them. Jaimoe, too, was impressed when he finally got to Muscle Shoals and heard Duane play. Additionally, Jaimoe felt that maybe he'd found someone who would compliment his own musical efforts.

In January, 1969, Duane called up his friend Berry Oakley from The Second Coming. Duane asked Berry to join him at Muscle Shoals. Duane wanted Berry to become acquainted with Jaimoe and his talent. Duane and Berry on guitar, while Jaimoe beat an innovative rhythm pattern, was unlike anything the experienced Muscle Shoals musicians had ever heard.

Raymond Berry Oakley III was born April 4, 1948, in Chicago. His father Ray worked for a real estate company, and his mother Margaret was a schoolteacher. Berry and his sister Candace spent their early years in Park Forest, Illinois. Berry was so into his Catholic religion that he served as an altar boy and considered the priesthood. "From early childhood, Berry had a passion for defending anyone in trouble and taking them under his protective wing until differences were resolved," says Candace Oakley.[1]

Berry got his first, acoustic guitar when he was fourteen. He took three Spanish guitar lessons with an instructor who played with the "Ted Viorita Band." Berry then became involved with the electric guitar, bought an amp, and started his own band. By high school, he was playing all night long at various clubs and bars in Chicago.

When Berry heard that pop artist Tommy Roe was looking for a bass player, the seventeen-year-old borrowed a bass, taught himself bass chording, auditioned, and got the job. Although he wasn't a huge fan of Roe's type of music, Berry figured that any professional playing was better than none. He moved to Roe's home base of New Port Richey, Florida, and played with the pop star for about a year.

Berry eventually made his way to Jacksonville, where he formed The Second Coming with some other Florida musicians. The name of the band had been selected tongue in cheek to poke fun at Berry's resemblance to Jesus. The Second Coming played blues, R&B, and good old rock and roll.

Duane Allman enjoyed jamming with Berry and The Second Coming. He was quite taken with Berry's enterprising approach to his instrument. Duane felt that Berry would bring some excitement and innovation to what was happening in the Fame studio. He asked Berry to come up to Alabama.

Duane had been intrigued with the way James Brown employed two drummers on stage, and thought a similar presentation would be interesting should his little side project grow into something bigger. He asked his Hour Glass buddies Paul Hornsby and Johnny Sandlin to come up to Muscle Shoals and see what they thought. They recorded several tracks, with Duane on guitar, Berry on bass, Hornsby on keyboards, and Sandlin on drums. "No Money Down," "Dimples," "Goin' Down Slow," and "Happily Married Man" were well presented and interesting, but Duane wasn't comfortable on vocals, and this showed.

"[The session] just didn't meet his criteria for what he wanted to do," recalls Phil Walden. He doesn't think that Duane really knew exactly what it was he wanted to do at that point. "He said, 'You know, I'm just lookin', Phil,'" says Walden. "'I think what I'm gonna do is just get in the car, and I'm gonna ride around for awhile. I'm just going to go to various Southern cities and just sort of sit in with the music scene and see what's going on. See if I can put together something that I have in my head.'" It was a sure bet that if whatever was in Duane Allman's head involved music, it was going to be something real good.

Over the next few months Duane talked with his friends about calling back his brother from California and forming a group. The idea met with resistance from Johnny Sandlin and Paul Hornsby. They'd been there, done that. They didn't want to relive the Hour Glass experience. Berry Oakley was interested but didn't want to abandon The Second Coming and his musical partner, guitarist Dickey Betts. Berry decided to return to Jacksonville. Jaimoe was certainly interested in Duane's idea, but a drummer and a guitarist did not a band make.

Duane was determined to make something happen. He enjoyed the studio work at Fame, but the session work was restrictive. Duane and Jaimoe decided to go down to Florida, get Berry involved again, and see what they could put together. Duane was a man on a mission. When Duane and Jaimoe got to Jacksonville, they stayed for a couple of weeks with Duane's old friend Butch Trucks. Soon Jaimoe and Butch were exchanging drumming theories and becoming the best of friends.

Claude Hudson "Butch" Trucks, Jr., was born on May 11, 1947, in Jacksonville. Butch began formal piano lessons when he was nine and also loved to sing. He served as youth director at North Jacksonville Baptist Church, played timpani in the Jacksonville Symphonette, and was named to the All-State High School Orchestra.

Butch decided that he wanted to focus on drums and played with two local bands, The Vikings and The Echoes. He formed a band with two other students while attending Florida State University in Tallahassee. The trio called themselves The Bitter Ind and traveled to Daytona Beach to play the many clubs that had cropped up there. While auditioning at The Martinique in Daytona, the band met Duane and Gregg Allman.

The Bitter Ind was successful as a folk rock band and was soon signed to Vanguard Records on the stipulation that it change its name. Vanguard felt that The Bitter End Club in Greenwich Village would likely have a problem with the

Berry Oakley, Allman Brothers Band bassist, 1970. Credit: W. Robert Johnson.

group's current moniker, so The 31st of February it was. The band cut an album, but it was far from successful, and the group's record contract was soon terminated.

Butch played with The Second Coming and other bands when he could, but he was dying to make something permanent happen for himself. After talking with Duane and Jaimoe, he was excited about the possibility in being in a venture with Allman. Duane was a musician he'd long admired. Butch had become friends with Berry Oakley from playing with The Second Coming in the local park during some Sunday afternoon jams. Butch told Duane that Berry was a pretty straight-ahead guy, and he didn't think Berry would walk away from his friend Betts. Butch, though, was ready to play.

Duane had been thinking along the lines of a power trio like Cream, but he soon realized that he wasn't going to be able to recruit Berry without inviting Dickey Betts to participate as well. Dickey, on the other hand, wasn't all that sure he wanted to leave the band he'd formed with Berry. Dickey didn't like having other people decide his future for him. He evidently wasn't thrilled with Berry and Duane's idea, but agreed when Berry suggested that the two of them jam with Duane and his friends when they played one of their Sunday gigs at Willowbranch Park.

Forrest Richard "Dickey" Betts was born in West Palm Beach, Florida, on December 12, 1943, and grew up in an atmosphere of country, string, bluegrass, and folk music. His father, Harold, played fiddle, and his uncles played guitars. When Dickey was five years old, he learned how to play a ukulele his father had come across in a neighbor's garage. The first song he learned was "Going Down the Road Feeling Bad." He was playing mandolin and banjo by the time he was ten. Soon Dickey was appearing in school talent shows. He tried music lessons when he was a teenager but didn't like to be discouraged from playing by ear. The lessons were dropped.

When Dickey was about sixteen, he decided to switch over to guitar. He bought a Stella guitar and a Gibson amp. Dickey lived to play music and soon was drumming as well. When he listened to Duane Eddy, B.B. King, Chuck Berry, and The Ventures, however, he realized that he longed to become proficient in the guitar. Besides, Dickey soon learned that playing the guitar was a good way to get girls to notice him. He bought himself a Gretsch, and there was now no stopping him.

One of the bands Dickey associated with was The Swingin' Saints. When the band was asked to tour a State Fair circuit, Dickey took to the road, playing dozens of shows a day, running the circuit. When he returned home, Dickey forged his birth certificate and started playing clubs. He settled for a time in Sarasota with a band he called The Jokers. This was where he met Berry Oakley. Dickey and Berry decided to form The Second Coming with Reese Wynans and Larry Reinhardt, and Dickey's wife Dale on vocals and keyboards. Berry convinced the other band members to go for broke and play some original compositions. He thought they could do better than playing only covers like most of the other local bands. Dickey went along with Berry's idea, and The Second Coming started to build a fan base.

Berry's idea to have Dickey play with Duane Allman was a good one. The musicians clicked immediately. One day soon after their park experience, the guys were casually jamming when everything simply came together. Duane, Berry, Dickey, Butch, and Jaimoe, with organ work by Reese Wynans, played every type of music they could imagine. They were stunned. The music was incredible. If this bunch of guys were to form the band that Duane was talking about, who knew where it could lead?

CHAPTER 2

Capricorn, Macon, and Idlewild South

1969-1970

During this time frame, the corporate world was changing, as were the personal lives of a myriad of musicians. Stax Records had long been a stronghold of quality rhythm and blues (R&B). Now Stax had left the Atlantic fold and had been purchased by Gulf & Western.

Atlanta's Jerry Wexler had been involved with R&B acts for quite a long time. He was very tuned in to the blues and Southern music. There was Stax in Memphis and Muscle Shoals in Alabama, but no studio or R&B scene in Georgia or the Carolinas. Furthermore, there was no major label support for R&B. Wexler then realized that the South was virtually untapped in regard to white soul and R&B production.

A year and a half had passed since Otis Redding's death, and manager Phil Walden had started to reassess his involvement with R&B. "I felt I had walked on the mountaintop with Otis," remembers Walden. "It just didn't quite have the same buzz it had had in that decade of the sixties." He didn't know exactly what he was looking for or what he wanted to do in the music industry. "I was looking for something that was new and something that was more rock-oriented than the R&B scene at that time," says Walden. He looked to his mentor, Jerry Wexler. Both men agreed there was a chasm in the South when it came to the production of R&B and rock music. Walden considered asking Wexler if Atlantic might be interested in fronting him the start-up money to open a studio in Macon, where that gap might be closed.

One day Walden was fishing in the Miami Gulfstream with Wexler on Wexler's Warner Communications boat, called "The Big A." The subject of the studio came up. "I said, 'Phil, I'll go you one better,'" remembers Wexler. "'I'll front you a label.'

I never went for the notion of making an ad hominem bet, 'This is my man and I'm going with you.' I had to know what he was bringing in. With Stax, it was the whole Stax roster: Booker T. and The MGs, Otis Redding. It was so successful. Muscle Shoals, it was the studio and the players. Atlantic was one of two [surviving, major] companies in history where the owners actually made records in the studio. The other one is Motown. The terrain was covered with independent record companies.

"But [Atlantic and Motown] couldn't make all the records ourselves. While we had talented in-house producers, we made records. It was quite a prolific source of music right there in-house, but it still wasn't enough and we needed more and more. We either had to grow or perish. All of our contemporaries, every single one of them, perished. There were some famous labels, MGM, Cadance, Chess, VJ . . . they're gone. So I was betting on Phil Walden, because I knew of his association with Otis Redding. I had an absolutely solid belief in [Walden's client] Duane Allman. In my opinion, he was the premier rock and blues guitarist of his time."

Walden was reluctant to go so far as to form a label, but Wexler assured him that he would do well if he did. Wexler certainly had his finger on the pulse of the music industry. His counsel was well based and insightful. Walden agreed to form the company. "Although neither one of us believes in astrology, we called it Capricorn because it's both our signs," laughs Wexler.

Walden was still interested in managing Duane, but he'd put everything on hold for the time being. Walden looked to establishing the Capricorn Studio. It would be located in his hometown of Macon. Capricorn would have an in-house rhythm section and songwriters, much the same as Stax. Among the first clients booked was Bonnie Bramlett, who had no recording band and who would benefit greatly from what Capricorn had to offer.

Since Paul Hornsby and Johnny Sandlin weren't interested in reforming Hour Glass or being a part of Duane's new association, Walden offered them something else. "He said, 'Well, if you won't be in this band, would you come and be in my rhythm section in my studio in Macon?" recalls Hornsby. "He said, 'I'll pay you guys a regular salary and then give you a percentage of the stuff you play on.' He thought he might build another Muscle Shoals-type thing. At that time the Muscle Shoals sound was big cause they had their own rhythm section. You had the Stax thing in Memphis, where Booker T. and The MGs were the house band, you know? He wanted to pattern his studio after that, with a house rhythm section. Every time he called, the offer got sweeter and sweeter. Finally Sandlin decided to do it, to come, and Pete Carr, and so they convinced me to come over to Macon with 'em."

"It was through the [Duane Allman and friends first session] that I met Johnny Sandlin, who became a major player for me and director of A&R, and as a producer at Capricorn," recalls Walden. "Also Paul Hornsby, who played a major role at Capricorn. He was the producer for Marshall Tucker as well as various other albums, as well as studio manager for us. Pete Carr I met through that, and Pete Carr later became a session player for Capricorn. The guys that Duane brought to that project all came to work for Capricorn in some other capacity. When I look back at Duane's influence in the original setup and the development of this company, it's unique. He was very instrumental in our success as a company. It was through his belief in the company and his support of the company that we were able to beat it out of the pack because a lot of labels sort of sprung up during that particular time."

Frank Fenter was serving as the managing director for Atlantic Records in Europe. Walden had met Fenter through his association with Otis Redding, and had brought Fenter into Capricorn as a minority partner. "We had some lean days in those early days," remembers Walden. "But I think the way we set it up, and the artists that we signed, and the whole communal Southern thing that Capricorn came to represent, Frank was very vital to that whole thing."

As the recording studio got underway, Walden received a telephone call from Duane. Duane informed his manager that he had, at last, put something together he thought Walden might be interested in hearing. The new venture was still in the formative stages, but Duane felt it had great potential.

Duane and Butch had been living with their girlfriends in a house in Jacksonville called "The Green House." Eventually Berry Oakley, Dickey Betts, and their girlfriends moved in. Duane was still under contract to Walden as a solo act, in spite of his desire to have a band. Walden had been encouraging Duane to move up to Macon where Capricorn and its studio were located. But Duane now had a band and the band would stay, for the time being, in Jacksonville. If Walden wanted to hear them, he needed to go down to Florida.

Walden agreed to check out Duane's new ensemble. When Walden and his business associates heard the new band in rehearsal, they were excited. "It sounded great," recalls Walden. "But it was basically an all-instrumental band.

Dickey Betts at Willingham Chapel, Macon, GA, 1969.
Credit: W. Robert Johnson.

And it seemed to playing a notch or two higher than the standard rock and roll bands. So there was some concern that this band was possibly too musical to fit into the current rock and roll scene."

As exciting as the music was, Duane recognized three things. He needed someone who really knew his way around the blues to handle vocals, as well as someone who could write some innovative songs for the band to perform. Also, he really wanted to work with his brother again.

Gregg Allman had been in California, mostly just hanging out. He hadn't been getting far with his music —when he took the time to focus on it. "They were just giving me the run around out there," Gregg says of his last days with Liberty. "I was working with their studio band and cut two songs . . . flops . . . I won't even tell you the names of those, they were that bad."

Duane decided to call Gregg. He wanted to convince his little brother that where he needed to be was back in Florida, working with this amazing new unit that Duane had put together. Duane didn't receive the resistance he'd expected. "There I was out in Hollyweird," Gregg remembers. "Didn't have many friends, and the sky was pink. I was about to put the gun to my head one Sunday evening, March 26, 1969. The phone rang, and it was my brother. He said, 'I got this band. . . .' That was such a blessing when he called me. And one thing I've never done before or since. I got on the freeway and put out my thumb. I hitchhiked all the way back to Florida."

Walden remembers this a little differently. He says that the group was already ensconced in a house on College Street in Macon when the call was made to Gregg. "Some several weeks after they arrived [in Macon], when we had an honest appraisal of the potential of this band, everybody felt it was fabulous music but that we needed a very strong vocalist," Walden recalls. "We finally made a phone call to Gregg. I think Duane, in fact, made the call and invited Gregg to come to Macon. He was in Los Angeles working on a solo project at the time. And he accepted Duane's offer. He came in, and it was magic from that point on."

When Gregg first heard the new band for himself, he knew that his brother was onto something big. Gregg was in. "The Brothers started coming together immediately," remembers Gregg. "I mean, after we got together, all in one room. I had a couple of songs. I just got on a roll, and I wrote 'Whipping Post,' and 'Black Hearted Woman,' and 'Please Call Home,' and a couple others. All in about a period of ten days. I was just real happy, you know, and I really belonged. There's nothing like that great feeling of belonging to something. Suddenly, with that, and a few blues songs and what have you, we had enough for a set. So everybody was sitting around. We're going, 'Well, now what?' I said, 'Well, let's go find the nearest big park, haul our stuff up there and just unload it, and hope to God somehow we can find outdoor power, plug in . . . and we did. We sent our roadies up there the day before. Of course, we went to Atlanta. We set up and you know, within three hours there was about 2,000 people there." The park was Piedmont, and the band was now The Allman Brothers Band.

One of the band's controversies has to do with whether or not Walden was interested in Duane's new band or simply wanted Duane to continue to work as a sideman with Walden's other artists. Gregg claims that Walden was primarily interested in his brother as a solo act at that time. "He wanted to just hire Duane," Gregg says. "My brother says, 'I'll have you know my little brother is in this band. It's The Allman Brothers *Band*. And we're all there, equal, or it don't happen. What's it going to be, boss?' The guy says, 'Bring it on.' He came up to Piedmont Park, saw the band, and so we moved to Macon, Georgia."

Walden, on the other hand, says that Duane needed to be encouraged to put a band together. "It was my idea," says Walden. "He was enjoying probably the most success he'd ever enjoyed in his career as a session player, so I was talking him out of that. I talked him into gambling with me on this other project."

Regardless of whose idea it was, the new band was exceptional. "It really started to gel and come together after Gregg's arrival," remembers Walden. "He was the perfect vocal complement to that wonderful instrumental aggregation that we had assembled. It was a band of Southerners that were united through their music. They had a lot of common ground between them. I think they became a melting pot for a lot of the music that came from the South. When you look back and listen to those early records, there's obviously a strong blues base, but a nice rock base. There are jazz influences, there are gospel influences, there are country influences. It all, sort of stirred together, came out a very unique brand of American music."

According to Walden, the first date The Allman Brothers Band played outside of the South was at the Boston Tea Party in Boston. The band was the opening act for The Velvet Underground. "A rather unusual bill," laughs Walden. "I had talked several major New York rock agents into attending this date. The general consensus was that they were a great musical band, but that there wasn't enough emphasis on entertaining. Several people suggested that Gregg needed to get out from behind that Hammond B-3 organ and be more up front, since Gregg was blessed with an abundance of good looks. This suggestion was not well received by the band. I don't recall exactly what Duane said, but I doubt if it would even be printable if I could remember. So, our first venture outside the South was a limited success."

The Tea Party gig didn't discourage either the band or Walden. The Allman Brothers Band took to the road to enable a wide assortment of audiences to hear its music. The band averaged between twenty-five and twenty-seven dates out of every month. They played whether or not they got paid. "If they were in a city and they had an open time and there was a park or someplace they could plug in and play for free, that's what they would do," recalls Walden. Relentless touring in an effort to break their act set the standard by which the members of The Allman Brothers Band approached their career for the next twenty years.

The band members were happy in their new home of Macon when they weren't on the road. They had little money and ensconced themselves in a two-room apartment at 309 College Street. They threw their mattresses on the floor and prepared to make some music. The sleepy little Southern town soon became a home away from home for the boys in The Allman Brothers Band.

Macon itself was an unlikely place to attract a bunch of long-haired musicians, but the little city had soul. Radio station WIBB had a popular show called "Night Ride." Hamp Swain, the show's host, would often feature live performances by different artists who passed through town. If artists had talent, they were welcome to appear on Swain's radio show to share it. A decade earlier, renegade performer Little Richard Penniman had let loose with a unique musical style. Little Richard lived in Macon, so he had ample opportunity to participate in Swain's show. Penniman made R&B a personal experience to Macon listeners.

One of the young men who listened regularly to Swain's show was Phil Walden. He enjoyed the same artists as Swain. Walden soon realized that he wanted to be a part of what he was hearing. When he'd opened his management and booking agency, his first act had been Johnny Jenkins and The Pinetoppers. One of The Pinetoppers was a local boy named Otis Redding. Redding was well on his way to becoming a huge star when his chartered airplane descended into the icy waters of Lake Monona, Wisconsin. While he dealt with the loss of Redding and devoted his attention to his other acts, nothing musically excited Walden again until his visit to Muscle Shoals to hear Duane Allman. Now he had brought Duane Allman and his Allman Brothers Band home to Macon.

The Allman Brothers Band members planned to continue to rehearse their music in front of audiences at free concerts in the city's parks, as well as wherever Walden could book them. They needed a couple of roadies to help them with their equipment. Although there was little money to be had, three young men came forward to take the job. They could tell that The Allman Brothers Band was going to go far. One of their friends from Jacksonville, Joseph "Dog" Campbell, offered to join the crew. Since there couldn't be two "Dogs" in the band, Campbell was quickly dubbed "Red Dog." Mike Callahan had served as a roadie for The Second Coming. Callahan was brought on board, as well as another friend named Kim Payne. Twiggs Lyndon, an associate of Walden's, would act as their road manager.

The band members played their music and waited for a recording contract to materialize. Walden didn't quite know what to do with The Allman Brothers Band. "He discovered Otis Redding, and he had Sam and Dave, Percy Sledge and Johnny Taylor . . . Joe Tex," says Gregg. "We were his first real white band. He didn't quite know at first, you know?"

There wasn't much money to be had at the time. The care and feeding of a bunch of young guys was expensive. One day the boys pooled their money and bought a single plate of food to share at a soul food restaurant in downtown Macon called "The H & H." Louise Hudson, the proprietor, felt sorry for the hungry musicians. She returned to their table with individual plates for everyone. The boys soon learned that they had a good friend in "Mama Louise." They could rely on Mama's kindness to provide them with free food when the times were rough. She continued to be their friend for many, many years. Mama Louise cared about the young musicians of Macon and supported them whenever they needed her. All of Macon's rock and roll musicians would come to love her in the years ahead.

The Allman Brothers Band rehearsed in an old Macon warehouse that Walden had purchased and planned to turn into an addition to his recording studio. The band members concentrated on blues and originals, mostly penned by Gregg. They enjoyed working out Gregg's songs, as well as adding their own signature to the old blues songs they knew and loved. "All of our Allman Brothers Records, if you'll notice, have one old contemporary blues song," Gregg points out. "Old songs like 'Trouble No More' and 'One Way Out.' 'Statesboro Blues' was written in, I think, 1932. 'Come On My Kitchen' was probably written about 1923, Robert Johnson. We'd take 'em and redo 'em, and they'd really always come out well."

The band found that it could come up with some really interesting material by improvising off someone's leads. The urban blues of Hour Glass melded with the psychedelia of The Second Coming to form a new, exciting blend of R&B, blues, and rock. Dickey Betts called it "Progressive Rock." Whatever it was called, The Allman Brothers Band was on to something important.

1969. Gregg Allman (center) with The Allman Brothers Band roadies Kim Payne (left) and Red Dog (right). Credit: W. Robert Johnson.

Something the band was also on to was psychedelic mushrooms. The band rehearsed all day and partied with psilocybin all night. The guys became such a fan of the mushrooms that they adopted a mushroom as their logo, and each had a small mushroom tattooed on his calf.

Some nights they would sit around the apartment listening to records by Miles Davis, Taj Mahal, John Coltrane, and Herbie Hancock. Other nights they would amble down to Rose Hill Cemetery to sit among the tombstones, smoking joints and playing guitars. One time Dickey was sitting in the graveyard writing a song about a girl. He didn't feel he could name the girl in the song, so he looked around to see what name he might be able to cull from one of the nearby tombstones. He saw the inscription "In Memory of Elizabeth Reed" and titled his song.

Duane continued to play sessions at Muscle Shoals when he wasn't rehearsing in Macon or out playing with The Allman Brothers Band. He enjoyed the diversion, and it brought in some money for the band. The Brothers continued to play their free concerts up in Atlanta, so the money Duane brought in was appreciated. The crowd at Piedmont was crazy about the band's music. The Brothers started to receive some very favorable press.

With Walden's recording studio off to a good start, he turned his attention to the label he'd promised Jerry Wexler. "The Allman Band," as it was referred to in the contract, was Capricorn Records' first act. The band members signed a five-year contract, allowing Walden 25 percent of the band's income. They would work with the entrepreneur serving as both their manager and label president. This would turn out to be a very interesting collaboration.

Walden knew the group needed exposure within the music industry. He encouraged the band to play New York City and the North whenever they had the opportunity. Enter Bill Graham and his Fillmore East. As with many events surrounding the Brothers, there is some controversy over Graham's introduction to the band. Writers in the past have attributed Graham's interest in the band to Walden's association with Otis Redding. Gregg Allman, on the other hand, claims that Walden had little to do with the band hooking up with Graham. "I think somebody met somebody that knew somebody that knew somebody that . . . kind of like that," Gregg says. "Cause Phil sure as hell didn't know him."

Regardless of how it came to be, The Allman Brothers Band opened at Graham's Fillmore East in New York City for Blood, Sweat and Tears in November, 1969. The Allmans' set was hindered by the fact that the audience was there to see the headlining act and had trouble comprehending the music the Brothers offered. Graham didn't care. He was enchanted with the band from the South and booked them time and again into both Fillmores, East and West.

While the Brothers enjoyed playing live, they knew it was time to put their act to the test and make a record. They worked long and hard on their first recording and at last were happy with what they had been able to create. *The Allman Brothers Band* was released in late 1969. The Allman Brothers had created their own blues, and

Gregg's vocals demonstrated that he was no stranger to the genre. The young man with the very old, soulful voice immediately caught the attention of all who heard him. No one could figure out where the boy had learned to sing the blues like that. Gregg himself doesn't understand the mystery. "Everything that touches your life, I mean sights, hear, smell, whatever, changes you in a certain way, you know," Gregg says. "You listen to a lot of different things. As well as listening to Ray Charles and B. B. King, I was also listening to Taj Mahal and Lightnin' Hopkins, Son House, and people like that. Little Milton Campbell was probably my favorite blues singer. He probably gets it down like nobody else."

The debut album was just as eclectic as the band that recorded it. The reworked songs were topnotch, and Gregg's originals were on an equal, if not higher, par. The album opened with an instrumental song off The Second Coming's set list, Spencer Davis's "Don't Want You No More." Two of Gregg's originals, "Not My Cross to Bear" and "Blackhearted Woman," quickly initiated the listener into the Brothers' music. "Trouble No More" demonstrated Duane's ability with the bottleneck guitar. Gregg's ethereal "Dreams," with Duane's slide enveloping his brother's vocals and breaking through for his own intricate contribution, carried the listener to an even higher level. That level is intensified with the closing song, "Whipping Post." Here all of the Brothers had the opportunity to show what they could do.

Thinking back on how the band had come together and the role Duane had offered him, Gregg was happy to have had the opportunity to contribute to the band and to the first Allman Brothers album. "[Duane] had the whole band assembled when I got there," reflects Gregg. "He called me and he said one of the best compliments I ever had. He said, 'Nobody here writes that much, and they don't sing that much. A little bit, but not much. I want you. With you [we can] round this thing up and send it somewhere. And I thought, let me hang up so I can get there. I took all my writings, which were about twenty-two songs. I think we used two of 'em. One of 'em was 'Dreams,' and one was 'It's Not My Cross to Bear.' I had already written those, but I don't know what happened to the other twenty. They probably came out in other songs. That's what most people . . . their theory on that is, when you're through with the stuff that you like and you'll be real tired at night and a song will hit you and you'll just say, 'Oh, screw it.' You know, when you'd be so tired. And I'm of the mind that it comes back to you." Gregg laughs, "I guess where the talent comes in is how to put it down on paper and set it to music, and not use too many words."

The vocals, the guitars, the drums, they are all there, bare and brutal. *The Allman Brothers Band* was an intense declaration of the band's philosophy and talent. It didn't go unnoticed. *Rolling Stone* magazine's Lester Bangs loved the album. He called the band, ". . . a white group who've transcended their schooling to produce a volatile blues-rock sound of pure energy, inspiration and love."[2]

While Walden was attempting to get the record out to those who would appreciate it, the Brothers were hitting the road to continue the effort to make people aware of their band and their music. "It took relentless touring to back up this album cause the debut album on Capricorn stopped at about 33,000 units," recalls Walden. "It probably would have discouraged most, but it didn't discourage us. It just sort of solidified the support behind the band. They continued to tour, and we continued to record and continued to try to spread the word about this band." "The band plugged themselves," says Gregg. "In 1970 I think we worked close to 300 nights." The hard work paid off. People were definitely beginning to listen to The Allman Brothers Band.

Whether on the road or at home recuperating, the boys listened to a variety of jazz, courtesy of Jaimoe. They started to experiment with jazz-influenced jams. While people sometimes came to the shows to see new guitar talent Duane Allman, the rest of the band was equally impressive. Each player was a consummate musician; there wasn't a slacker in the bunch. Gregg had begun to draw a lot of attention because of his vocals. There wasn't a better bass player than Berry Oakley. The twin drummers offered diverse and intricate backbeats and solos. Dickey Betts's guitar playing complemented everyone. And the songs were spectacular.

Dickey seemed to remain in Duane's shadow until he finally felt comfortable enough to share the stage equally with Duane. Although people may have initially come to see the boy genius, Dickey's talent couldn't be ignored. Dickey developed dual guitar riffs that kept even Duane on his toes. His songs were also a major contribution to the band's music. Duane wasn't stingy with his audience. He let Dickey rip and acknowledged Betts's contribution to the band, both on stage and off.

In the spring of 1970, Berry's wife, Linda, rented a huge, fourteen-room house in the historic district of Vineville near downtown Macon. Berry, Linda, and their baby daughter, Brittany, moved in with Duane; his girlfriend, Donna; and their baby daughter, Galadriel. Gregg and his girlfriend, Candace, Berry's sister, also moved in. Berry dubbed the house "The Big House." He wanted a place where everyone could stay, eat, and make music together. Berry bought a huge dining table and supervised the meals, as well as helped to plan and prepare them. He then purchased a pool table so everyone would stick around and socialize. According to Candace "Berry was the self-appointed father and master of ceremonies to everyone."[3]

As traditional as life in The Big House seemed to be, things were getting pretty wild on the road. The guys in the band were doing their share of drugs and certainly not turning away the volumes of groupies that they were now attracting. There was a thin line between acceptable behavior and full-on rock and roll debauchery, but the band was having a good time.

On April 30, 1970, Twiggs Lyndon stepped way over the line. Lyndon and Angelo Aliotta engaged in a fight as Lyndon attempted to collect money owed the band by the owner of Aliotta's Lounge in Buffalo. Lyndon stabbed Aliotta three times. Aliotta was dead within the hour. The band members saw to it that Lyndon was appointed a lawyer, then jumped in their Winnebago and took off for their next gig. Lyndon was eventually tried for the murder, found not guilty by reason of insanity, and sentenced to six months in a mental hospital. He was replaced as road manager by Willie Perkins. (Several years after the incident, Lyndon returned to the music scene as road manager for a band called The Dixie Dregs. While on tour with The Dregs in 1979, Lyndon was killed while sky diving when his parachute failed to open.)

The Brothers were concerned about Lyndon's fate, but they continued to impress audiences out on the road. Music, after all, was the focus. "We just try to make the audience be consumed by what we're doing and if we can make that magical kind of music happen," Dickey said. "They [the audience members] don't know what's happening exactly, except they know that we're really focused on what we're doing, and it sounds good, and the energy is good. What they will do is forget about this and forget about that and have fun, just simply have fun for two or three hours."[4]

By mid-1970, it was time to come off the road and record another Allman Brothers Band album. The second record would be titled *Idlewild South*, after Dickey's Georgia farm. The Brothers knew they needed a strong effort, and the recording of this next album took much longer than the first, almost seven months. It had been decided that the recording would be done at Criteria Studios in Miami under the production of Tom Dowd. The band had quite a few gigs scheduled and ended up flying down to Miami whenever it had a break from appearances. Dowd, through his association with Atlantic Records, believed that he was keyed in to what it was The Allman Brothers Band hoped to achieve on vinyl. He'd worked closely with Jerry Wexler as engineer to Wexler's production on important R&B recordings by Percy Sledge and others. Dowd was right: almost immediately he sensed the direction in which the members of The Allman Brothers Band wanted to take their music. Because of his studio expertise, Dowd appeared to be the producer who could help them get there. "He just heard us and took a real liking to us," remembers Gregg. "He kind of came and rescued us." Dowd's experience, coupled with his excellent ear, benefited the band in more ways than one. Dowd was definitely an asset to both Gregg's development and that of The Allman Brothers Band.

"Everything from Jackie Wilson to, well, name 'em, he's worked with 'em," says Gregg. "He worked for Charlie Byrd and John Coltrane, and, oh God, all of 'em. He's shown me a lot of different stuff. Cause see, I didn't play Hammond organ til I got in The Allman Brothers. I knew a little bit of piano, chords-wise. He showed me other versions of stuff like that, which this far down the line sounds like something real, real trite, but at the time he showed me, it really helped me. Like when you make a chord, you gotta use the first, third, and fifth. But you can put the first on top or you can put the third on the top. If you want to play a seventh, you can put the seventh in the middle or on the bottom. It really gives it that different sound, but it's still laying three chords and there's just another, different way to do it. That's how I got into that."

Idlewild South not only pays tribute to Dickey's farm by its title, but opens with a song he wrote to celebrate the family atmosphere of the band. "Revival" is a fast-paced number that fully utilizes both Dickey and Duane's guitars. Gregg's "Don't Keep Me Wonderin'" contains some outstanding harmonica playing by Thom Doucette. An exciting interlude is provided when Duane plays his slide off Doucette's harp.

The Allman Brothers Band, 1970. (Back, left to right) Gregg Allman, Jaimoe, Butch Trucks. (Front, left to right) Thom Doucette, Duane Allman, Dickey Betts, Berry Oakley. Credit: W. Robert Johnson.

Gregg wrote a song for the album that remains one of his favorites to this day. While Kim Payne received credit as co-writer, especially for his contribution of the line "The road goes on forever," Gregg's "Midnight Rider" is fairly autobiographical. The song's first appearance on *Idlewild South* is nothing short of riveting. Gregg's vocals were top-notch, and Berry's bass added a flavorful background. Duane's pedal-steel-like solo wrapped itself around the drums, and Dickey's guitar contribution was sweet and full-on. It is no wonder that "Midnight Rider" quickly became a fan favorite, both on record and in live performances. "I've always liked that song," says Gregg. "I don't seem to get tired of it."

Another showpiece featured on the album is Dickey's "In Memory of Elizabeth Reed," the song whose title he took off the Rose Hill Cemetery marker. "Liz Reed," as it has come to be known, is a long, spiritual, melodic jam that employs musical peaks and valleys that have been unrivaled in both their complexity and soulful simplicity. The real Elizabeth Reed, ironically, died just down the street from The Big House in 1935.

Berry's lead vocal on the blues number "Hoochie Coochie Man" is both fun and powerful, as is the guitar and bass work. The album closes out with Gregg's touching rendition of "Please Call Home." The album was outstanding. *Idlewild South* became The Allman Brothers Band's first hit record. The Allman Brothers Band was a success.

CHAPTER 3
Jacksonville, Florida
1970

Little did a quintet of high school buddies from the "Shantytown" area of Jacksonville, Florida, know that when they formed a garage band designed to play teen centers and skating rinks, they were beginning a journey that would result in great musical success, altered lifestyles, and ultimate personal tragedy. Ronnie Van Zant, the leader of the band, had a vision. His desire to make it in the music industry was so strong that those associated with his dream couldn't help but be as dedicated and as driven.

Born on January 15, 1948, to Marion and Lacy Van Zant, Ronnie was the second of the six Van Zant children. He was known as one of the meanest, toughest kids in town. According to his family, Ronnie felt destined to somehow dig his way out of the barrenness that constituted his lower-middle class neighborhood. Ronnie felt he could rise to great heights of achievement through the music that he heard in his head and felt in his soul.

Ronnie loved to sing, and he was particularly fond of singing in the bathtub. He immediately picked up on whatever songs he happened to hear, but that wasn't always a good thing. One time his mother had to go down to school to counsel young Ronnie against singing "Beer Drinkin' Daddy" in the classroom. While still in junior high school, Ronnie decided that music was going to be his life's work.

In 1964 Ronnie heard that some of his fellow students at Lakeshore Junior High were putting together a band named Us and holding auditions. Ronnie showed up and announced that he was their new singer. No one felt it would be particularly prudent to fight with him over his declaration, so it was quickly decided that he would be the band's vocalist. Fueled by the musical inspiration he found in the melodic rock ballads of Free's Paul Rodgers, Ronnie started to develop a plan.

He would surround himself with the best musicians he could find and through hard work, something that Ronnie had been thoroughly exposed to through family ties and Southern roots, that band would succeed.

Only one obstacle seemed to stand in Ronnie's way when it came to a career in music: his own adolescent dream of a career in the big leagues of baseball. Sandlot and Little and Minor League baseball was a major attraction to the boys in Jacksonville. There wasn't a lot to do other than fish and hang out with friends. Ronnie played American Legion ball with the Lakeshore Rebels as a centerfielder and one year managed to earn the highest batting average in the league.

One day at the baseball field, a ball that sixteen-year-old Ronnie hit bounced off the head of young Bob Burns, one of the neighborhood kids. He'd been watching Ronnie's team play in the company of his twelve-year-old friend, Gary Rossington. The blow knocked Burns unconscious. Ronnie felt terrible about the accident. Over the course of a few weeks, Ronnie befriended the younger boys. They discovered that they all shared an interest in music. Burns was a drummer and Rossington, a guitar player.

Gary Rossington, born in Jacksonville on December 4, 1951, had at first been drawn to baseball as a possible career. His ambition had been to play second base for the New York Yankees. But after seeing the Rolling Stones on television, he thought that a career in music might suit him better. He and Burns decided to form a band.

Rossington and Burns were at first interested in playing the drums, but soon realized that a band with two drummers and no guitar players wasn't going to be too successful. Gary switched to guitar after saving his money to purchase a Sears Silvertone. His sister was dating a local musician named Lloyd Phillips, who was happy to show Gary how to play his new instrument.

Bob Burns remained a drummer, Gary now played guitar, and Larry Jungstrom, a friend of theirs, had been recruited to play bass. They called their band You, Me and Him. Gary later purchased a Les Paul Sunburst, which he named after his widowed mother, Berneice. Gary was ready to rock and roll by the time he met Ronnie Van Zant.

Ronnie, Gary, and Bob decided to form a band. Baseball would have to wait. A trio seemed ineffective in the era of the powerhouse bands of the late 1960s. The boys realized that they would have a better chance of attracting attention if they added a second guitar player. They'd heard of teenage guitar picker Allen Collins and thought they would ask if he would like to join them.

Larkin Allen Collins, Jr. was born on July 19, 1952, in Jacksonville. After his parents divorced while he was quite young, Allen focused his need to keep his mind in incessant motion on learning everything he could about race cars. He spent many summer nights at the Jacksonville Raceway.

When Allen's interests grew to include music, Eva, his mother, saved to surprise him with his first guitar, a Sears Silvertone. Allen's stepmother, Leila, taught him to play it. By the time Allen met Ronnie, Gary, and Bob, he already knew that what he wanted out of life was to be a rock star.

Allen played his guitar tirelessly, learning all he could in preparation for the fulfillment of his dream. Everyone who heard the young player knew that he had a special talent. Bass player Leon Wilkeson later regarded Allen's contributions to music as "incredible." "I think if Eric Clapton were to be sitting in the audience watching him, he'd be a little nervous," says Wilkeson.

Ronnie and Gary thought Allen would be perfect for their new band and went looking for him. When the boys spotted him on the street and called to him, however, Allen took off running. He'd heard bad things about Ronnie and figured he'd done something that Ronnie intended to beat him up over. After Ronnie

and Gary caught up to Allen, they convinced him that they wanted nothing more than to ask him to be in their band.

It was decided that Larry Jungstrom would be a part of Ronnie, Gary, and Bob's new effort along with Allen Collins. After performing at local parties under a variety of names, including My Backyard and

One Percent, 1970. (Left to right) Larry Jungstrom, Ronnie Van Zant, Allen Collins, Bob Burns, Garry Rossington. Credit: W. Robert Johnson.

The Noble Five, Ronnie finally dubbed their venture One Percent. "Only 1 percent of people who try to play music for a living succeed," he told classmate Charlie Faubion. "And I plan to be in that 1 percent." Gary recalled that they decided on the name after seeing a Hell's Angels movie. The bikers had tattoos that said 1%, because, according to one of the characters in the movie, 1 percent of the world are bikers. Regardless of how the name came about, One Percent it was.

The boys of One Percent liked to hang out at The Comic Book Club. They would often stay until the wee hours of the morning soaking up the music. "Allen Collins had a paper route," Johnny Van Zant, Ronnie's brother, remembers. "My dad worked for the *Florida Times Union* too, as a branch manager and a paper delivery guy. [Allen] would come from The Comic Book Club and fall asleep in front of the branch in his car with all his papers. We'd be done throwing our paper route and come back and Allen would be laying there still asleep. So we'd have to help him throw his."

The time the boys spent at The Comic Book Club was invaluable. The talent was stellar, and there was a lot to be learned. The One Percent band members not only enjoyed the bands that passed through, but were sometimes given the opportunity to play. They practiced their craft and waited for a break. Like local heroes Duane and Greg Allman before them, One Percent played every recreation center and small club in North Florida that would have them for years. Their taste in cover songs primarily included those of The Yardbirds, Beatles, Stones, Creedence Clearwater Revival, Illinois Speed Press, and Cream. Free and Bad Company had always been favorites of Ronnie and Gary, and they started to write songs reflecting those influences. "[Ronnie] thought Paul Rodgers was one of the best singers in the world," recalls Ronnie's widow, Judy. "The drive that Free and Bad Company had in their songs, the heavy bass and the guitar, that's really where the Free thing came in."

Ronnie's commitment to succeed was confirmed when he recognized that his band's balls-y rock/blues/funk was welcomed and enthusiastically received wherever One Percent performed. Allen continued to astonish people with his talent, and Gary was already developing a signature sound. "A lot of people compare [Gary] to Mick Ralphs or Paul Kosoff of early Free," says Billy Powell, One Percent roadie and later Skynyrd piano player. "He listened to [them] a lot, and he kind of got that style . . . laid back picking style. He established his own identity with that."

A 1967 win in a Battle of the Bands contest resulted in the band landing a gig as the opening act for a popular flavor-of-the-day band, The Strawberry Alarm Clock. The date brought One Percent even more recognition as an up and coming rock band. People who were part of the local music scene started to pay attention.

In 1968, the boys saved and borrowed enough money to release a single on the Jacksonville-based Shade Tree label. The A side was a tune called "Need All My Friends," while the B side was a song the band wrote titled "Michelle." The record received a little local play, but not much was heard of it outside of Jacksonville.

Ronnie had married a girl named Nadine when he was eighteen, and by this time the couple had a baby daughter, Tammy. Ronnie's devotion to playing music every night proved to be too much of a strain on the relationship and eventually cost him his marriage. Ronnie was disappointed that the marriage had failed, but his dedication to making the band work grew ever stronger.

While attending Lee High School, Ronnie, Gary, and Bob had been warned repeatedly by Coach Leonard Skinner to cut their long hair or face the consequences. The boys would slick down their hair with Vaseline, but even that didn't seem to help. Their consistent refusal to comply with his demands didn't amuse Coach Skinner, and he suspended the boys from school on more than one occasion. The battle between Ronnie, Gary, and the coach was well known in local circles and was the cause of much insider snickering. Ronnie and Gary finally just quit going to school.

Allen had the same experience while attending Forrest High School. One day his father was called to take him to a barber to get him a "real" haircut. Because the ensuing disagreement between father and son seriously damaged their relationship, hair length was a sore spot with Allen as well.

One night in 1970, Ronnie decided on a whim to goof with the audience at a show at The Forrest Inn. He frequently kidded with the band by introducing them as something other than One Percent, and that night was no different. On this particular evening at The Forrest Inn, Ronnie evoked Coach Skinner's name and introduced the band as Leonard Skinner. The audience roared its approval. The new name seemed to represent what the band was willing to sacrifice to play their music. Changing some vowels to protect the innocent, One Percent was now Lynyrd Skynyrd.

CHAPTER 4

Pop Festivals, Georgia Rhythm, and "Layla"

1970

On July 4, 1970, the rock-loving community of Georgia came together in Byron for the 2nd Annual Atlanta Pop Festival. More than 300,000 people turned out to hear Jimi Hendrix, Bob Seger, Johnny Winter, Spirit, B.B. King, Richie Havens, and their hometown heroes, The Allman Brothers Band. Duane Allman was given a standing ovation as he tuned his guitar before the band's performance began.

The Brothers' appearance at the festival wasn't without its problems, though. The tarp covering the stage started to collapse and needed to be repaired while the band was still playing. The rest of the band moved away to allow the crew to complete the job, while Jaimoe and Butch Trucks launched extended drum solos. The quick thinking kept the crowd's attention firmly fixed on the stage. After this short inter-lude, the Brothers returned to captivate the audience for more than two hours. The Pop Festival was a success, and The Allman Brothers Band, a standout act.

The band started to receive requests to appear at a variety of major music festivals and events. The Brothers performed at The Isle of Wright Festival that year, and in December opened for Canned Heat at Bill Graham's Fillmore East. The Fillmore East appearance was magical. The Allman Brothers Band, called back for repeated encores, didn't relinquish the stage to the headliners until 3:30 in the morning.

About the time The Allman Brothers played the Fillmore East, the boys in Lynyrd Skynyrd—Allen Collins, Gary Rossington, and Ronnie Van Zant—were realizing that the time had come for their band to expand their base beyond their own backyard.

They'd been rehearsing in Bob Burns's carport, but the continual complaints from his neighbors had forced the band to look elsewhere for someplace to perfect its music. Someone turned the band members on to an isolated farm just outside of Jacksonville where a little shack on the property would soon become the home of Lynyrd Skynyrd. Because of its extreme temperatures—mostly hot—the band's new rehearsal hall was named "Hell House."

For the Lynyrd Skynyrd band members, 1970 turned out to be an eventful year. Allen Collins married Kathy Johns, and his bandmates were included in the wedding party. Kathy asked all of them, including her husband-to-be, to wear wigs to cover their long hair to appease her parents.

Something magical happened during Allen and Kathy's wedding reception. Allen had written a song with Ronnie Van Zant and wanted the band to play it during this special occasion. This was the first time "Freebird" was performed in public. Although the song played that day was a little different from the "Freebird" that would later rock the airwaves, a rock and roll classic had been born.

Also in 1970, Phil Walden's brother Alan decided that Lynyrd Skynyrd was promising enough to warrant his management attention. Walden took the band up to Muscle Shoals to cut a demo. Jimmy Johnson recorded several songs, including "Freebird." He was impressed with what he heard and encouraged the musicians to return to the studio when they could afford to record an album's worth of songs.

Lynyrd Skynyrd borrowed money from home and returned to Alabama to complete its album demo. Rickey Medlocke, another Jacksonville boy, was recruited to play the drums on two tracks, "One More Time" and "Coming Home." Medlocke also laid down some work on other songs, including "Freebird" and "Simple Man." The band would re-record these two songs at a later date. A bass player named Leon Wilkeson also participated in the session. Alan Walden shopped the finished product around, hoping a record label would see the band's potential and take the group under its wing. Capricorn was interested, but Ronnie didn't feel he wanted his band to be signed to a Southern label that was devoting most of its time promoting the South's largest act, The Allman Brothers Band.

A single, "I've Been Your Fool," was released on a local label to generate some interest in the music industry, but nothing came of it. The public wouldn't hear the remainder of the songs on the demo tapes until long after they were recorded.

The members of Lynyrd Skynyrd didn't, by any means, give up on their dream. They turned to creating new music.

Ronnie, Gary, and Allen had started to devote a lot of time to writing their own compositions by this time. Ronnie kept the band busy rehearsing original songs and perfecting its musical style. "Ronnie ran Skynyrd like Stalin ran Russia," says Wilkeson. "Very, very disciplined. He was a genius. He had a heart as big as all outdoors. He'd give you the shirt off his back, and the last place you wanted to be was on his bad side. But it always paid off."

Lynyrd Skynyrd started to play gigs outside of Jacksonville. Walden helped the band obtain bookings in various parts of Florida and up into Georgia. Soon they were playing in bars and high schools throughout the South. "We had this big, box truck that we used to haul our equipment in," remembers Rickey Medlocke. "We rode in the very back of it, and we'd stack equipment up toward the front. Then we'd put mattresses toward the back and lay on the mattresses. I remember one night we were leaving to go to Nashville to play a club called The Briar Patch. We were all in the back of the truck. The two roadies were up front driving the truck. We were all in the back, and Ronnie and I were looking down the highway. We had the door open a little bit, looking down Interstate 10 as we were leaving Jacksonville. I looked over at Ronnie and I said, 'Man, there's nothing like this, is there?' He goes, 'You know what, Rickey? One of these days we aren't going to have to worry about none of this bullshit. We'll have it made in the shade.'"

About the time Skynyrd was hitting the road and The Allman Brothers were starting to receive national attention, radio was embracing a couple of amicable pop songs. "Spooky" and "Traces" were light, straightforward, and fairly easy to perform. Consequently, they quickly became popular with cover bands. Just about anybody who listened to music was aware of the tunes. The songs had been recorded by an act called The Classics IV.

The Classics IV was composed of a group of musicians who had been hired by producer/songwriter Buddy Buie to perform his cache of pop ballads. The Classics IV wasn't so much a performing, touring band as a collection of excellent musicians Buie brought together to record some hits. Producer Bill Lowry had introduced Buie to Dennis Yost and the Classics IV.

"[Co-writer] J.R. Cobb and I literally set out to write standards," says Buie. "We were very big fans of Burt Bacharach and Hal David. Very big fans of the Tin Pan Alley writers. It was right in the middle of the whole English thing, and we wanted to write a standard. We devoted our songwriting careers at the time to trying to write a standard. It's kind of a lofty goal, and usually you don't reach your lofty goals. . . ."

Buie and Cobb's instincts were correct and both "Traces" and "Spooky" were huge. "I'm real proud of ['Traces,'] of the fact that it is the thirty-fourth most performed song in the history of broadcasting," says Buie. "To put that in perspective, 'My Way' is fifty." Buie might have been at a point in time in his career where he wanted to write standards, but the truth of the matter was he was in the business for the music, not for the rewards.

Buddy Buie was born in Dothan, Alabama, where he shared his love of music with Bobby Goldsboro, his boyhood friend. When Goldsboro formed a group called The Webs, Buie jumped in to manage the band and provide it with original material. After Goldsboro and his band started to realize some regional success, Buie not only continued to manage his friend, but also formed a business association with Goldsboro through a firm involved with concert promotion.

Country/pop pioneer Roy Orbison became acquainted with The Webs and asked if the members would be interested in becoming his touring band. Buddy renamed the band The Candymen and signed on to manage Orbison's tour. The Candymen included two young men who would figure prominently in Buie's future, Dean Daughtry and Robert Nix. Rodney Justo was soon added to the group on vocals. Two albums were recorded, *The Candymen* in 1967 and *Bring You Candypower* in 1968.

Buie eventually decided that he would like to produce, and he relocated to Atlanta. Daughtry and Nix quit The Candymen and cast their lot in with Buie to work with musicians Barry Bailey, Paul Goddard, and J.R. Cobb as Buie's session band. Daughtry and Cobb performed as part of the band, and the resulting Classic IV hits established Buddy Buie as a man who not only had an ear but knew how to get it done. Buie soon was producing and experiencing great success with B.J. Thomas and Billy Joe Royal.

"Back in around 1968, or '69, I started working with Buddy Buie," remembers engineer/producer Rodney Mills. "He started recording at Lefevre Sound, where

I was working. "[There were] several session musicians that Buddy used all the time, and sometimes after we'd get through with a recording session we'd just kind of let the band jam, instrumentally." Buie enjoyed producing but considered something that would more involve his sessionmen.

In 1970 Buie got an idea. "There had been the British invasion, and everybody was talking about Clapton and all these guitar players," Buie remembers. "I said, 'My goodness, I work everyday with guitar players. Barry Bailey and J.R. Cobb are incredible guitar players, and those guys kinda emulate the sound of Southern players, who are influenced by Black players, who go back to the church roots and all that, you know?'"

If Buie were to work with the session musicians that he'd been using on other people's records, they might enjoy some success as a band of their own. "We'd been making pop records, and I had a lot of success with The Classics IV," recalls Buie. "We had so many hits. This was a studio band, and we were just tired of doing it and wanted to really try to go together and not make records for other people, but make records for ourselves."

Buie thought the combination of Bailey and Cobb on guitar, Daughtry on keyboards, Goddard on bass, Nix on drums, and Justo on vocals could be hot. They could call themselves The Atlanta Rhythm Section. "My main goal was to have a band founded in songwriting," remembers Buie. "That the songs be as important as the playing. Cause we had good players and we had good writers. It was kind of a creative workshop."

The band would record at Buie's Studio One in Doraville, Georgia. Buie's studio was state of the art. Studio One would come to play a major role in what would soon be referred to as Southern Rock.

Miami's Criteria Studio was also becoming very popular. Jerry Wexler was now living in Miami and had been working with a band called The Dixie Fliers. He worked out an agreement with Mac Emmerman, the owner of Criteria, to provide Criteria with the first MCI tape machine and control panel. "We bought three of them because our engineer, Tom Dowd, helped these MCI people develop this first eight-track," recalls Wexler. "We bought one for Criteria Studios, one for Muscle Shoals, and one for our studios at Atlantic in New York. Soon, everybody else followed us down. The Bee Gees, Eric Clapton. . . . Before that, the only person of note who recorded at Criteria was James Brown, and they'd do a lot of commercials there. So that became a big recording center."

Duane Allman was about to become well acquainted with Criteria. He'd continued to expand his musical connections outside of the band, and he was delighted to play with any musician worth his time. The opportunity to play with Duane was something that most musicians who were familiar with his music availed themselves of in an instant.

Delaney Bramlett, of the duo Delaney and Bonnie, had been in Europe playing with Eric Clapton for several years. Delaney was unaware of Duane and his impact. "I was about to produce my first record on Delaney and Bonnie," remembers Jerry Wexler. "I was working out of Criteria Studios and living in Miami at the time. Delaney called me and said, 'I need a slide player on a couple of the tunes. Could you get Ry Cooder?' Ry couldn't make it. He was busy. So I said, 'Delaney, don't worry about Ry. I've got somebody that you'll be very happy with.' So I brought Duane Allman in to play on this record, the record called *From Delaney to Bonnie With Love*."

Meanwhile, Delaney's old band, which consisted of drummer Jim Gordon, bass player Carl Radle, and keyboardist Bobby Whitlock, was in London working with Eric Clapton and George Harrison on Harrison's album *All Things Must Pass*. After completing their session with Harrison, Clapton, Gordon, Whitlock, and Radle began playing local clubs as Derek and The Dominos.

"It was while we were in the studio doing [*From Delaney to Bonnie With Love*] that Eric came down to Criteria to record with The Dominos and [Clapton and Duane Allman] met in the studio," remembers Jerry Wexler. The next thing, of course, was "Layla."

Tom Dowd had been called in to produce Clapton's next album, and Dowd and Clapton joined forces at Criteria in the summer of 1970. Duane had been a fan of Eric Clapton's for a long time. Clapton had been intrigued with Duane ever since he heard Duane's guitar on 'Hey Jude.' Dowd knew that both guitarists were anxious to meet each other and was happy to arrange such a meeting when The Allmans came to town for a gig in August.

Duane and Clapton, at times accompanied by others in the band yet mostly by themselves, spent the next day and night together. They jammed, explored, and celebrated the rhythm and blues (R&B) and blues music they both loved. Dowd was able to record some of the magic laid down during that first jam. Gregg Allman would later comment that the first jam with Clapton was some of the best guitar playing of Duane's life.

Clapton enjoyed jamming with Duane, but he was there, after all, to record an album. Duane was ecstatic when Clapton asked him to contribute some of his wizardry to the song "Tell The Truth." Duane played second lead with his slide, while Clapton was inspired enough to engage in some slide playing himself. The second song, "Key to the Highway," was recorded almost by accident. The tape wasn't rolling during the first run-through of the song until Dowd noticed the omission and quickly had the engineer jump on it. The first take was perfect.

At this point Clapton seemed committed to sharing most of the album's guitar leads with Duane. Duane was thrilled. He thought that he would be playing on only one or two songs. Duane interrupted his work with Clapton only for a few days to play some dates with his own band. He returned to record several more songs for the album, which would later be titled *Layla & Other Assorted Love Songs*. Included in that session was the title number, "Layla." Clapton, as is now known, had written the song about his despair over his love for George Harrison's wife, Patti. The song was written as a soft, slow ballad, but when Duane heard Clapton play it, he felt that the song lacked energy. Duane felt the song had more potential as a mercurial rock and roll hymn resolutely blanketed in the desolation and frustration of Clapton's unrequited passion. Duane played the song's signature riff, while Clapton's haunting vocals wrapped themselves around Duane's driving, yet poignant leads. It would be here in "Layla" that Duane's counter-melody would be compared to the tears of a bird, foreshadowing Lynyrd Skynyrd's future dedication of "Freebird" to their guitar hero.

The end result of the recording of "Layla" was nothing short of a masterpiece. Those who knew Duane Allman had been the man in the lead were delighted that the skinny guitar player from the South had at last been given a forum for his unbridled talent.

CHAPTER 5

Success

1971

A decision was made when Duane Allman returned to The Allman Brothers from his Dominos session. It was time for another album. The band members felt strongly that the only way they were going to be given their due as an exciting and innovative entity would be to record a live record. The Brothers were fine in the studio, but they really cooked in front of an audience, improvising and playing off one another.

Bill Graham was happy to involve his Fillmore East for the occasion. The hall was booked for March 12 and 13, 1971. Four shows would be taped by Criteria's Tom Dowd, and the band would decide later which songs to use.

One night the band played until the very early hours of the morning. They were exhausted by the Fillmore effort, but they felt great. For Gregg Allman, the recording of the Fillmore concerts was a turning point. "I guess the first time I realized I was in it for good was when we got to the Fillmore," Gregg says. "It was that long. I just thought, 'Well, you know, this'll probably go on for a couple of years, and I'll either go off playing clubs, and other people doing other kinds of business, and hopefully some of us saved what money we got.' And next thing you know we had another damn record on the charts."

The Allman Brothers were beginning to recognize their niche. Although they would always strive to be more creative, they felt their years of struggling musically finally fell into place. "We were becoming accepted by the audience," remembers Gregg. "That was the best thing about the whole thing because I started feeling like

The Allman Brothers Band, ca. 1971. (Standing in back)
Berry Oakley. (Front, left to right) Butch Trucks,
Dickey Betts, Duane Allman, Gregg Allman, Jaimoe.
Credit: Kirk West/Allman Brothers Band Archives.

we had made some progress. Maybe had our foot in the door. No better feeling than that."

The Allman Brothers Band At Fillmore East is one of the classic rock and roll live albums, if not *the* classic rock and roll live album. Everything came together for The Allman Brothers Band that weekend; the members were able to demonstrate exactly what it was that made them the icons they were well on their way to becoming.

Willie McTell's "Statesboro Blues," the song that inspired Duane to put a bottle on his finger and play slide, ignites the album as the opening cut. The Elmore James classic "Done Somebody Wrong" follows, with excellent alternate leads from Duane and Dickey Betts and powerful, soulful vocals by Gregg. Harpist Thom Doucette made an appearance with a harmonica solo.

An extended organ solo focused on Gregg's newly acquired keyboard talents for T-Bone Walker's "Stormy Monday." While Gregg was proficient on guitar, he claims he switched to the organ out of necessity. "There was a need-be factor," he says. "There started getting to be so many guitar players around me that I had to change over or I was pretty well out of the band."

"You Don't Love Me" is a lengthy piece of funk that gave several of the musicians the opportunity to strut their stuff. Duane's solo on this old blues number was exceptional. An eerie quiet came over the audience as it listened in rapt appreciation of Duane's talent, and the silence is palpable on the record.

"Hot 'lanta" is an original composition that enabled Berry Oakley to show what he could do through his animated and unqualified bass guitar playing. Berry worked hard at perfecting his craft. The amazing twists and turns he demonstrates on this song clearly illustrate that he, even at this early juncture, was one of the best bass players in rock and roll.

"In Memory of Elizabeth Reed" follows, grown even more otherworldly when presented live. Dickey and Duane play off one another as if involved in a mysterious and intimate coupling. Duane's solo is intricate and soul-piercing. "Whipping Post" is a showcase for Gregg's guttural, spiritual vocals. "Mountain Jam" closes out the album.

After Dowd assembled *At Fillmore East*, it contained several lengthy cuts. Because of this, producer Phil Walden decided to make it a double album. "Atlantic informed me that they weren't interested in a double LP by a band that had yet to sell 100,000 albums," remembers Walden. "Then I informed them that we had this brilliant marketing scheme that we wanted to sell it for $6.98 because we were trying to project this image of The Allmans as sort of the people's band. We felt that a special price for a developing band like The Allmans would be a good marketing tool."

It took some fancy talking with Jerry Wexler, but Walden and Capricorn were finally convincing enough to obtain their backing. The only condition was a reassurance that they would make a special arrangement with the song publishers so that expenses could be limited. There came a question from Atlantic that perhaps the longer songs on the album should be edited. "A short song would probably be six or seven minutes," recalls Walden. "But we convinced him that that was all part of The Allman Brothers."

The album was released in July and was an immediate national hit. *At Fillmore East* not only was a showpiece for The Allman Brothers Band, but a masterwork that would soon find its way into the record collection of nearly every serious rock and roll aficionado. "From that point on," says Walden, "It was a pretty dramatic rise by The Allmans."

The Allman Brothers Band was happy with the results of their first albums, but the road was where they felt they belonged at that moment in their career. The Brothers played more than 275 dates in 1971. Joe Dan Petty, Willie Perkins, and Tuffy Phillips had joined the crew by this point, but the tours were long and hard and life with The Brothers unpredictable. Kim Payne had been shot by a police officer and charged with resisting arrest in Macon the week after the band had returned from recording the *Fillmore* album. Payne wasn't able to be as much help as he wanted, but he did what he could.

On March 22, the band and three of the roadies were arrested in Jackson, Alabama, for possession of heroin, marijuana and PCP. The charges were later reduced to disturbing the peace. The band paid more than $5,000 in fines and expenses related to the charge.

Bill Graham felt that the Fillmores had run their course, and the time had come for them to be closed. He asked The Brothers to headline the closing of Fillmore East the weekend of June 26, 1971. The show on the night of the 26th turned out to be another legendary date in rock and roll history. The band members were totally in sync after taking the stage at 2 A.M. and didn't quit playing until nearly 7 in the morning. Some of the members of the band and people in the audience felt it was a near religious experience. "It was a big jam," remembers Gregg. "People would go on and off stage. We played about five or six hours that night. That was probably the height of The Allman Brothers Band . . . the original Allman Brothers Band as we know it."

After playing the Fillmore, Duane was asked to stay in New York City to add his guitar to some Herbie Mann tracks. Mann was working on his "Push Push" album. Duane had long been a fan of Mann's and enjoyed being on hand for the session.

On the weekend of July 4, 1971, The Allmans were scheduled to appear at the Newport Jazz Festival in Rhode Island. The band was honored to be on the Sunday night bill with such acts as B.B. King, Ray Charles, T-Bone Walker, and Joe Turner. Unfortunately, a riot broke out during the show the night before The Allman Brothers Band's appearance. The remaining days of the festival were canceled.

The band members were disappointed that they hadn't been able to perform at Newport, but their frustration at having been denied the opportunity to play at so prestigious an event turned to happiness when *At Fillmore East* was released and appeared at #13 on the *Billboard* Album Chart. The record sold as quickly as it climbed the chart. Within weeks The Allman Brothers Band had its first gold record.

About the time The Allman Brothers Band was celebrating its gold record, Capricorn Records was signing a band from Florida called Cowboy. Originally called Easy, Cowboy consisted of Scot Boyer, Tommy Talton, and Pete Kowalke on guitar; George Clark on bass; Bill Pillmore on piano; and Tomm Wynn on drums.

"I auditioned Cowboy in Johnny Sandlin's living room," recalled Walden. "They set up and just played acoustically and sang beautiful songs and these incredible harmonies. These were some fabulously talented young musicians." The band had a Poco/Nitty Gritty Dirt Band sound, full of beautiful melodies and lots of acoustic guitar. The members of Cowboy also knew how to rock out, although most of the songs they selected to put on their upcoming album were either entertaining, carefree tunes or gentle melodies.

Although Cowboy didn't take to the road with as much activity as its contemporaries, the band's appearances were well received. "In a way," wrote C.A. Bustard in the Richmond *Times-Union* of Cowboy's July 25, 1974, show at the Mosque, "Cowboy has treated American rock stylization in much the same way that Traffic has developed on the British model. The jazz flavoring is surprisingly effective, even in the horniest of the group's songs."

Capricorn released the Johnny Sandlin-produced *Reach For The Sky* in February, 1971. Unfortunately, Cowboy soon dissolved. Several of the members, Boyer and Talton in particular, became important Southern Rock session players and songwriters. Boyer and Talton later released an album of their own.

In addition to Cowboy, Capricorn was looking to break in another act. Wet Willie was about to begin the process of making their mark on the Southern Rock scene. From today's vantage point, it seems there isn't a Southern musician alive who isn't a fan of the "blue-eyed soul" band from Alabama. "A really great band," says The Outlaws' Hughie Thomasson. "A fun band. Their songs were just fun. There's no other way to describe it. They had a good time playing, you could tell it. It carried over to the audience." Wet Willie not only cared about its audience, but loved the music the band developed and offered as their own.

Jimmy Hall was the frontman of the band that would become known as Wet Willie. Jimmy knew from an early age that he wanted to be on stage performing music. His family had always been involved in the musical events of the Baptist church in Mobile, and his mother often played piano there. "She played all styles, from honky-tonk and boogie-woogie, to church hymns and gospel, and got all of us kids involved in church choir," remembers Jimmy. "I was interested in singing from a very early age. I did *HMS Pinafore* in the fifth grade. I had a lead in that, and the bug bit me pretty hard right there. I knew I could do that, enjoy it, and was pretty good at it."

Jimmy's brother Jack became involved in some local garage-type bands. Jimmy hung around his brother, learning all he could. Jack had decided that making music was the way he wanted to spend his free time, and soon Jimmy made up his mind that he did, too. Jimmy picked up the saxophone in the seventh grade and joined the school marching band.

Both Hall brothers were influenced by the myriad of musical styles that they'd been hearing, everything from classic rhythm and blues (R&B), to soul music, to British rock and roll. "I considered some of the old blues to be recycled through the British invasion," recalls Jimmy. "The Rolling Stones, The Yardbirds, some of those groups. I liked the way they presented it. It was hip. I liked the bravado about them. They were also like an encyclopedia of R&B and blues. I think they turned a lot of kids on to people like Willie Dixon and Muddy Waters because they were recycling, doing some of the old blues thing and making it accessible to the general public. It made me go back and look at the originals."

On Jimmy's sixteenth birthday, brother Jack bought him a Chromatic harmonica. Jimmy learned how to play it, blues style, by listening to Jimmy Reed, Slim Harpo, and Little Walter. He later studied contemporaries like Johnny Winters. "[Johnny] proved that here was a white guy, as Stevie Ray Vaughn was later, who just blew everybody away," recalls Jimmy Hall. "Had a real feel for roots music, for blues." John Hammond and Taj Mahal would also influence Jimmy's playing.

Jimmy and Jack formed a band they originally called Fox, changing its name to Wet Willie in 1969. The band consisted of five excellent musicians: Jimmy on vocals, harp, and sax; Jack on bass guitar; Rick Hirsch on guitar; John Anthony on keyboards; and Lewis Ross on drums.

Rick Hirsch had a friend named Frank Friedman who was a staff writer with Capricorn Records. Friedman had been encouraging the band to come to Macon and check out the musical atmosphere. "We thought about other scenes, Muscle Shoals, other producers, but Capricorn Records, The Allman Brothers. . . ." remembers Jimmy Hall.

Wet Willie developed some material to present in a showcase but lacked a full set of originals. Frank Friedman helped the group round out its presentation. When Phil Walden and Frank Fenter heard the band, they were knocked out.

In 1970 Wet Willie got the call. Would the group be willing to relocate to Macon and sign with Capricorn Records? Oh yeah. When Walden entered the picture, the Wet Willie band members felt that they'd teamed up with someone who would help them achieve their dream of gaining entry into the professional world of music on a higher level. "He was a man with a vision," says Jimmy Hall. "Phil was always miles ahead of the competition in a lot of ways. He fueled the fire and helped everybody move along."

Looking for something different from his in-house-produced Allmans, Walden called on Eddie Offord to produce Wet Willie's first album. Offord had been working with Emerson, Lake and Palmer and Yes, but was very interested in recording the Southern boogie band. Walden and Offord thought that they might be looking at America's version of The Rolling Stones.

Wet Willie was released in 1971. The record was composed of Wet Willie originals, supplemented by some of Frank Friedman's songs. Although the album was well recorded and well played, it never really took off like Capricorn and the band had hoped it would.

Wet Willie, in the meantime, had started making live appearances. The band members took to the road nonstop, playing their brand of R&B for anyone who would come to hear them. Over the course of their time together, the members of Wet Willie would tour with The Allman Brothers Band, The Grateful Dead, Grand Funk Railroad, and Aerosmith, among others.

When Wet Willie wasn't on the road, the band members were home in Macon. They all lived together in a large two-story house. The band enjoyed the musicians' community and spent time at the Big House with The Allman Brothers Band. "The camaraderie among the bands was pretty comfortable," remembers Jimmy Hall. "It was a brotherhood of people there who helped each other when you needed some guidance in a certain way or needed advice on equipment. If we were on the same show together, 'If you need help with anything . . . we'll help you unload your truck or we'll jump on stage and jam with you if you're so inclined.' There was a lot of interaction that way."

The boys in Wet Willie were welcomed by Mama Louise and her H & H Restaurant as yet another contingent of young people who needed her help. "Food is nurture for the soul," reflects Jimmy. "Food represents home, welcome, a lot of things. Well, to a lot of guys who were away from their home and hanging out in town with not a lot going on, this restaurant . . . which could have been a cultural closed door, a black restaurant with soul food. The Allmans Brothers had opened the door and would go in there and eat and Mama Louise . . . if you didn't have enough money, she didn't care. She made sure everybody ate, and you paid her later. She'd take care of you. She was a patron of the arts, and it became a social hangout. It had one of the best jukeboxes that I can remember."

The community of Macon outside the Capricorn coalition was at first cautious in its view of the musicians. "Macon wasn't a big city," says Hall. "Wet Willie used to do concerts in the park on Sundays [in Macon]; we used to do that in Mobile. We had to break the ice. The Allman Brothers helped do that. There were always things that we did for the community, fund-raisers, giving back to the community. It wasn't long before the environment there welcomed all of us long-haired musicians into the city as a viable part of the community." Within a very short time, Macon, Georgia, was becoming the musical capitol of Southern Rock.

CHAPTER 6

Tragedy

1971

The private lives of the members of The Allman Brothers Band were becoming as intricate as their musical career. Duane Allman had divorced Donna, his common-law wife, and had moved in with Dixie Meadows, a woman from Mississippi. In September Gregg was married to Shelley Kay Winters. Dickey Betts was in love with Sandy Wabegijig, and the other band members were involved in their own relationships. Berry Oakley remained married to Linda.

Gregg had been introduced to heroin earlier in the year, but Duane wouldn't allow any intravenous drug use among the band members or the roadies. Heroin was allowed only as long as it was inhaled. The same rule applied to cocaine. As with most rock and roll bands, there was a surplus of women, drugs, and partying, but the band remained focused on the music.

In October, 1971, The Allman Brothers went down to Criteria Studios to record some tracks for its next album. One of the songs the guys laid down during that visit was "Little Martha," a short instrumental Duane had written for Dixie. The music wasn't flowing in the studio as well as it had in the past. For maybe the first time, drugs seemed to be getting in the way of the creativity.

Duane had been in New York City visiting with his friend John Hammond and headed back to Macon to attend Linda Oakley's October 21 birthday party. Dixie Meadows and Candace Oakley spent the morning of the 21st baking Linda a birthday cake at Duane and Dixie's house while Duane slept in. He decided to join the women when they went over to the Big House in the afternoon and followed them on his Harley.

After helping the kids carve jack-o-lanterns in the backyard, Duane and Dixie decided to go home to change for the evening's festivities. Berry and Candace decided to go with them to pick up the cake and Linda's presents. Duane rode back on his motorcycle, and Dixie and Candace followed him. Berry brought up the rear in his car but was preoccupied and took a wrong turn somewhere along the way.

The speed limit was 35 MPH on Hillcrest Avenue, but Duane loved to push his big Harley Sportster and might have been traveling faster. Dixie and Candace could see Duane a couple of car lengths ahead of them when he reached the intersection of Hillcrest and Bartlett. They also saw a flatbed truck, which was determined later to have been driven by Charles Wertz. The truck was just beginning to make a left-hand turn in front of Duane's motorcycle.

Duane saw the truck and swerved to allow the truck room to maneuver its way past him. It looked like this could be accomplished without any problem until the truck suddenly stopped in the middle of Duane's lane. There was little for him to do to avoid hitting it. Duane attempted to scoot pass the truck, but he hit some part of it as he sped past. Both Duane and the bike bounced into the air, twisting and turning. The motorcycle landed on top of Duane and then skidded about 90 feet.

Dixie and Candace ran to help Duane and found him unconscious. Remarkably, he appeared to have only a few scratches and maybe a broken arm. Candace ran from house to house attempting to get someone to call an ambulance; eventually Duane was taken to the Medical Center of Central Georgia. After he was examined, it was determined that he had massive internal injuries, including a ruptured coronary artery, a lacerated liver, a collapsed lung, and severe head trauma.

Duane was rushed into surgery while his friends gathered in the hospital, anxious to be told that everything was going to be all right. Berry paced and prayed while Gregg was summoned to the hospital. Duane's body couldn't be repaired. Within three hours he was dead. He was just twenty-four years old. Gregg was stunned and unbelieving when Red Dog gave him the news. Duane, his brother, his surrogate father, his mentor, his friend, was gone.

The other guys in the band were equally dazed, but no one was more devastated than Berry. Although they'd known each other only a few years, Duane had been like a brother to Berry. "Berry was a fine bass player and a fine organizer," says Gregg. "He always kept us laughing and kept us very motivated. He was a real motivated guy. He really was. If there wasn't some stuff happening, he'd start it. That's why him and my brother were so tight. That's why the day my brother died, Berry died the same day. Just a matter of time, though."

No charges were filed against Charles Wertz. Wertz claimed that when he entered the unpaved road at Bartlett, he stopped to avoid the potholes ahead of him. He thought that Duane had time to slow down while he maneuvered his way around the holes in the road.

Duane's casket was placed in a room at Snow's Memorial Chapel. The funeral was held in the chapel on November 1. Hundreds of Duane's friends attended, many having flown in to Macon from all over the country. Duane's Les Paul guitar was set up in front of his casket, and the band's equipment was placed behind it. Jerry Wexler delivered the emotional eulogy.

The remaining members of The Allman Brothers Band, Gregg, Jaimoe, Berry, Butch, and Dickey, accompanied by their old friend, harp player Thom Doucette, walked to the front of the chapel, picked up their instruments, and began playing "The Sky is Crying." They followed that song with several numbers Duane would have loved: "Key to the Highway," "Stormy Monday," and "In Memory of Elizabeth Reed."

The band was joined by Delaney Bramlett and Dr. John as everyone joined hands to sing "Will The Circle Be Unbroken." Gregg sang two songs by himself, then the rest of the band joined him for the final song. Dickey reached over and picked up Duane's guitar. The band played "Statesboro Blues." When the final strains of the music had faded, Dickey placed the Les Paul back in front of the casket. Duane's friends and family were now left with their memories. Because of legal difficulties regarding Duane's estate between Duane's ex-wife, Donna, and his current love, Dixie, Meadows, his burial was deferred.

The Allman Brothers Band had been scheduled to play Carnegie Hall on November 25. The musicians flew up to New York as a five-piece band to keep their commitment. They knew that Duane would have wanted them to play the date.

The thought of replacing Duane was out of the question. Dickey would play lead guitar for most of the songs now instead of sharing that position with Duane. The band returned to the studio to finish its new record, although many of the songs that would appear on that album were songs that Duane had recorded with them or songs that had been taken from the *Fillmore* tapes. The Allman Brothers Band would endure.

CHAPTER 7

Reaching For the Charts

1972

In 1971, Lynyrd Skynyrd member Ronnie Van Zant married Judy Seymour, a Waycross, Georgia, woman who had been introduced to him through Gary Rossington and Skynyrd's roadie Dean Kilpatrick. Judy had been sharing a house on Riverside Drive with Dean and another woman, just down the street from the Allmans' early residence, "the Green House." Judy's house was called " the Gray House."

Ronnie was working days at his brother-in-law's auto parts store when Gary introduced him to Judy. They dated for awhile and eventually moved in together. Ronnie was fortunate to find someone who not only understood his ambition, but supported it wholeheartedly. "I always said that if you're going to be involved with a musician, you might as well just know right from the get-go that that's the most important thing in their life," says Judy. "You have to accept that, and if you can't, then you need to get out because you can't take it away from them. It would kill them."

Dean Kilpatrick was a special and unique individual who believed in Ronnie's band from the beginning of the dream. Dean had met the band through its appearances at The Comic Book Club, one of his hangouts. The band members enjoyed hanging with Dean because he had varied interests and always had something to talk about.

Dean, born May 30, 1949, was an artist, and the Jacksonville music community enjoyed the pictures Dean drew of various band members and their friends. Art wasn't just a casual hobby with Dean. He'd spent several months working in a monastery in Florence, Italy, restoring damaged works of art as part of former First Lady Jackie Kennedy's Committee for the Restoration of Italian Art.

Dean knew how to dress, and the guys were always asking him for pointers about their clothing. And about women—the ladies loved Dean. He wrote songs, but sharing them with the public wasn't something Dean felt comfortable with. Now he was Skynyrd's Number One roadie.

Ronnie's commitment to his new family, along with support from Judy, meant he had to work even harder if he was going to take his career a step further. "That was in the days when long hair wasn't cool," recalls Judy. "He'd have to put this wig on everyday to go to work to sell auto parts and then he'd come home and at night they would rehearse. It was real frustrating to him. I just said, 'Well, I'll work. You quit. You concentrate on the music.' We struggled for awhile, but it worked out fine." Ronnie Van Zant was now a full-time musician.

Even though the members of The Atlanta Rhythm Section had given up doing sessions, they were full-time musicians. It wasn't long before Buddy Buie and his band struck a recording deal with MCA. The band was finally able to record its own record.

When *Atlanta Rhythm Section*, the group's first album, was released in early 1972, it received mixed reactions from within the music industry. There was no argument that the band was composed of some excellent musicians, but the fact that they'd been studio musicians and that the band had been "manufactured" rankled some people. Still, what difference did it make *how* the band came together? The proof was in the music, and there could be no denying that the music was good.

The Rhythm Section's Barry Bailey had long been recognized as an exceptional guitar player. He started playing on a Sears Silvertone at the age of twelve and later performed with high school bands, such as The Imperials, The Vons, and Wayne Loguidice and the Kommotions. By 1966 Bailey was opening for The Yardbirds and jamming with Bo Diddley and The Byrds. His amazingly swift fingers had been duly noted by every musician who happened to cross his path.

Band member Dean Daughtry has attended Huntington College on a music scholarship before becoming involved with The Candymen. The experience with The Candymen served the other musicians in the band well, as did their long list of session work. All the members of The Atlanta Rhythm Section were respected as being the masters of their craft. It would be interesting to see what they would come up with next.

Wet Willie had already recorded its second effort. Eddie Offord had returned to cut *Wet Willie II* in 1972. The band cooked when they performed in concert, yet the albums lacked the magic that they so easily conjured up onstage. The band had recently introduced Donna Hall and Ella Avery, two backup singers called The Williettes.

The first two albums sold moderately, mostly to those who had the opportunity to hear the band live. Everybody seemed to like the band, but the members of Wet Willie still needed that hit record to get noticed as contenders. They weren't about to give up. The band's third album, *Drippin' Wet*, was recorded live at New Orleans' Warehouse on New Year's Eve, 1972. Capturing the band's live sound and releasing it on record were just what Wet Willie needed. *Drippin' Wet* hit the charts. The Wet Willie sound was definitely Southern Rock, but it was also a hybrid of R&B, blues, rock, and funk. "We called it rock and soul back then," says Jimmy Hall. "It was very up, feel good, party down music."

Phil Walden enjoyed working with Wet Willie. "All these bands," Walden recalls, "were just really very talented, very nice people. Everybody just sort of fit in to our little family. Jimmy Hall and his brother . . . their sister worked as a receptionist at Capricorn before she finally went on the road as a Williette. She used to work at the office during the daytime and answer phones and then at night do session work. We've always attracted bands that have other members from the same family. Allman Brothers, Marshall Tucker, Wet Willie . . . I never really thought about that, but in the '70s we really were that way."

Capricorn was about to invite another family-oriented band into its family-oriented company.

Toy and Tommy Caldwell, ca. 1955. Credit: Abbie Caldwell Collection.

CHAPTER 8

Spartanburg, South Carolina

1965-1972

Marshall Tucker was one of those brother acts that was about to
hit Macon and the country in a big way. One of the fun things about
Marshall Tucker is that no one in the band has that name. Just as
Lynyrd Skynyrd has to contend with uninformed fans claiming to
like "his" music, so, too, do the Tuckers. But I'm getting ahead
of the story.

Like The Allman Brothers Band, Marshall Tucker was formed and led by two
brothers, named Toy and Tommy Caldwell. Also like the Allmans, the founding
siblings considered their bandmates to be part of their musical family. There wasn't
a marginal musician in the bunch. The Caldwells' idea of putting together a group
to play a magical blend of rock and roll, country, jazz, and blues was an idea well
received by the boys who would play with them.

Toy and Tommy Caldwell's roots were set firmly in the soil of Spartanburg,
South Carolina. The Caldwell family included music as a part of its day-to-day life.
Toy P. Caldwell, grandfather to Toy and Tommy, played banjo, piano, guitar, and even
xylophone. The boys' parents, Virginia and Toy Sr., sang together on the radio as
part of station WSPA's entertainment family. Toy Sr. played guitar and wrote honest
and heartfelt country melodies. But this wasn't the only legacy he passed along to
his sons.

Toy Jr., born on November 13, 1947, was the oldest of the three sons of Virginia
and Toy Sr. Toy watched his daddy's playing closely. As soon as he was old enough
to hold a guitar, he emulated his father's unique thumb-picking style. Toy kept his

guitar close at all times, and he learned to play the songs of Hank Garland, a Nashville songwriter and noted session musician. The teenage Toy would become lost in the reverie of the songs he was either attempting to learn or already creating on his own.

Toy's talent for writing surfaced early on. In his early teens, he and his friends used to spend time on nearby Silver Lake. His buddies would throw out a word or subject, and Toy would come up with a song that centered on it. Toy would often skip school to sneak away to Greenville to hang out and listen to guitarist/keyboard player Rudy "Blue Shoes" Wyatt. Wyatt would be instrumental in helping to land Toy's first studio opportunity.

Toy's passion for the guitar was of great interest to his younger brother, Tommy. Tommy, born November 9, 1949, had learned his father's thumb-picking as well. Tommy grabbed Toy's guitar on those rare occasions that it wasn't in Toy's hands to try out a few of his own rock and roll ideas. It didn't take long for the boys' parents to realize that the only way they were going to keep peace in the house was to get Tommy his own guitar. Tommy decided to devote his efforts to learning the bass. He soon became proficient on the bass, but wasn't truly happy unless he could participate in Toy's musical activities. Soon the friendly competition between the two brothers elevated into a need for each of them to form his own garage band. The bands rehearsed mostly cover songs, with Toy's band throwing in some original material.

Toy had started singing, but guitar was his first love. "He had a strange style," Paul Hornsby later commented. "He didn't play with a pick like 99 percent of the other guitar players. He used his thumb. That was very strange because there's a lot of things you can't do with your thumb. You don't get that clarity of sound, like a lot of your chord work and stuff. It was a unique thing. He attacked a guitar. He had a distinctive sound, and he didn't play like anybody else."

In the seventh grade Toy put together a unit for a junior high school talent show called "Magar's Madmen" with Kenny Magar and Franklin Wilkie. The Motown-influenced Ramblers became Toy's first band. Another Spartanburg picker named George McCorkle was brought in when Magar left to pursue his own projects.

George McCorkle's roots were in 1940s swing music, the music his parents preferred to listen to. Western Swing pioneer Bob Wills and the sweet harmonies of the McGuire Sisters trio were often heard around the McCorkle house. When

George first picked up the guitar, he studied the blues guitar of B.B. King, the surf-sound instrumentals of The Ventures, and the sophisticated country/classical picking of Chet Atkins. He started writing his own music by the age of nine. When the British invasion came along, the teenager listened to The Beatles, The Rolling Stones, and Jimi Hendrix. McCorkle brought a little bit of everything to The Ramblers.

Robbie Cobb, Reggie Gosnell, Wallace Huckaby, and David McCutcheon joined Toy, Wilkie, and McCorkle in the new group. A lot of rehearsals were held. Although a few dates were played, the band never really got off the ground.

By 1965 Toy, McCorkle, Wilkie, and McCutcheon decided to recruit drummer Ross Hannah and form a band that would reflect the music of the day. The Ramblers became The Rants. The boys were only junior high school students yet they managed to land quite a few fraternity party gigs. The Rants played excellent South Carolina beach music, and their reputation as a party band grew.

Wilkie and Toy's friend Rudy Wyatt was regularly playing the Club Jarmata with a group called The Wylde. Wyatt fixed up The Rants with two friends of his who worked at the Mark V Recording Studio in Greenville. The band went into the studio to cut a demo and recorded "Seven Lonely Days" and "Hey Little Girl," among other songs.

Mark V's Willie Hammond introduced John Hurley to The Rant's sound. Hurley was producing The Gentrys and working with Dusty Springfield at the time. Hurley liked what he heard and asked The Rants to record a couple of more tunes. The boys missed school to go into the John Foster Studio in Nashville to cut the demo. The gamble they made by cutting classes almost paid off. Hurley called them upon their return home to tell them he'd gotten them a deal with Mercury/Polygram. For whatever reason, however, the deal never went through.

In the meantime, Tommy's bass guitar was rapidly developing. He also was using the thumb-picking style he'd learned from his father. "Tommy was playing with his thumb, and most of the other bass players either used a pick or used their first two fingers," says Paul Hornsby.

When he was about thirteen, Tommy got together with another local boy named Doug Gray. Tommy and his friends had heard around town that Doug could really sing. As a boy, Doug was known to entertain customers down at the drug store by singing along with the juke box records of Elvis Presley and other popular singers.

Tommy felt Doug had a real talent when he finally heard the boy sing. One day Tommy and a friend rode their bikes over to Doug's house to ask the thirteen-year-old Doug if would like to join Tommy's new band. "He said, 'I'm Tommy. You want to come over and sing for us?'" Gray recalls.

Harold Douglas Gray was born in Spartanburg in 1949. Doug remembers listening to radio station WLAC as far back as laying in his crib. B.B. King is the first artist who comes to his mind when he talks about his musical roots. Doug performed the laugh from The Ventures' surf hit "Wipe Out" at his first talent show at the age of seven and started a band called The Guildsmen while still in elementary school. He tried to soak up whatever music he was exposed to and went to local concerts on a regular basis. Doug attended The Pabst Blue Ribbon Jazz Festival with his family and went to see Nat and Cannonball Atterly with his teen-aged friend Toy Caldwell.

Doug prefers female singers over male singers, though. His taste runs the gamut from Dionne Warwick and Minnie Ripperton, to Mariah Carey and Chaka Kahn. Doug is a soul singer who doesn't let gender get in the way of his appreciation of good music.

Doug doesn't feel the bands from the South were all that influenced by Mick Jagger-type personalities. The reason seems simple to him. "Hey, somebody'd cut you, you know?" he laughs. "We were afraid to act that way when we were young."

One of the pivotal points in Doug's early musical development was attending the Second Annual Atlanta Pop Festival in Byron, Georgia. Gray dropped acid and sat on the roof of an ambulance to enjoy the show. He watched the likes of Jimi Hendrix, The Chambers Brothers, and The Allman Brothers Band perform their magic.

Doug wanted a career in music and was delighted when Tommy approached him with his idea for a band. Tommy and Doug joined together with Ross Hannah and Randy Foster to form The New Generation. The band covered everything from Motown to some of the songs that the current British acts were making popular.

Doug Gray proved to be a powerful, soulful singer. His version of "When A Man Loves A Woman" was a big hit with The New Generation's fan base. "They were tight even then," remembers Jim Brown of Spartanburg. "Multiple layers blended, folded and swirling around, topped off by the best white blues voice I've heard to date."

Tommy and Doug wrote a song called "Because of Love, It's All Over," and recorded it at the Reflections Studio in Charlotte in 1965. The record was released on the small Sonic label and receive some local radio airplay. Tommy and Doug quickly became hooked on this music thing. It seemed nothing could get in the way of the music. They were wrong.

Because these Spartanburg boys had been raised in a community where honor and country were of utmost importance, it probably never occurred to them attempt to dodge the draft or deny their country's request for volunteer soldiers. The Vietnam War loomed large over the United States and in 1966, the day after he graduated from high school, Toy was on his way to Parris Island as a Marine. He was soon in Vietnam. George McCorkle went into the Navy, and Doug Gray enlisted in the Army after his high school graduation. Shortly after arriving in Vietnam, Gray was promoted to Sergeant.

Nine months after Toy was discharged from the Marines, in September, 1969, he married Tommy's longtime classmate, Abbie Goode. Toy loved his wife and his new married lifestyle. He also still loved his music.

Toy and Tommy joined with their friend Steve Smith to form a trio and play music together. They were able to book a few dates at some of the local clubs. For some reason, though, Smith soon left the little band.

Toy decided that the time had come for him to form a real band with his little brother. He realized that Tommy had a talent for the bass and also for songwriting. The two brothers were anxious to see what kind of music they could make. It was decided that Tommy would play rhythm guitar. The Toy Factory consisted of Toy, Tommy, Wayne Cassantra, and Ross Hannah, with Doug Gray on primary vocals. When Tommy left for basic training in the Marines in the fall of 1969, Franklin Wilkie played with the band. They called themselves The Toy Factory.

Tommy Caldwell didn't go to Vietnam. Although he joined the Marines in 1969, he hurt his leg during basic training. He was eventually released from service on a medical discharge and was once again ready to rock and roll.

George McCorkle had formed a band in early 1970 called Pax Parachute. Pax had been McCorkle's idea simply as an entity to play some music with his friends. Eventually some other friends were brought in to play: Wayne Cassantra and Freddie Brown. McCorkle had been working with a drummer named Ronnie Edwards, but

Edwards suddenly found himself drafted. McCorkle heard about drummer Paul Riddle through word of mouth. Riddle was from Drayton, South Carolina, and had a gig playing jazz/swing-oriented drums at a local dinner club. He'd been heavily influenced by Charlie Parker and Miles Davis. Riddle didn't know a lot about rock and roll, but he knew all kinds of twists and turns and was a very interesting drummer.

Tommy Caldwell approached McCorkle and Riddle after hearing them play at The Sitar Club. Tommy mentioned to McCorkle that he wanted to return to music. McCorkle introduced him to Riddle. "[Tommy] said, 'Well, heck, let's get up there and play one and see what it sounds like.' That was in the middle of our job, our gig, so the three of us got up on stage and started playing. The next day we decided to put it together."

Tommy decided that what he really wanted to do was play bass, and bass it was. McCorkle, Riddle, and Tommy were now a trio, with Tommy and George handling the vocals. The main thrust of the music was original material, contributed mostly by Tommy and McCorkle. There wasn't a lot of interest in a band that refused to cover other artists, but the members of Pax pursued as many dates as they were offered.

It wasn't long before Toy and Tommy decided that what they most enjoyed was playing music together. Tommy returned to The Toy Factory. Ronnie Edwards and David Ezell, another friend, occasionally participated, and Carol Cox eventually joined the band as a keyboard player. George McCorkle played with his friends for a while, but then left the band to try his own wings.

The band members continued to play English blues, but they also incorporated American R&B, contemporary rock, and many of Toy's original songs. Toy had already written what would later be known as his masterpiece. "Can't You See" was a huge hit with The Toy Factory's fans.

The enthusiastic regional following of The Toy Factory resulted in something incredible. After opening for The Allman Brothers during a gig at The Sitar, The Toy Factory was selected to open on the southeastern leg of the Brothers tour. The band was on a roll. The group began its road experience as a rock and roll band traveling through several states in a Tom's Peanut truck.

Toy took a job at the Spartanburg Waterworks to supplement his income; he worked there during the day and played his music at night. He likely knew that the talent within The Toy Factory would soon erupt into something significant.

The Marshall Tucker Band,1972. (Back row, left to right) Tommy Caldwell and Doug Gray. (Middle row, left to right) Toy Caldwell and George McCorkle. (Front row, left to right) Paul Riddle and Jerry Eubanks. Credit: The Collection of George McCorkle.

It was decided that McCorkle and Riddle would come over from Pax Parachute and join Toy, Tommy, and Doug Gray. Another old friend of theirs named Jerry Eubanks was recruited to broaden the sound of the new venture. Eubanks was a saxophone player in the high school band, but Toy thought it would be cool if he played flute. Eubanks immediately set out to learn the instrument.

Toy polished up a new version of "Can't You See." He added some other songs that he'd written and felt would get a good workout by the band: "Take the Highway" and "Hillbilly Band" were among them. The universality of Toy's songs was the appeal of the band, according to the members of Marshall Tucker. "When he [Toy] wrote songs, he wrote them for himself, but he wrote 'em in such a simple way that everybody understood," says Gray. "'Can't you see what that woman's been doing to me' had nothing to do with a woman. It really didn't, as far as I'm concerned. It had something to do with the torment of a relationship."

The members of the new band started rehearsing in earnest. At the suggestion of their friend Cecil Corbett, they booked time at Muscle Shoals to cut a demo. Unfortunately, the demo wasn't all they envisioned.

Shortly after their arrival home from Alabama, the band was booked into their favorite local club, The Sitar. The Sitar attracted a lot of excellent touring bands and was a favorite of the Caldwell and friends creation. But the band members didn't know at the time that The Sitar was about to play a major role in their history. The group was popular right from the start. It had a great sound going and certainly a lot of confidence. "When they came out there [on stage] it was just like, 'Hey man, we're here to play some damn music, so hold on to your seat.'" says Paul Hornsby.

One night Capricorn's Wet Willie played The Sitar. During the sound check, Wet Willie experienced equipment problems. Winston Squires, the club's owner, made a call to Toy Caldwell asking Toy if he could loan Wet Willie an amp. Toy agreed to bring over two amplifiers.

Jimmy Hall called Toy up to the stage near the end of the show. Toy slowly climbed on stage with a little Fender Twin amp and plugged in his Les Paul Deluxe. Toy was ready when Hall indicated he could take a short guitar lead. "Toy cranked up the volume on his little Twin and ripped off a few licks," remembers Terry "Chainsaw" Collins. "The small modified amp sounded as big as a Marshall stack. The players in the band knew then that this kid was for real."

Toy Caldwell and his guitar blew away everyone present. They wanted to hear more. Toy was asked to bring his band in to open for Wet Willie's next show. Jimmy Hall told Toy and Tommy that The Toy Factory was exceptional. "We heard this band, and it was just a special sound," remembers Jimmy Hall. "There was a band with two brothers, just like my brother and I in our band. We said, 'These guys need a break.' We'd see what we could do to help them."

Hall suggested they cut a fresh demo and would make sure that someone at Capricorn Records gave it a listen. The boys went back up to Greenville's Mark V Studios and cut "Can't You See," "Take the Highway," "Ramblin'," and "Low Down Ways," along with some other original tunes.

Toy Caldwell was developing into a phenomenal songwriter. "I've always called Toy Caldwell a manly writer," says George McCorkle. "He writes manly. It's really stuff that relates to the average person. Not anything above or lower."

Tommy and Toy took the tape down to Macon. Mike Holland, who was doing A&R at Capricorn, listened to the tape and then shared it with Frank Fenter, Phil Walden's partner. Fenter was impressed enough by what he heard to have Walden listen to it.

The boys from Wet Willie invited The Toy Factory down to Macon where they could play a gig at Grant's Lounge so Walden and Fenter could check out the band's live sound. Grant's Lounge was very popular with the Macon music crowd. "[Grant's] became just a mecca . . . our version of The Whiskey-A-Go-Go, I suppose," remembers

Paul Hornsby. "A little funky hole in the wall, but you could walk in there in the '70s and see about anybody in the world playing there."

The band rehearsed at the Burwell Building at the corner of West Main and Daniel Morgan Avenue in downtown Spartanburg for its big record company debut. One night during rehearsal, Tommy picked up a key fob with a tag attached that read "Marshall Tucker." It had been suggested that "The Toy Factory" wouldn't work as a name for the new group, and the band had been desperate to come up with something else. Tommy looked at the fob and suggested that the band call itself "Marshall Tucker." Why not? Nothing better had come to mind. Marshall Tucker it was.

Marshall Tucker was, in fact, a very real person. Although Tucker was blind, he led a very full life. He attended the South Carolina School for the Deaf and Blind. Tucker and his friend Eddie Pack had rented the rehearsal hall in the Burwell Building as a place to tune and store pianos. "It never bothered me that they used my name," Tucker told the Spartanburg *Herald Journal* in 1995. "I'm just glad they made good."

The members of The Marshall Tucker Band made an appearance on "The Merv Griffin Television Show" after they became successful. In the course of the conversation, one of the boys mentioned that they thought the "real" Marshall Tucker was dead. The "real" Marshall Tucker heard about the remark and asked his nephew, an attorney, to write a letter to Griffin. Tucker informed the popular television host that he was, indeed, still alive. For the next several weeks the show's closing credits read, "Marshall Tucker is alive."

The Marshall Tucker Band was ready when it was time for the gig at Grant's Lounge. "It was a tiny, tiny stage," laughs McCorkle. The band members were impressed with the Macon music community and the support they were given that night. "I remember people treatin' us good," recalls Gray. "There was a camaraderie of people that were not necessarily fans, you know? They were 'hurrah' people. 'Hurrah, let's go.'" Marshall Tucker's set was very well received.

Phil Walden liked what he heard. "They had this very powerful sound that was rock, but with these incredible country influences. Toy Caldwell's songs and very unique thumb-picking guitar sound of his. . . . He was one of the great, great guitarists, I believe, of this era. A magnificently talented man."

Walden and Fenter decided to offer The Marshall Tucker Band a contract. The boys decided that they needed to think about what they wanted to do. They were anxious to sign to Capricorn, but as with his other acts, Walden wanted to act as Tucker's manager and publisher as well. The boys finally agreed that the arrangement Walden proposed could work out. Within a week, they were back in Macon to sign on the dotted line.

Marshall Tucker entered the Capricorn studio in the summer of 1972. Staff producer Johnny Sandlin had been tapped to produce the new act, but Sandlin didn't feel confident that he was the best man for the job. So Sandlin asked his partner Paul Hornsby if he would take the band into the studio; Hornsby responded positively. He'd already produced two excellent albums by Eric Quincey Tate and the band Sundown.

Hornsby was challenged by The Marshall Tucker Band and their interesting blend of music. "They had no experience in the studio," Hornsby laughs. "They were all South Carolina shit-kickers with a lot of energy, but they didn't know what to do with it. They were the greatest bunch of guys I'd ever met. They were extremely eager to please, to do anything, to experiment, to try anything in the studio. Anything that you did for them, it was like, they'd thank you ten times, you know? It was a wonderful relationship."

Hornsby worked with the Spartanburg boys for two months, recording their songs on a sixteen-track console. They worked an average of sixteen hours a day laying down tracks, re-recording them, adding, and subtracting. Hornsby was impressed at the way the members of Marshall Tucker listened to his input and offered their own ideas. They were eager to learn and didn't balk at anyone's suggestions. The band also felt comfortable working with Hornsby. "[On] 'Take the Highway' there's that Melotron. . . . [Hornsby] had a big impact on the band," McCorkle claims.

Tucker's material was original, and the use of Toy's unique guitar and Eubank's flute put an additionally magical spin on Marshall Tucker's sound. Some very exciting tracks appeared on the album. It opened with "Take the Highway." Toy had written the tune as a ballad, but by the time it reached vinyl the other Tuckers had added their parts and jazzed it up. Toy didn't mind. He liked it even better.

The second song on the album was destined to become a rock standard. The boys had featured "Can't You See" for several years in their shows. The forcefulness of the guitars and Toy's emotional, intense vocal were finally captured on tape. Marshall Tucker knew it had recorded something special.

"Hillbilly Band" was the first Toy Caldwell song the new band had learned. It was a fun song that they often opened their shows with, yet they ran into problems when they attempted to lay down the track. Several takes were discarded. It didn't seem to be transferring well to tape. It was decided at the time that distancing themselves from the troublesome song was probably a good idea. The song was a favorite of the band members, and they eventually returned to successfully place it on the album.

"See You Later, I'm Gone" offered a unique challenge to the band. Tommy played drums on a track for the first and last time. Toy took up the pedal steel for this one. "Ramblin'," a concert favorite from the beginning, would continue to be one of Tucker's most requested songs. A gospel tune titled "My Jesus Told Me So" was included, as well as Toy's tribute to his wife, "Ab's Song."

By the end of the studio time, so much work had gone into the album that no one at Capricorn was sure what they had in the can. Capricorn didn't know if they wanted to release the self-titled *The Marshall Tucker Band*. The record was played for a couple of other labels to test the waters as to whether or not the master should be sold. Finally, someone convinced Walden that releasing *The Marshall Tucker Band* was the thing to do.

Capricorn had made the right decision. It wasn't long after the album's release that the flute-laced, dynamo-guitar-riffed opening track, "Take the Highway," was being heard on newly popular FM album-oriented radio. The album gradually climbed the *Billboard* chart and ultimately reached #29. It was eventually certified gold.

CHAPTER 9

More Tragedy

1972

The Allman Brothers Band had returned to the studio to see if it could score another gold album. *Eat A Peach* was released in February, 1972. According to Butch Trucks, one of the band's drummers, Capricorn was originally going to title the album *The Kind They Grow in the South*. It was retitled *Eat A Peach For Peace* when the band members recalled Duane Allman telling a reporter that what he and the band would do for the revolution, if there was one, was "eat a peach for peace." The title was shortened to *Eat A Peach*, and the album read "Dedicated to a Brother."

The album opened with one of Gregg Allman's most melancholic songs to date. "Ain't Wastin' Time No More" not only addressed the issue of his loss, but also underlined his commitment to carry on and honor his brother's legacy. Dickey Betts demonstrated that even though he'd never been called on to play interesting, if unadorned, slide guitar, he could do it. He drew on what he knew as a musician. He wasn't trying to replace Duane, but rather continue the Brothers' innovative approach to their music in his own way.

"Les Brers in A Minor" followed, an intricate instrumental that Dickey wrote. Berry Oakley's bass line was prominent and unyielding. Musically, Berry remained a vital member of the band.

The third song was "Melissa," Gregg's sweet yet emotionally troubled tribute to love and death. He'd recorded the song with Duane, and it was one of the songs he sang solo at his brother's funeral.

The members' introductory statements made, the album segues into material from the Fillmore sessions. Sonny Boy Williamson's "One Way Out" sizzles from the initial riffs of Dickey's guitar through to Gregg's insistent and swaggering vocal. "Trouble No More" and "Stand Back" follow. "Blue Sky" introduced Dickey's debut as a vocalist on a song so sweet and pure it can only be classified as country, Allman Brothers style. A forceful version of "Midnight Rider" comes next, and then the album returns to Duane's studio-recorded "Little Martha." "Little Martha" was Duane's song for Dixie, although the title came, once again, from a monument for a little girl who died and was buried at Rose Hill Cemetery. Two album sides of "Mountain Jam," the most ambitious rendition yet, close the album.

Gregg and Berry, the two brothers Duane had left behind, buried their grief with drugs and withdrew into their own heartache. While Gregg, no doubt, was cognizant of his own depression and subsequent drug obsession at the time, he also was aware of Berry's reaction to the pain caused by the loss of his closest friend. "He was pretty bad after that," Gregg remembers. "He was never the same."

Despite their personal anguish at the loss of Duane, the members of The Allman Brothers Band was pleased to be rewarded for its musical effort when *Eat A Peach* climbed to #5 on the *Billboard* chart. Their musical merit was also recognized when the band was asked to headline the Mar Y Sol Festival in Puerto Rico in the spring of 1972. The Allman Brothers Band continued to be a viable force in the music industry.

Several of the band members had children born to them that year, including Gregg's son Devon. Although happy events took place, a blanket of sadness still remained. The band looked to Berry for leadership, but he was still enveloped in his own grief. He seemed overwhelmed by the responsibilities of keeping the musical machine operational. Although Berry made a valiant effort, he received little support from the various entities involved in the business of The Allman Brothers Band. He grew increasingly frustrated and continued to mask his heartbreak and disillusionment in alcohol and drugs. Berry didn't seem as steady and predictable as he had in the past. He was known to be a less than proficient driver and surprised his friends when he bought a motorcycle. That had been the very vehicle that had carried away the world as he knew it.

On a different front, Berry and the band were doing well. The Allman Brothers Band at last started to realize substantial financial rewards for its musical endeavors.

The band took some of its royalty money and bought a 440-acre farm in Juliette, Georgia. The guys looked forward to riding horses and kicking back at the ranch when they weren't on the road.

By the time the next Allman Brothers Band album was due, Phil Walden had sold Capricorn's distribution to Warner Brothers. This necessitated some changes in the way the label did business, as well as some creative reconstruction. Since Tom Dowd continued to work for Atlantic, a new producer needed to come in to work for the Allmans.

Johnny Sandlin continued to work with Paul Hornsby in the Capricorn Studio and was appointed to shepherd The Allman Brothers Band through its fourth album. Sandlin felt that while Duane shouldn't be replaced, perhaps the addition of a piano player would boost the sound of the band in Duane's absence. Sandlin suggested Alabama keyboard player Chuck Leavell. The band members agreed to give Leavell a try.

Leavell had previously been in The Misfits, a band that had earned quite a regional following around Tuscaloosa. He'd joined forces with Hornsby to form a band called Southcamp after Hour Glass was shelved and Hornsby returned to Alabama. Shortly after Hornsby left Alabama to take the studio job at Capricorn, he called Leavell down to work on an album with a new group named Sundown.

Leavell landed a gig playing on the road with Capricorn artist Alex Taylor through his association with Hornsby. Taylor often opened for The Allman Brothers Band, and Leavell's exposure to the Allmans live act was exciting to him. After Taylor left the label, Leavell took a job touring with Dr. John.

Immediately after the end of the Dr. John tour, Sandlin called Leavell to ask if he would like to do a little work with Gregg Allman on a solo project. Leavell jumped at the opportunity. When Leavell arrived to rehearse with Gregg, however, he found himself playing with the entire Allman Brothers Band. The guys must have liked what they heard because Leavell was soon asked to join the band on piano.

Around this time, some of the Brothers began to feel that they weren't receiving the royalties that others of their stature were getting from their record labels. They'd entered into the unique position of having their manager serve as their label president as well, and there was no one to negotiate for them. There is a controversy surrounding whose idea it was, the band's or Walden's, to increase the band's royalties at this time, but a new 12 percent rate, $100,000 advance contract was signed with Walden on November 1, 1972. Publishing remained with Walden's No Exit Music, with higher rates and royalties.

Even with all of the inner turmoil, the Brothers performed well. A show at the Academy of Music in New York City that year was exceptional. "The lasting impression from this show was Dickey's performance," says fan Mark Baird. "It seemed to be a daunting task to carry on without Duane, but Dickey was up to the challenge that night. He put on a show that practically stunned me and left me shaking my head in amazement at his talent."

In early November, The Allman Brothers Band, with new member Leavell, flew up to New York's Hofstra University to appear on Don Kirschner's "In Concert" television show. The band debuted Dickey's new song, "Ramblin' Man," giving their usual, excellent performance.

After the group returned home from New York, Berry booked Macon's Ad Lib Club for a show he planned to put on with local musicians. On November 11, the day of the show, Berry and Kim Payne rode their motorcycles up to the Idlewild South farm. On their return to Macon, they stopped to see Tuffy Phillips. As they headed back to the Big House for a rehearsal, Berry and Kim drove down Napier, goosing each other and other vehicles with their bikes. Payne navigated the difficult curve at Inverness Avenue and looked back to make sure that Berry, not the most proficient of bike riders, wasn't having any problems. This was when Payne saw the Macon city bus that had just passed him slam on its brakes and swerve to avoid colliding with Berry's motorcycle.

The bus driver's quick thinking was of no avail. Berry, later determined to have had a .24 blood alcohol count, slammed into the middle of the bus. He bounced back into the rear of the bus and flew into the air as his bike went with him. The motorcycle landed on Berry 58 feet away from the bus. He was unconscious by the time Kim reached him, but only for a minute or two. He stood up, bleeding from his nose and a cut on his lip. Berry told Kim that he was okay and examined his bike. He just wanted to go home. Berry walked around and talked to the police, who advised him to go to the hospital. Berry declined and instead caught a ride back to the Big House with a friend who passed by and saw the accident.

Although Berry went right up to bed when he got home, he once again refused to go to the hospital. He suddenly turned incoherent and started hallucinating. That was it. Berry was carried down the stairs and placed in Leavell's car to be taken to the Medical Center of Central Georgia. Unbeknownst to Berry, he had severed a number of key blood vessels in his head, causing irreversible damage to his brain. He died within the hour.

A service for Berry Oakley was held at the Macon Catholic Church and a private memorial service was conducted at Hart's Mortuary. As they had only a short year before, the band members played music for a brother they'd loved and lost, with Johnny Sandlin on bass.

Donna Allman, Linda Oakley, and Berry's sister Candace selected adjacent plots in Macon's Rose Hill Cemetery for both Berry and Duane. It had taken more than a year to straighten out the legal problems that would allow *someone* to bury Duane. Now Duane would lay next to Berry Oakley, his friend, his brother, for eternity.

Linda Oakley designed special headstones that reflected the young men's devotion to their family and their music. Special inscriptions were etched into the stone: an entry from Duane's diary and a quotation that reflected Berry's philosophy. At the foot of the graves were two small angels kneeling in prayer. The angels represented Galadriel Allman, Duane's daughter, and Brittany Oakley, Berry's daughter.

Berry's loss was felt by everyone who knew him. There was no denying that he was a compassionate and unique individual. "Berry believed in fair play and honesty and helping his fellow man," wrote his sister Candace. "Perhaps more important than his accomplishments are the values and morals that like fibers held him together on his journey."[5] He would be greatly missed.

The Allman Brothers Band was scheduled to play with The Grateful Dead in Houston the weekend of Berry's death, but canceled the appearance. It was too soon. The music would have to wait just a little longer.

As with Duane, the band members knew that Berry would want them to stay together and continue to make their extraordinary music. The band couldn't, however, play that music without a bass player. Auditions were held, and the band finally asked Lamar Williams to join on bass. Williams was a childhood friend of Jaimoe's from Gulfport. His father was a professional gospel singer. Williams was drawn to the music and the rhythm in the bass guitar. He taught himself how to play the instrument, and by 1964 was playing in a band with Jaimoe called George Woods and The Sounds of Soul. After Williams was drafted in 1968, he continued to play with a Special Services band. When he was discharged, he joined a group from North Carolina called The Fungus Blues Band. Williams, like Chuck Leavell, was offered $400 a week to play bass for The Allman Brothers Band's new album.

Capricorn had been working on an album of Duane's material and released *Duane Allman: An Anthology* at the end of November, 1972. The two-record set includes selections from throughout Duane's career, from Hour Glass to Muscle Shoals sessions, the Clapton sessions and The Allman Brothers Band. It was a thoughtful tribute to a musician missed by everyone who seriously cared about rock and roll.

The Allman Brothers Band prepared to welcome the new year by performing at the Warehouse in New Orleans on New Year's Eve, 1972. Although it was the group's first gig without Berry, the evening went well and the band accepted additional bookings. The guys were soon playing large arenas and outdoor stadiums, making more money than they ever had before.

Capricorn was pleased with the current status of The Allman Brothers Band, yet knew that most of the Brothers' fans were still tuned in to the music that the band had made with Duane and Berry. The record company released a double-record set titled *Beginnings*, which was a compilation of the first two Allman Brothers Band albums.

The band members were making enough money now to form a corporation and make investments. Phil Walden continued to be their music business partner. As was their pattern when new ideas were formulated, there would be changes in the structure of the band's extended family. Joe Dan Petty left the crew to perform with a group of his own. Kim Payne, Mike Callahan, and Tuffy Phillips were fired, allegedly for excessive drug and alcohol abuse; Walden demanded that they be replaced after an incident during which they threw a label executive off the stage. The Allman Brothers Band as a unit, however, continued to prosper.

CHAPTER 10

Pronounced Leh-Nerd Skin-Nerd, the "Godfather," and Brothers and Sisters

1973

The members of Lynyrd Skynyrd decided that they should play Atlanta if they were going to crack the music industry. They were booked into a club called Richard's, where they soon were performing nearly every week. The audiences were enthusiastic when they heard Skynyrd's raucous music.

Through word of mouth, Skynyrd was fortunate to land a gig at an Atlanta club called Funnochios in 1973. Bob Dylan protégé and super-session man Al Kooper happened to be at the club one night when Skynyrd was playing. Kooper had recently formed his Sounds of the South label as an Atlanta-based alternative and competitor to Phil Walden's successful Macon-based Capricorn Records. Kooper felt an exciting sound was developing in the South. "There were a lot of bands that didn't get to be heard that were really good," says Kooper. "Moses Jones, Hydra, Eric Quincey Tate . . . but there were only so many pieces of the pie. If Capricorn didn't buy into you, there was nowhere to go."

Kooper liked what he heard in Skynyrd and returned to hear the band five more nights that week. "This was the time of Genesis, ELP, King Crimson," Kooper recalls. "These were thought and skill bands, but they sometimes lacked heart and soul. I remember thinking if someone came along with a great rock and roll band right then, they'd clean up. Lynyrd Skynyrd was a panacea to the problem."

Kooper signed Lynyrd Skynyrd as his first Sounds of the South act. Almost immediately he was shepherding the band into Buddy Buie's Studio One. "Skynyrd was years ahead of their time," says Kooper. "They were twenty year olds playing like thirty year olds. I'm not interested in producing anybody I can't learn from."

A major change occurred within the band before any tracks were laid down. Larry Junstrom was replaced by Leon Wilkeson, a bass player the boys had known in Jacksonville; he was a welcome addition to Lynyrd Skynyrd. Leon Wilkeson was born April 2, 1952. He was a fan of Paul McCartney and The Beatles and decided by the time he was twelve that playing bass guitar suited him as an ambition. Wilkeson's parents purchased a Sears Silvertone guitar with the amp built into the case for their son, and the lessons began.

One day Wilkeson was approached by his next door neighbor, Betty Jo Ann Morris. Betty Jo Ann just happened to be Ronnie Van Zant's sister. Betty Jo Ann asked the fourteen-year-old Wilkeson to give guitar lessons to one of her sons. When she heard what the young guitar player could do, Betty Jo Ann told Leon that her brother Donnie needed a bass player for his band, The Collegiates. Leon auditioned and joined the band. His father made him quit, however, when his grades began to drop. Evidently the marks came back up because Wilkeson began to play with other garage-type bands. He eventually dropped out of high school and became affiliated with a Zombies cover band. Leon started to realize that he was beginning his life's work.

Wilkeson decided that he wanted to stay focused on the bass guitar and attempted to soak up everything he could learn about the instrument. He listened to McCartney, Chas Chandler of The Animals, Jack Casady of Jefferson Airplane, and John Paul Jones of Led Zeppelin. "I went and just really researched anybody that had the balls to stand on the stage and pluck one of them things," Wilkeson remembers. "Not steal licks, but just to learn."

Wilkeson became involved with a group called The King James Version with fellow Jacksonville native Dru Lombar. There were problems in the band, and Wilkeson began to think he might want to work somewhere else. He asked for an audition when he heard that Larry Jungstom was leaving Skynyrd and the band was looking for a replacement. He jammed with the band for a while and then stood back to see what might develop.

One night Wilkeson went to listen to Donnie Van Zant and Skynyrd roadie Billy Powell rehearse their band Alice Marr. "In walks Mick Jagger, Keith Richards, and

Brian Jones from Lynyrd Skynyrd," Wilkeson recalls. Ronnie told Wilkeson that his playing had been impressive and asked if he'd be interested in filling Skynyrd's bass position. He was.

Ronnie then laid the ground rules. "'One thing I gotta tell you about playing with this band,' Ronnie said," Wilkeson recalls. "'I'll put it to you in terms of sports and baseball. You know when a professional ballplayer steps up to the plate, he's got several choices. He can bunt, he can try to hit a single or a double or a triple. The basic requirement of everybody that plays in this band is, every time you step up to the plate, you gotta put it out of the park. Every time. Gotta be a home run.'" Wilkeson nodded his head and said, "Okay. When do we start practicing . . . 10 minutes?" He was happy to be in the band. "They were just hip, man," he says. "They were the real deal."

Wilkeson enjoyed playing with the band and took to the road like the other band members, but changed his mind about a professional career as the time drew near to record an album. "I just thought I was too young," he recalls. "I just had haunting premonitions about becoming famous, you know, having my mug on a cardboard album cover. I didn't feel I was ready for it yet. So I went to work for Farm Best Dairy Products."

The band members were taken aback. Kooper was ready to record their album and now they didn't have a bass player. Their thoughts immediately turned to a guitar player they'd met years before; they asked former Strawberry Alarm Clock guitarist Ed King to come into the band on bass. Kooper was pleased with their choice. "Ed was the icing on the cake," Kooper remembers. "He knocked out the whole back door."

Ed King was born September 14, 1949. He grew up in Southern California in the small San Fernando Valley towns of Panorama City and Glendale. King's early influences were Duane Eddy and the other guitarists associated with the surf music of the early 1960s. Ed started to pay attention to Duane Allman and Pete Townshend, The Who's guitarist, as he got older. "Duane Allman was an amazing guitar player and a huge influence on me," says King. "I saw him play on October 9, 1971, at the Santa Monica Civic and October 12 at The Whiskey. He was dead two weeks later. I couldn't believe it."

In 1967 King founded the Strawberry Alarm Clock with his friend Mark Weitz. King wrote the music for that band's huge radio hit "Incense and Peppermint," but the record company supplied the lyrics. King's credit didn't appear on the finished product. His association with The Strawberry Alarm Clock wasn't one of his favorite career activities.

In 1971, King and Weitz heard that a bogus Alarm Clock band was touring Florida. Figuring they had nothing to lose, the two decided that the real band might as well tour. A band named One Percent opened for the group on one of its Florida dates. This might have been when Ed was introduced to Ronnie Van Zant, but the impact Ed's guitar playing had on One Percent wouldn't be forgotten. "Actually, out of every guitar player that's ever been in this band, I think Ed was the best," says Billy Powell. "He could play classical, I guess, if he wanted to. He's grouchy on the outside, [but] he had a heart of gold on the inside."

Kooper was pleased with the band's guitars. He felt that Allen Collins was Claptonesque, and Gary Rossington had a sound not unlike blues/Tex Mex virtuoso Ry Cooder or Free's Paul Kosoff. Ed King reminded Kooper of Elvis Presley's main guitar man, the much respected James Burton. Burns was doing a good job on drums. Kooper himself would contribute mellotron, organ, and mandolin when they were indicated.

Lynyrd Skynyrd, 1973. (Standing, left to right) Bob Burns, Allen Collins, Ronnie Van Zant, Billy Powell, Ed King, Gary Rossington. (Seated) Leon Wilkeson. Credit: Sounds of the South/MCA Records/Judy Van Zant Jenness Collection.

Two other guys who were there from the beginning of Skynyrd's career would prove themselves invaluable to the band. Dean Kilpatrick had, of course, signed on as a roadie as soon as the band hit the road. Dean became one of Skynyrd's best friends and a most trusted family member. "He was nothing but A-1 class, First Class," Leon Wilkeson says. "And he came in handy," Wilkeson chuckles, "because a lot of people mistook him for Allen."

Kevin Elson was also a member of Skynyrd's early crew. He had an incredible ear and was able to assist the band in several ways both on and off the road. Elson soon became the band's sound man.

Billy Powell had signed on as a One Percent roadie. He'd pitched in and lugged amps and wired mikes with the

Lynyrd Skynyrd, 1973. (Standing, left to right) Bob Burns, Kevin Elson, Allen Collins, Leon Wilkeson, Ronnie Van Zant, Gary Rossington, Ed King.(Seated, left to right) Dean Kilpatrick, Alan Walden, Billy Powell. Credit: Judy Van Zant Jenness Collection.

other two crew members. His position in the band, however, had recently changed. Billy Powell was born June 3, 1952, in Corpus Christi, Texas. His father, Donald, died of Hodgkin's disease while a lieutenant commander in the Navy, stationed in Italy. The family moved to Jacksonville where Billy's mother, Marie, took a civilian job at the Naval Air Station. Powell had been picking out tunes on the piano since he was a toddler. His mother bought him a piano when he was six, and he began taking lessons. His devotion to music was a comfort to him during the three years he spent in an academy for Navy kids. When Powell was kicked out of the academy, he enrolled in Jacksonville's Bishop Kenney High School. During high school, he took lessons from four different piano teachers. After he graduated, he majored in music theory at Jacksonville Community College.

It was the music of The Beatles that gave Powell the spark to believe he might be able to make a living through his piano playing. He worked toward achieving that goal, but in the meantime he knew that being involved in the local music scene would serve him well. He decided to take a gig with One Percent, wiring amplifiers and doing whatever else needed to be done.

Kevin Elson had introduced Powell to the band. One night after One Percent played a prom at The Bolles School in Jacksonville, Elson mentioned to Ronnie, Allen, and Gary that they might be interested in listening to some keyboard playing that Powell had worked up to fit into "Freebird." "I sat down and played my version of

'Freebird,' and they just all three dropped their jaws," remembers Powell. "Ronnie went, 'Wow, you play piano like that and didn't tell us?' I said, 'I never dreamed you'd ever want a piano player in the band 'cause you've been so long without one.' Then that's when Ronnie said, 'Would you like to join the band as keyboardist?' Then my jaw fell to the floor. That was like an instant dream come true. Just like that, I was in the band."

There was a small problem with Powell's playing, however. He claims he was very technical and had to learn from the other band members how to feel the music. He listened to Emerson, Lake and Palmer, Billy Joel, British rock pianist Nicky Hopkins, Elton John, drummer Nigel Olson, noted keyboard player Bobby Whitlock, and whoever else he felt could help him learn to play rock and roll. Powell had been playing a little bit with Alice Marr, which included Donnie Van Zant, Don Barnes, Bill Pelkey, and Larry Steele, but the band's actual gigs were few and far between. Powell wasn't thrilled about Ronnie's remark that he was an "educated fool" in regard to his playing. He gave it all he had to learn what it was that would make him fit in with Lynryd Skynyrd's type of music.

Powell looked forward to interweaving his piano with the guitars. "With three of 'em, there's always something happening with guitar, and it's really hard to find all the little entry spots to fill in the spaces in between," Powell laughs. "I had to play in between the lines, and I think that established the band not only as a guitar army, but [me] as a real good keyboard player." Powell was free to pursue his own sound. Like the other members of the band, the music came first. "Ronnie always said, 'You guys just play your instruments, think of music, and I'll do the business.'" he recalls. "And that's the way it was. We knew we could trust him. We knew we could count on him, and we knew he had the head for it and he did. He was father, founder, and leader of Lynyrd Skynyrd."

The band was now in place and ready to record. Lynyrd Skynyrd entered Studio One to record its 1973 debut album, *Pronounced Leh-Nerd Skin-Nerd*. The band members weren't particularly nervous. This was the moment they'd been waiting for.

Al Kooper instructed and led the inexperienced members of Lynyrd Skynyrd through the intricate stages of selecting songs and getting them onto tape. "Al had a vision," says Ed King. "He knew how the band should be presented and how it should be recorded."

Kooper and the band clashed periodically, but the results were well worth any temporary animosity. Kooper was well known and experienced. He'd worked with the best: Dylan, Hendrix, The Stones, electric blues guitar master Mike Bloomfield, and other superstars. Kooper's experiences caused him to have definite opinions on what would and wouldn't work.

Ronnie, although considerably less experienced, knew what he wanted from his band. He and Kooper sometimes disagreed. It was not only their approach to music, evidently, but a shared nature. "Ronnie butted heads with everybody," according to Judy, his wife. This seemed to be especially true when it came to what he felt was best for Lynyrd Skynyrd. Ronnie, well known as a taskmaster by the other band members, respected Kooper enough to have him intricately involved. "He can get moody at times," said Ronnie, referring to Kooper. "But when he gets moody with us, we get moody with him. And there's seven of us. We don't put nothin' on record unless we like it too."[6]

Most times Kooper liked it just fine. Sometimes not. Ed King remembers Kooper being less than enthusiastic about the inclusion of the song "Simple Man" on the album. The band members, however, loved the song and wanted to find a place for it. They decided to record it whether or not Kooper approved. "Basically, Ronnie led Kooper over to his Bentley, opened the door, and told him to get in," King recalls. "After shutting the door, Ronnie stuck his head in through the window and said, 'When we're done cutting it, we'll call you.'"

Kooper says he doesn't remember it that way. He claims he didn't have anything against the song; he just preferred other songs when it came time to select what was going to be included on the album. The in-studio differences of opinion were loud and frequent, yet Ronnie didn't hesitate at all when he was later asked if Kooper would continue to be involved with the band's music. "If it was left up to us, and we're sure it will be," said Ronnie, "Al Kooper will be doing it again."[7]

Throughout the recording of the album, Gary made good use of his Les Paul. Allen mostly played his Gibson Firebird. From time to time, though, Gary would use a Gibson SG and Allen would alternate between his Firebird, a Gibson Explorer, a Fender Stratocaster, and a Telecaster. King favored a Stratocaster as well but employed a variety of other guitars when the mood hit him.

The band members continued to rehearse while recording and touring. "Ronnie ruled the band with an iron hand," recalls King. "We'd go to that little house and work from 9 o'clock in the morning to late at night. I'd look forward to what we were going to do, what we were going to write."

The songs included on the album set the standard for the band's future recordings. The selections were mostly culled from real-life experiences. "Gimme Three Steps," for example, is a tale based in reality. Ronnie and his friends had been in the W.T. West Tavern one day when the incident played out much the way it is relayed in the song. Other album standouts are "Tuesday's Gone," "Mississippi Kid," and "I Ain't The One." "Simple Man" harkens back to Ronnie's roots. "It kind of says it all, doesn't it?" muses Leon Wilkeson.

The album's musical piece de resistance is the anthem that became the hallmark of Skynyrd's live appearances for the next thirty years. Allen Collins's soaring tribute to freedom utilized everything that was available to him within his guitar forum. "Freebird," which was later dedicated to Duane Allman, was almost a classic from the first time it was heard at Allen's wedding. Collins's playing of the song on the album was spectacular. "Certainly Allen's legacy is the guitar solo in 'Freebird,'" says guitarist Jeff Carlisi. "[He] will always be remembered for that. It'll live forever. It's a classic, but it went way deeper than that. It was the spirit and the passion that he had every time he picked up a guitar. He became that guitar."

While the album was recorded for Sounds of the South, the record was distributed by mega-label MCA Records. Skynyrd was excited to have that kind of support. The band members couldn't wait to see what would happen to their record when it was released. *Sounds* magazine called the record "a raw blend of blues, hillbilly country and British boogie packed with typically Southern flavor: moaning slide guitar, country pickin' mandolin, aggressive guitars, driving rhythm section in straight 4/4 and dry, thirst parched vocals."[8]

While Ronnie Van Zant's vocals were being noticed, another vocalist was preparing to come to the forefront of a newly popular band. By 1973, Ronnie Hammond had replaced Rodney Justo as The Atlanta Rhythm Section's singer. "His voice just fit our music so much better," says Buddy Buie. "I love Ronnie's voice. I like writing for him. He doesn't have a great range, but his voice is so warm. He means what he says when he says it, and I like that part."

Hammond's debut into the world of music wasn't driven by an overwhelming desire to sing songs as the frontman for a band. Originally from Macon, he initially played drums, guitar, and keyboard for a hometown group called The Celtics. Ronnie enjoyed hanging around the recording studio and soon was working as an engineering assistant. Hammond took a job as an engineer with Rodney Mills at Lefevre Studio after graduating from high school.

When The Atlanta Rhythm Section happened to hear what Hammond could do with a vocal, Ronnie was hired as Justo's replacement. "I recognized the talent Ronnie had when he was just in high school," recalls Mills. "I knew from the first time I ever was around him and worked with him a little bit he had a lot of talent. Ronnie is a very gifted musician. He's one of these guys that can play a little bit of several different instruments, and I've always loved his voice."

Hammond's first album with The Atlanta Rhythm Section was *Back Up Against The Wall* in 1973. Ronnie might have been new to the band, but his contribution to its sound was immediate. *Back Up Against The Wall* received notice. A lot of that notice was because of the band's new singer.

Someone else who was starting to receive notice within the music industry was a guitar-picking, fiddle-playing South Carolinian named Charlie Daniels. "I got started what would be considered a little late for most people," says Daniels. "But once I had learned to play a little bit and did a little bit of entertaining, that was all I ever wanted to do." By 1973, Daniels had been recording and touring with Marshall Tucker for a couple of years and counted The Allman Brothers, Wet Willie, and Lynyrd Skynyrd among his friends and musical associates.

Maybe because there was a fiddle involved, or maybe because of his much publicized simple approach to life, Charlie Daniels's music has too often been categorized as country. The truth of the matter is that there isn't a form of music that Charlie hasn't tackled. He has done it all: country, rock, pop, gospel, bluegrass, instrumental, and ballads. There's probably even a rap song somewhere in there. Yet to a man, the Southern Rockers considered Charlie one of their own.

Charlie Daniels was not only welcomed into the Southern Rock family, soon he was serving as the genre's unofficial "Godfather." Maybe that was because he was a bit older than the young musicians he played with or maybe it was just Charlie's style. The rowdy rock and rollers who had seen and done it all knew that Charlie had good counsel on how to survive life on the road. He was, and is, a good friend to the boys in the bands. He played with them, collaborated with them, nurtured them, kicked back with them, partied with them, and grieved with them. There isn't a musician who has crossed his path who doesn't have the highest respect for Charlie Daniels.

Charlie himself isn't comfortable with any title, let alone "Godfather of Southern Rock." "There's a lot of people that would deserve that a whole lot more than I did," he says. "I'm very honored that somebody would call me that, but I don't feel I deserve it." A lot of people would disagree.

Charles E. Daniels was born in Wilmington, North Carolina, on October 28, 1936. Unlike many of his contemporary Southerners, he didn't come from a particularly musical family. His father played a little mouth-harp, but he mostly liked to sing. Charlie liked to sing, too; he especially liked hymns. Charlie did listen to a lot of radio. "They played all different types of music," he remembers. "They played country music before daylight a lot of times, then they played music for housewives in the morning. In the afternoons when the kids came home from school, they started playing whatever the popular music was of the day. I just came up liking a lot of different kinds of music."

A neighbor showed Charlie how to play guitar when he was fifteen, and he was hooked. He formed The Misty Mountain Boys in the ninth grade. While he initially played little but bluegrass and country, he started fooling around with the pop tunes of the day and found that audiences were hungry to hear that type of music performed live. When Elvis hit the scene, rock and roll was the music that Charlie's young audience clamored to hear. He was more than happy to oblige.

Charlie formed The Rockets in the summer of 1956. He sharpened his skills while performing songs by Chuck Berry, Fats Domino, and, of course, everything that Elvis was making popular at the time. The Rockets started out entertaining the marines at Camp Lejeune, but the band soon expanded its base to the clubs in Washington, DC, and WRVA's Old Dominion Barn Dance out of Richmond, Virginia.

The Rockets met songwriter Bob Johnston while going to see what opportunities might await them in California. Johnston arranged for the band members to record an instrumental they'd written called "Jaguar." Shortly after their arrival in California, they were excited to learn that their record would be released on Epic. The name of the band was then changed to The Jaguars. "Jaguar" received a good deal of airplay, and Epic offered to release a second instrumental, "Exit 6." The Jaguars and their music were starting to take off when Epic learned that two of the members of the band were underage. The label executives had no choice but to send the boys home.

By 1962 Charlie was working with a group called The Jesters and basing himself out of El Paso, Texas. He stopped to visit Bob Johnston in Nashville later that year while on a trip home to Carolina for the holidays. The two wrote a song called "It Hurts Me." Johnston was able to place the song as the "B" side of Elvis's single release of "Kissin' Cousins." The record hit the charts and climbed to #29.

Charlie was certainly pleased with the success of "It Hurts Me," but he didn't stop to think about it much. He returned to working the clubs and bars, this time with a new incarnation of The Jaguars. The Jaguars played clubs throughout the Midwest and South but really didn't catch fire. Charlie left the band in 1966 and took a job as an organ player in a Newport, Kentucky, lounge.

Johnston knew that Charlie was one tremendously talented picker and suggested that he might find work in Nashville. Charlie enjoyed the session work he was quickly able to procure. He learned a lot playing with such diverse artists as country balladeer Marty Robbins, banjo-playing Flatt & Scruggs, folk singers/songwriters Pete Seeger and Leonard Cohen, Al Kooper, and Ringo Starr.

Charlie became acquainted with Dino Valenti, Quicksilver Messenger Service's singer/songwriter, while working sessions. Through this association, Charlie was hired in 1969 to produce The Youngbloods' album, *Elephant Mountain*. He'd been surprised yet pleased when he found himself under consideration for the position. Producing an album hadn't been something that was on his mind. "The Youngbloods approached Bob [Johnston] about recording 'em, and Bob didn't have time to do the project," recalls Charlie. "He sent me out to talk to them, and we got together." The Youngbloods must have been pleased with his work. They asked him to produce their next album as well. *Ride the Wind* was released in 1970.

Charlie also had the pleasure of working with Bob Dylan on Dylan's *Nashville Skyline*, *New Morning*, and *Self Portrait* albums in 1969 and 1970. Charlie got on well with Dylan and found him to be not only warm, but in possession of a wonderful sense of humor. Dylan was impressed with Charlie's guitar playing and asked specifically for him to be included in the sessions.

News of Charlie's talent traveled throughout the music community, and he was offered a contract from Capitol Records for a solo album. *Charlie Daniels* was released in 1970, without much fanfare and without much airplay. Charlie had been around the music industry long enough to know that an album without a touring band couldn't get far. He put the disappointment of *Charlie Daniels* behind him and looked to the future.

Charlie knew that there was a place for his talent in contemporary music. He'd worked hard to develop a variety of styles and surely that would be appreciated. He decided to form a band that would reflect the versatility of his music.

Charlie was savvy enough to know that album rock was the popular genre of the day. He'd been introduced to Neil Bogart, president of Kama Sutra and Buddah Records, and felt that there might be a place on that label for his new venture. Charlie formed a band. When Bogart heard what they could do, he agreed that an album by The Charlie Daniels Band might do well for Kama Sutra.

Te John, Grease and The Wolfman was released on Kama Sutra in the fall of 1972. While the album attracted some attention from the radio and public, it wasn't the breakthrough album that Daniels and Bogart hoped it would be. Charlie's real introduction to the radio-listening, record-buying public would have to wait until the next time.

The next time came quickly enough. *Honey In The Rock*, released in 1973, contains a song that captured attention and provided Charlie with his first hit record. "Uneasy Rider" was the saga of a long-haired hippie type who was forced to kill some time in a redneck bar in Jackson, Mississippi, while he awaited the fixing of a flat tire. The story was meant to be humorous, but a lot of people felt they could identify with the emotions experienced by the man in the song as he dealt with the prejudiced reactions between two distinct elements of contemporary American society. "Uneasy Rider," the title a takeoff on the popular hippie film *Easy Rider*, hit the pop charts and made its way into the Top 10.

Another act with ties to Bob Dylan and Nashville was Barefoot Jerry. "Probably more people are aware of Charlie Daniels's line [in "The South's Gonna Do It Again']" than they are with our music," considers Barefoot Jerry's Wayne Moss. Charlie sang about the people in Tennessee digging Barefoot Jerry. It's true that the talent of the musicians who composed that entity was almost a well-kept regional secret. Still it seems the musicians who haven't, somehow, been associated with the members of Barefoot Jerry are few and far between.

Musician Wayne Moss arrived in Nashville in 1959 from South Charleston, West Virginia. In 1960, Moss opened Cinderella Studios in Nashville. Cinderella caught on fast. To this day, Cinderella doesn't have a listed telephone number, but musicians from all over the country come to Nashville to avail themselves of the studio. Mickey Newbury's first-time recording of "American Trilogy" was recorded at Cinderella, as was Charlie Daniels's *Whiskey* album and Linda Ronstadt's *Silk Purse*.

Moss not only operated the studio, he played on sessions for the acts that booked time both at his studio and other Nashville studios. Moss became known for his bass and guitar proficiency. He played with Chuck Berry and Fats Domino, as well as on Roy Orbison's "Oh, Pretty Woman," Tommy Roe's "Sheila," Tammy Wynette's "Stand By Your Man," and Bob Dylan's *Blonde On Blonde* album.

One night in 1969 during a recording session of The Monkees, at RCA's Studio "A," the studio musicians started jamming on their own and became excited about what they were hearing. By the time the night was over, the players discovered that they'd written half an album's worth of songs. It was decided that the session men would form a band.

Area Code 615 was named after Nashville's telephone access number. The band consisted of Wayne Moss, Charlie McCoy, Mac Gayden, David Briggs, Kenneth Buttrey, Bobby Thompson, Buddy Spicher, Norbert Putnam, Elliot Mazer, and Weldon Myrick. The group members had an abundance of talent. "We go down to the roots of rock and roll," says Moss.

McCoy was predominantly known as an exceptional harmonica player. He would play with Peter, Paul and Mary and Bob Dylan; record more than thirty albums; serve as musical director for the television show "Hee Haw"; and develop the ever-popular Nashville Number System. Gayden wrote "Everlasting Love," which has been a #1 hit record for various artists for four decades. Buttrey has played drums and percussion on Jimmy Buffett, Bob Dylan, and Neil Young records, among others', and has appeared in Elvis movies with McCoy. Putnam produced the first million-record-selling folk album, *Blessed Art* by Joan Baez, as well as steered Jimmy Buffett, Dan Fogelberg, and others to successful albums.

The band members released two albums for Polydor, *Area Code 615* and *Trip In The Country*, but they never toured. They had no desire to tour as a band and made only two serious public appearances: on the Johnny Cash television show and at Fillmore West. *Trip In The Country*, however, was nominated for a Grammy.

Area Code 615 lost its recording contract in 1970 because the guys wouldn't tour in support of their album releases. Then they decided to put together a band called Barefoot Jerry. The name came from Barefoot Jerry's Grocery in Townshend, Tennessee. The real Barefoot Jerry liked to sit around his country store, playing the fiddle and telling tall tales. The front of the store was featured on the covers of the re-releases of the group's first and second albums.

Barefoot Jerry initially consisted of Wayne Moss on bass and guitar, Mac Gayden on lead guitar, Kenneth Buttrey on drums, and Charlie McCoy on a variety of instruments, most notably harmonica. John Harris, who had recorded with Mickey Newberry and Alex Harvey, among others, played keyboards.

The band was almost immediately signed to Capitol Records. The group's first album was *Southern Delight*. "The original intent of the band was to play nice, relaxing, original music," says Moss. Once again, little was done to promote either the record or the band.

By the time the band's second album, *Barefoot Jerry* was released, the band was on the Warner Bros. label. The title tune from that album was released as a single. According to Moss, "It bubbled under the Top 100."

Over the course of their career as a band, Barefoot Jerry counted some twenty-three musicians among its band members. Most of them went on to make significant musical contributions. They continue, to this day, to work with the finest talent. Barefoot Jerry band members included: Russ Hicks, who has played steel guitar with country artists Ronnie Milsap; Mickey Gilley; Tom T. Hall; Marty Robbins; Don Gibson; Bobby Thompson, the writer of the musical theme for the television show "Hee Haw"; Buddy Skipper, musical director of "Music City Tonight;" Jim Colvard, who played guitar on such records as Dave Dudley's "Six Days On The Road" and "Why Me Lord" and who would become a part of Porter Waggoner's television band; Terry Dearmore, who played with Brewer & Shipley; Kenny Malong, who taught percussion to the U.S. Navy Band; Nashville session drummer Si Edwards; Jim Maxwell, producer for Andre Crouch; Buddy Blackmore, who wrote for country singer Randy Travis; Warren Hartman, who currently works with Kenny Rogers; Moby Grape's Dave Doran; Steve Davis, who went on to write immensely successful country songs; Barry Chance, who played guitar with country songwriter Joe Stampley; John Moss, a drummer who was also Barefoot Jerry's road manager for eleven years; Mike McBride, who plays bass with renegade country artist Johnny Paycheck; Fred Ewell, who played banjo, bass, and guitar on "Nashville Now;" Jim Isbell, who has played drums with Al Hirt and Jerry Lee Lewis; and Buddy Sprecher, who works with Crystal Gayle.

Barefoot Jerry released several other albums over the years on Monument Records: *Watchin' TV, You Can't Get Off With Your Shoes On, Keys To The Country*, and *Barefootin'*. The albums continued to offer a wide variety of musical genres. Eventually, however, it became time to move along. The boys in Barefoot Jerry had other fish to fry.

To this day, Barefoot Jerry is relatively unknown outside of the music industry. "We received more critical acclaim than we [had] fans," says Moss. "If we'd picked out one type of music and stuck with it, maybe they would know it was us. Barefoot Jerry is hard to categorize. We played instrumental, folk, gospel, rock. We had to adapt to the styles of [the various] sessions we played on, so we became interested in a lot of different types of music. It might have been a bad career move, but it never got boring because we were always changing. But we went in so many different directions, they didn't know it was Barefoot Jerry when they heard us on the radio."

Moss and McCoy currently own and operate their own publishing company. The guys in Barefoot Jerry were happy when Monument re-released their first two albums, and now all six of their albums are available on CD through Barefoot Jerry's website. Although the band is no more, the music lives on both through the reissues and through the many contributions the band members continue to make.

There was, of course, more to a successful career than hit records. On July 28, 1973, another special event in rock and roll history took place. The Allman Brothers Band, The Grateful Dead, and The Band performed at the Watkins Glen Summer Jam in upstate New York. The outdoor concert was adequately and effectively directed by promoter Bill Graham, former owner of the Fillmores. The event was bigger than Woodstock. More than 600,000 people constituted the Jam's audience. It was, to date, the largest rock and roll event in the history of the genre. The Brothers played a three-hour set as headliners. The Dead and The Band joined them at 2 A.M. to jam for another ninety minutes. The crowd dug it, big time.

The Allmans' *Brothers and Sisters* was released a few days after Watkins Glen. The album showcased a different Allman Brothers Band in more ways than one, yet the first cut of the album, "Wasted Words," offered the band's fans some familiarity through Gregg's ragged yet effective vocals. Dickey Betts's slide playing easily envelops Gregg's voice just as Duane's used to do, yet the presentation is very much Dickey—and exceptional at that.

The next cut is Dickey's country-rooted "Ramblin' Man." The song had been written in the kitchen of the Big House. Some of the lyrics were inspired by a friend of Dickey's who built fences and would ask Dickey how he was doing whenever he saw him. Dickey would reply, "I guess I'm doing fine." Berry plays bass on the song, and Dickey's guitar is complemented and challenged by Les Dudek on twin harmony. "Ramblin' Man" was the last song Berry Oakley had recorded.

Lamar Williams debuted as the Brothers' new bass player on "Come and Go Blues." Williams showed no hesitation to make his mark. The song left no doubt that the band had made a wise decision by hiring Williams. Gregg's "Jelly Jelly" is a drowsy blues number that closes the first side.

Side two opens with a rocker. Although Dickey wrote "Southbound," Gregg performs the insolent vocals. Chuck Leavell demonstrated what he had to offer here, and Dickey contributed three short guitar solos that cooked.

The second song is Dickey's transcendent instrumental, "Jessica." He wrote the song as he watched his daughter Jessica playing while he attempted to create a melody that could be played with two fingers, a la Django Reinhardt. Les Dudek again provides some fascinating guitar, but the changing tempos and blissful gentleness are pure Dickey. The song envelops the listener within its amazing weave and remains one of Dickey's classics to this day. Concluding the album is "Pony Boy," a rousing country-blues number that is enhanced by Dickey's bottleneck, Williams's upright bass, Chuck's piano, Butch's drums, and Tommy Talton's acoustic guitar. Everyone's playing is superb. "Pony Boy" is one of those songs that leave an audience clamoring for more. It is a perfect ending for an exceptional album.

Brothers and Sisters had hit written all over it. The record climbed quickly up the charts, reaching #1 by the first week in September, and stayed at the top of the charts for six weeks. In the meantime, "Ramblin' Man" had been released as a single and provided The Allman Brothers Band with its first Top Ten hit when it reached #2 on the *Billboard* chart.

Other good things happened for the band. The Allman Brothers' New Year's Eve, 1973, show at San Francisco's Cow Palace was broadcast live and was a major radio hit. *Billboard* magazine awarded the band its 1973 Trendsetter Award. *Rolling Stone*, the magazine the band loved to hate, gave the group a cover and named it Band of the Year. The Brothers were now superstars.

Gregg decided that he wanted to release a solo record and asked Johnny Sandlin to produce it. They titled the album *Laid Back*. Gregg worked with Scot Boyer, Tommy Talton, Bill Stewart, Jaimoe, Paul Hornsby, Chuck Leavell, and David Newman. The songs selected included a transitional version of "Midnight Rider" that surpassed any previously recorded versions in depth and emotion. Also included was a re-worked "Please Call Home," a ballad titled "Queen of Hearts," Rufus Thomas's "Don't Mess Up A Good Thing," and a temperate number called "Multicolored Lady."

Two other songs stand out on the album as a testament to Gregg's transcendent vocal appeal. Jackson Browne's "These Days" is given a depth even Browne hadn't realized in his own recording. The album concludes with "Will the Circle Be Unbroken," the Carter Family song that had come to mean so much to Gregg and the other members of The Allman Brothers Band.

When *Laid Back* was released in the fall of 1973, it became obvious that Gregg was an effective and exciting musician as well as a captivating vocalist, independent of Duane and the band. The resulting effort is melancholy and reflective, yet at the same time demonstrates that Gregg had something important to say outside of his involvement with The Allman Brothers. The album would remain one of Gregg's favorite solo efforts.

Ed King, ca. 1974. Credit: MCA Records/Judy Van Zant Jenness Collection.

CHAPTER 11

Hit Singles and New Arrivals

1974

When Lynyrd Skynyrd toured in support of *Pronounced Leh-nerd Skin-nerd*, the band members found that the anthem "Freebird" was an immediate monster hit with their new audience. "The first time I heard 'Freebird' I knew that kids would want to hit their heads against the wall," recalls Al Kooper. "Freebird" received major FM radio play when it was released as a single in 1974. It eventually found its way up to #19 on the *Billboard* Singles chart.

MCA was behind Lynyrd Skynyrd all the way. Although the executives at the company had little in common with the redneck boys from the South, they sensed that this "little old band from Jacksonville," as Leon Wilkeson called them, was something special.

Alan Walden had been replaced as the band's manager by this point. Peter Rudge of Sir Productions, whose company managed tours for The Who and The Rolling Stones, was a man with many connections in the music industry. He was called in to take over the business aspects of Lynyrd Skynyrd. "Walden got a real nice buyout, though," claims Ed King.

It was time for yet another change. King remembers Wilkeson's return to the band vividly. King was living with Ronnie Van Zant at the time. One night Ronnie

Leon Wilkeson, ca. 1974. Credit: MCA Records/Judy Van Zant Jenness Collection.

came to King and put his arm around Ed. "He told me, 'You're the worst bass player,'" remembers King. King acknowledged that bass wasn't his primary instrument and suggested that he be moved to guitar and Wilkeson be asked back into the band. "Leon is my favorite guitar player," claims King. "He's a great player." Ronnie obviously agreed and approached Wilkeson with the band's offer.

Ronnie had sent Ed King to Wilkeson during the recording of *Pronounced* to learn Wilkeson's bass parts for "Simple Man." Wilkeson had continued to keep in touch with the band's music and, independent of the band's intentions, had decided that he wanted to continue to be a part of Lynyrd Skynyrd. One day Bob Burns and Billy Powell came to tell Wilkeson that Ronnie was out fishing and wanted to talk to him. Wilkeson, intrigued by the summons, found Ronnie down at the dock.

As Ronnie fished, he told Wilkeson that King preferred to play guitar. Next, Ronnie asked Wilkeson if he would be interested in taking back the bass. Leon didn't have to think about his answer before he accepted the offer. Ronnie then handed Wilkeson his fishing pole. "He says, 'Cast the line over there by them lily pads floating on the water,'" Wilkeson chuckles. "So I very, very scientifically, carefully obeyed his command. He says, 'I guarantee you're going to catch a fish, like less than a minute.' So I caught a fish. I'm holding up a fish, looking at Ronnie, going 'I consider that a good omen.' He said, 'I do, too . . . see you at rehearsal tomorrow.'" Leon Wilkeson was back in the band.

In an extraordinarily beneficial career move that would provide the band with strong national exposure, Lynyrd Skynyrd was added as the support act on The Who's *Quadrophenia* tour beginning in December, 1973. "We didn't know we were even on the tour until the day before it started," remembers King. "We knew it was being worked on, but Pete hadn't given his approval yet." By the time the tour began, more than 100,000 copies of *Pronounced* had been sold. The figure was sure to rise quickly as the tour continued.

Skynyrd took advantage of this exceptional opportunity to show off its three-guitar assault. The band's unique sound, coupled with the raunchy lead vocals of the exuberant Ronnie Van Zant, introduced the rock and roll world to a Southern musical aggression that couldn't be ignored. "We were prime," says Billy Powell. "We were 100 percent that [first] night and every night, as far as that tour. Where The Who wasn't." The Who was having trouble keeping Keith Moon, its eccentric drummer, off heavy drugs and into the music. The people in the audience might have come to the show to see The Who, but the opening act from Florida grabbed their attention from the get-go and commanded them to listen.

Ronnie's intense yet laidback presentation wasn't something rock audiences had previously experienced. His aggressive, barefooted performance demonstrated that while he was there to do b usiness, he approached that business with a certain nonchalance. Ronnie said in interviews that the reason he performed barefooted was because he liked to feel the heat of the stage. Brother Donnie Van Zant laughs at that notion and says, "My mother couldn't ever get him to

Ronnie Van Zant, ca. 1974. Credit: MCA Records/Judy Van Zant Jenness Collection.

wear shoes." Ronnie's widow, Judy, might have a more accurate theory. "He had a pin in his ankle, for a little football injury at school," Judy says. "These little pins in his ankle, that's what kept him out of the draft, actually. I think he was just comfortable without shoes and I think he probably did it a few times, and it kind of became one of those things like the gambler hat [that he always wore onstage], you know?" Ronnie inadvertently had created a gimmick for himself.

The crowds went wild when Skynyrd tore into the music. The brutal, no-holds-barred guitar aggression encouraged the audience members to participate in the show by working themselves into a frenzy that clearly defined their reaction to the band's assault on their senses. Males and females alike yelled, whistled, and stomped their approval of what Skynyrd was offering up. If they happen to know the lyrics, they sang along. If they didn't, they were content to boogie in their seats and in the aisles. For the hour or so Skynyrd was on the stage, everyone in the audience was a rebel.

The combination of Skynyrd's undiluted attack on the songs, along with the audience's anticipation of another raucous Who performance, occasionally created offstage chaos. The crowd rarely remained in its seats and more often than not would surge forward to get closer to the stage. Security guards were kept busy pushing fans back and protecting those on stage from being assaulted by their devoted congregation.

During the tour's first show at San Francisco's Cow Palace, Billy Powell was mugged by both a security guard and impresario Bill Graham for failing to reveal his stage pass. "Bill Graham came running down the stage, down this ramp from the stage, and punched me in the mouth," Powell remembers. "I mean with full momentum. Knocked me about ten feet." Graham didn't realize that the kid arguing with the security guard was actually a member of the opening act. It was an interesting start for Skynyrd's first major tour.

Strange happenings aside, the band was thrilled to open for one of the biggest rock and roll bands in the world on a national tour. Skynyrd was given only eight inputs into The Who's mixing board, which didn't make for a crisp, intelligible sound. Although the band was allotted only thirty minutes to play, the experience was incredible. "It scared us at first on our first gigs. We were supporting The Who," Ronnie remembered. "And our first night we were playing too fast; the tempos were all wrong. After awhile we got to know The Who. They had a great influence on us. They're the type of people who tell you what you're doing wrong. By the end of the tour we were playing good and still getting our asses kicked by The Who."[9]

While the experience was a once-in-a-lifetime opportunity, it took its toll on Skynyrd. "We were terrified and told things like no band has opened for The Who that hasn't been booed off stage," recalls Wilkeson. "That's when we commenced to drinking. We decided to take the bar atmosphere on stage. Had a little portable bar up there, and everybody was drinking then. Problem was, we never stopped."

The band members were drinking well beyond the limits of social acceptability, even in the permissive rock and roll environment. They were a little nervous about and quite overwhelmed to be appearing with a band they would have paid money to see only a few months before. They didn't handle their enthusiasm for performing on such an important bill as well as they would have liked. It wasn't unusual for something to happen that would have mortified them under other circumstances. King remembers Roger Daltry coming into Skynyrd's dressing room one night at the precise moment a bottle of beer was being hurled across the room. "The beer went all over his famous leather vest," King recalls. "But he was okay about it."

Another interesting non-musical interlude occurred during the tour. On one date the band was booked to play Willie Nelson's annual picnic in Tulsa, Oklahoma. "We were supposed to be picked up by this chartered plane in San Francisco," Judy Van Zant Jenness remembers. "It was supposed to go to L.A. to pick up Waylon [Jennings] and Willie. Everybody was real excited, including the guys in the band. And when we got there, all we picked up was Hell's Angels that were their bodyguards at that time. Waylon and Willie weren't even on the plane, and everybody in the band was just freaking out. Ronnie told everybody not to say a word. It was the first time I've ever seen them sit so quiet from L.A. to Tulsa, Oklahoma."

Having somehow survived its first major tour, Skynyrd returned to the studio to record its next album. *Second Helping* was once again produced by Al Kooper. Among the tracks is "Sweet Home Alabama," a tongue-in-cheek little number that Ed King co-wrote with Ronnie Van Zant. King recalls how he first "heard" the song. He always keeps a guitar by his bed, and one night the music permeated his sleep. "I woke up, wrote down the music, complete with all of the guitar parts, and then played it for Ronnie," King remembers. Ronnie put the lyrics to it, and the band recorded it five days later. "[Ronnie] had an incredible feel for what would work and knew what he wanted to say," King believes.

"Sweet Home Alabama" was recorded in one night. Engineer Rodney Mills was impressed by the way the recording came together. "The main guitar solo on that was a first take all the way through by Ed," recalls Mills. "I can remember the amplifier he did it in. It was a Fender Twin, and he did the solo. I don't know how many people in the band were in the control room when he did the solo; everybody was just jumping up and down. They thought it was great. Al Kooper wanted him to do it again, and the whole band just kind of said, 'What are you talking about?' I think we may have recorded another solo, but I think we kept the very first one. I think that was the one that Al used on the record."

King remembers that Kooper wanted to change the key of the guitar but that the band backed King's original vision of the music. Ironically, since Steve Gaines, who joined Skynyrd later, couldn't play it the way Ed did, the version that is now performed in concert is played the way Kooper heard it.

Either Kooper or the band thought it would be a great idea to supplement the song with female backup vocalists. The engaging vocals of Merry Clayton and Clydie King of The Sweet Inspirations were added to the track, setting a precedent for The

Honkettes, a trio of girl singers that Skynyrd would employ in the future. Kooper says he was pleased with the end result.

Whenever "Sweet Home Alabama" was played in the South, accompanied by the unfurling of Skynyrd's traditional backdrop, a huge Confederate battle flag, the reaction of the audience was always the same: thunderous, enthusiastic, and immediate. Neil Young's song "Southern Man" had offended Southerners by seeming to accuse all people born in the South of being racists and terrorists. Since Young's observations obviously weren't accurate, Southerners were delighted when Skynyrd squared off with Young to defend their honor by releasing "Sweet Home Alabama" with its direct references to Young's faux pas. Skynyrd fans overwhelmingly supported the idea that the Southern man, or woman for that matter, didn't need Neil Young around to point out the problems of their society.

"We thought Neil was shooting all the ducks in order to kill one or two," Ronnie told *Rolling Stone* regarding the creation of the answer song. [10] The band felt that Young's lyrical content was somewhat typical of the myopic "Yankee" belief that all Southern men should be held responsible and accountable for the verbalizations and actions of a racist minority. Just the same, the boys in the band held Young in high regard for his musical achievements. "Neil is amazing, wonderful . . . a superstar," said Ronnie Van Zant. "I showed the verse to Ed [King] and asked him what Neil might think. Ed said he'd dig it; he'd be laughing at it."

Radio liked "Sweet Home Alabama." When the song was released as a single to generate additional interest in the new album, it charted at #8. "It's been paying the rent for twenty-four years," says King. Industry insiders began to see that Lynyrd Skynyrd was starting to make its mark.

In the fall, soon after the release of "Sweet Home Alabama," Skynyrd hit the road supporting The Marshall Tucker Band. "Ronnie and I was in this head shop in L.A.," remembers Tucker's singer Doug Gray. "We were standing there, and all of a sudden on the rock station their song plays. I said, 'Well, I guess that's it for y'all opening the show.'"

Some in the rock press were cautious about Skynyrd's new album when it was released in 1974. *Rolling Stone* claimed that "*Second Helping* is distinguished from their debut album only by a certain mellowing out that indicates they may eventually acquire a level of savor faire to realize their many capabilities."

One of the standout songs on the album is a soulful ballad titled "Curtis Lowe." "The song 'Curtis Lowe' was really based upon my dad," says Rickey Medlocke. "They didn't want to say actually Shorty Medlocke cause he'd probably get hassled by people. He was a big influence on myself and other people. My dad was a musician all his life. He grew up on a sharecropping farm in northwest Georgia. The share-cropping farm across the road from them was a black family. At the end of the week, they would have meals together and they would play together. [Later] my dad would play these old 78 records of Blind Lemon Jefferson, Mississippi John Hurt, Huddie Leadbitter, and Robert Johnson. All these old black players." Like the fictional Curtis Lowe, Shorty Medlocke influenced a new generation of blues and country singers, Ronnie Van Zant among them.

"Workin' For MCA" had been written for the band to present to the record label during a showcase at a Sounds of the South press party. The song's sassy references to making sure that the band be paid its due from the Yankee slickers were just cheeky enough to get the attention of those in charge. The label executives loved it. They were going to keep their eye on this band.

Second Helping hit #12 and was certified gold. Lynyrd Skynyrd was only the second Southern band to achieve that honor. Skynyrd was now well on its way to stardom.

The Skynyrd boys were overwhelmed with the reception they received both on the radio and in concert—not that they felt they didn't deserve it, but the adulation and attention weren't something that they'd been raised to expect. The boys were gratified that whatever success they'd been experiencing was based on their commit-ment to being themselves. What you saw was definitely what you were going to get. Lynyrd Skynyrd wasn't a manufactured band. The Skynyrd band members were proud to be representing their homeland and the honesty and integrity they believed it to possess. The songs represented commitment to honorable living and the right-eousness found in a deep commitment to family. If there were references to drinking and rowdy behavior, that was a part of the Southerners' package as well. The Lynyrd Skynyrd boys would never pretend to be anyone other than who they were, no matter how many records they might be able to sell. They were selling records left and right just by being themselves.

Ronnie Van Zant's persona as a rebel country boy was developing, accentuated by the distinctive Texas Hatters headgear he wore. Tattoos were prevalent with all members of the band. Ronnie had two: an eagle with its wings spread over an American flag and a scroll with his father Lacy's name on it.

Back home, Skynyrd's notoriety for brawling and drinking had been understood and grudgingly accepted. With the musicians' newfound success, the excesses they'd enjoyed as rowdy young men in Jacksonville expanded to rock stars on a rampage. Having a reputation as good ole boys who reveled in guzzling whiskey and loved a raunchy bar fight was good press, but it soon became a personal problem for the boys in the band. They were frequently arrested for brawling. Ronnie picked fights at the drop of a hat when he'd been drinking.

"When he got drunk," claims Billy Powell, "he was definitely in the Dr. Jekyll and Mr. Hyde syndrome. He knocked my teeth out twice." The second time that happened, Billy needed a six-piece bridge and decided Ronnie should pay for it. Ronnie didn't have a problem with that. "He's going, 'I'm sorry, Billy. Here's the check, man.' And he's laughing the whole dadgum time. He thought it was really funny." says Billy. "[But] when he was straight, he was just a all around good guy. He really was, and that's what I hope everybody remembers him for."

Living with this sudden, dramatic realization of the American Dream was confusing and difficult for the guys in Skynyrd. Descending head-first into the world of rock and roll debauchery, the toll of the endless stream of groupies, too much Jack Daniels, and very little sleep soon had the members of the band continually at odds with one another. Their inter-band fist fights became legendary, especially since the bandaged hands, busted teeth, and broken noses and arms of virtuoso guitar and keyboard players were difficult to hide. "We made The Who look like church boys on Sunday," said Ronnie. "We done things only fools'd do. I was abusin' myself on the road, because, after all, man, if it ain't fun, it ain't worth it."[11] Enjoying the spoils of their new-found wealth, the boys didn't waste any time purchasing fancy cars and were even

Billy Powell, ca. 1974. Credit: MCA Records/Judy Van Zant Jenness Collection.

quicker running them into ditches and trees. Some band members found drugs to be a welcome departure from the whiskey and champagne rampages.

But the guys bowed to no one once they were on stage. "Even Eric Clapton didn't intimidate them," remembers Judy Van Zant Jenness, referring to the night Lynyrd Skynyrd opened for Clapton in Memphis. They believed wholeheartedly in their music and felt no band was better when it came to doing what they were doing. They'd earned every bit of their success simply playing their music. "We are just simple, common people who are not trying to be big actors," Allen Collins told *Creem* magazine. "We're trying to get people off, just trying to be good."

Allen Collins, ca. 1974. Credit: MCA Records/Judy Van Zant Jenness Collection.

Ronnie Van Zant continued to nurture the band that was now his dream come true. "Ronnie was a great leader of a great band," says Outlaws guitarist Hughie Thomasson. "He took his music very seriously and made sure the rest of the band did, too." Even though Ronnie was wholeheartedly participating in the wild life on the road, he tried to encourage the others to focus on the music when it was focus-on-the-music time. "[Ronnie] was a ramrod in the band," says Charlie Daniels. "And kind of a spark plug. He was just the personification of what Lynyrd Skynyrd was all about."

Buddy Buie, the spark plug for The Atlanta Rhythm Section, was disappointed that *Back Up Against The Wall* didn't make the breakthrough that he and the band had hoped for, despite the attention Ronnie Hammond's vocals received. The band terminated its contract with MCA and signed with Polydor.

Third Annual Pipe Dream was released in 1974. The band hoped that this record might be the one that would do the trick. Following in the steps of Southern Rockers before them, The Atlanta Rhythm Section boys took to the road to promote the album. They figured if their records weren't going to receive the airplay needed to introduce them to their audience, appearing on a bill where they could show what they could do might be the answer.

The band's efforts paid off. "Doraville," a catchy, bass-driven song about the Atlanta suburb where Studio One was located, was released as a single off *Third Annual Pipe Dream.* It played well on the radio and eventually made its way to the Top 40. The band members began to think that they might have a chance at succeeding and putting all the naysaying to rest. The group remained on the road, and at the very least, the audiences recognized "Doraville."

Wet Willie was about to receive more recognition than it ever dreamed possible. In 1974 the band members recorded *Keep On Smilin'*, their fourth album. Donna Hall and Ella Avery had been brought in as The Williettes to provide background vocals. Donna, Jimmy and Jack Hall's sister, had participated in their earlier albums. as well as worked with Marshall Tucker, Cowboy, and others. Donna now hit the road with the band. The success of the Williettes within Wet Willie's sound later influenced Lynyrd Skynyrd to bring its own female backup singers to the party in the form of The Honkettes.

Having proven that there was an audience for Wet Willie's music, Phil Walden and the band decided to work with a producer who could capture the group's onstage appeal. Tom Dowd was brought in to aid in the effort. Having Dowd on board worked. The band was both astonished and delighted when "Keep On Smilin'" was released as a single and quickly climbed to #10 on the *Billboard* Singles chart.

"Keep On Smilin'" was a personal song for co-writer Jimmy Hall. "I actually had moved outside of Macon to a little farmhouse with my girlfriend," remembers Hall. "Some of those experiences, and some relationship problems at the time with my girlfriend, fueled the lyrics. Thus the lines, 'City boy to country man' [and] 'Are you a farmer, are you a star?' I was looking at the country side of life and enjoying it. The quiet. Growing a garden. I had put the lyrics together, and it was a steady flow. I didn't have a song form in mind. I just had these words when we went in to start preproduction on the album. So I was sitting around with Rick Hirsch, and I said 'What have you got?' He said, 'I've got this little instrumental, a little riff that I want you listen to.' It was kind of reggae, and I liked it.

"We fooled around with it a little while, and I said, 'Let's see what I've got. Something that might work with that. [I] pulled out the lyrics. It went fast in the way it gelled. In a couple of rehearsals it started falling together. I could tell that it was pretty special. I liked the positive message; it was autobiographical. Rick liked it. We liked the way it was a little Van Morrison-ish. We played it for Tom Dowd, and he just was knocked out from the very beginning. He had a sense about it that it was a special song. It was one of the first things we recorded for that album. Everybody was jumping up and down. I'll never forget hearing it on the radio for the first time. That's when it more or less hit me that this was a song that was maybe one in a lifetime."

Hall wasn't the only one who felt that "Keep On Smilin'" reflected his emotions. "There are so many stories around it that have come to me," he says. "People that were positively influenced by it or helped them through a hard time. It had a positive, uplifting appeal to people."

The success of Wet Willie gave others in the Southern Rock fold hope for their own success. After The Marshall Tucker Band's first album was released, its members assessed what was going on in their lives. Toy Caldwell had been working at the Waterworks in addition to playing with the band. He returned home to Spartanburg every night after regional gigs and was wearing himself out. Tommy prevailed upon Phil Walden to give the band more of an advance so that Toy could quit his job. Walden agreed.

The daily life of Toy Caldwell and the Tuckers took a turn for the better. With the success of *Marshall Tucker Band*, it was easy for Walden to book Tucker as the opening act for the now extremely hot Allman Brothers Band on a national tour. At first Marshall Tucker was just another hot band, without a clearly defined regional identity. "We never thought of them as a Southern band," remembers New York fan Steve Avery. "We didn't think of them as country, either. Especially with their flute. But Lynyrd Skynyrd, with that big Confederate flag behind them. . . ."

Toy and Tommy Caldwell, 1974. Credit: Doug Gray/Michael B. Smith.

Backstage with Marshall Tucker, ca. 1974. (Standing left to right)
Paul Riddle, Doug Gray, Toy Caldwell. (Seated left to right)
Jerry Eubanks, George McCorkle, Tommy Caldwell. Credit:
The Collection of George McCorkle.

Regardless of how Northerners perceived the members of The Marshall Tucker Band, they were thrilled to share the bill with the Allmans. "[The Allman Brothers] was the best band, playing-wise, excitement-wise," says Doug Gray. "They didn't move; they just played their asses off. I thought it was the best band in the world. 'What am I doing here?' That was what it was like."

The exposure that the Allman dates brought Marshall Tucker was just what the band needed. Soon word of mouth, bolstered by the verbal support offered by Gregg Allman and Dickie Betts, had the name Marshall Tucker on lips all over the country. The Brothers were playing sold-out arenas and coliseums, and the boys from Spartanburg were suddenly in the thick of it. Soon they were receiving requests to open for other major acts, and the musicians traveled around the country playing wherever they were asked. Commenting on life on the road in a Dodge van crammed with seven people, Gray says with a laugh, "You learned how to drive with the band, you learned how to cry with them, you knew their emotional problems that everybody had, you know? You knew what was going to make it work."

The electricity that flew off the stage when the Tuckers took it was sometimes intimidating, even for the most established acts. Marshall Tucker opened for Three Dog Night one night at the Forum in Los Angeles. The Tuckers were surprised to learn that their set was limited to fifteen minutes. "The night before, we blew their ass away," George McCorkle remembers. "They gave us seven foot of stage, maybe ten foot of stage. We had fifteen minutes to play, and that was it. Then get off."

Debating whether or not it was even worth going out, the boys decided that some exposure was better than none. They ripped through "Take the Highway" and "Ramblin'" and left the stage. The crowd went nuts, and the Tuckers were allowed to return for an encore of "Can't You See." Three Dog Night paled in comparison.

"Kicked their ass again," laughs McCorkle. "[The time limitation] probably didn't have anything to do with the band or the musicians at all."

The success of that show, however brief, was indicative of every show Marshall Tucker played that year. "When the Tucker band was on, when everybody was feelin' good, playin' good, that was a hard band to have open for ya," McCorkle muses. "Because we were so hungry. We didn't intentionally want to hurt anybody, but we knew what we had to do. When the switch went down, we went to work." Marshall Tucker did, indeed, take the highway. The group ended up playing more than 300 nationwide dates in 1974.

Marshall Tucker played New York City for the first time at a place called Kenny's Castaway. The venue held about sixty people. On August 12, 1974, the group returned to the city to perform at the Wollman Rink with John Hammond and Grinderswitch. The show went well. *Variety* claimed that that the "combo may not be as flashy and raunchy as other groups, but they're one of the tightest."[12]

Just a few months later, the Tuckers returned to play Madison Square Garden, opening for The Allman Brothers Band. Something happened to George McCorkle during that time in New York City that hadn't happened to him anywhere other than in his home town of Spartanburg: he was recognized on the street as being George McCorkle from The Marshall Tucker Band. "Scared me to death," remembers McCorkle. "You think, 'Well, hell, we just a little small Southern band from Spartanburg, South Carolina. And here's somebody that I don't even know recognizes me in New York City.' That was a real turning point for me in understanding the impact the band really did have."

Marshall Tucker's music was well received wherever it was heard. The combination of musical styles and the variety of instruments caused a lot of excitement among audience members. Fan Randy Davis remembers how the musical personalities and stage presence of the band were exciting for those who saw the guys perform. "Toy would take off on his guitar, and the rest of the band would hold on and enjoy the ride."

The exposure was great, even if the financial rewards were slim and sometimes nonexistent. McCorkle claims the band looked at the big picture rather than got depressed over what they weren't making. "I remember many nights counting the money in the van, going from town to town, and ending up with one penny, after you've fed everybody, and the hotel was paid for, and the van was gassed up," remembers McCorkle. "You had one penny. I remember seeing, I think it was Joe McConnell, our road manager, rolled the window down and slung [the penny] over a bridge in the river. That's all we cleared. So you just accept that, and go 'all right, we're goin' to make some more tonight. Here we go.'"

The Tucker boys played music. That's what they did. The alternatives, working at the Waterworks or at the cotton mill, weren't choices they cared to make. "My father, when I was ten years old, took me to the cotton mill," reflects Doug Gray. "He said, 'All right, we're going to walk down here and see if you want a job on the weekends.' So guess what, I really started singing good then."

While deeply involved in this onslaught of performances, The Marshall Tucker Band returned to the studio to cut its second album. Paul Hornsby produced *A New Life* at Capricorn Studios in early 1974. He was concerned with the fact that the band was tired and had very little time to pull something together. The first album had been such a hit that the follow-up was expected to be exceptional. "I always liked being prepared and knowing what I was going to cut when I went in," says Hornsby. "But you could never do that with them. You had to take what you got. But they always pulled it off. I was always amazed when they'd come out of the studio, and there'd always be a gem in there somewhere, you know?"

"I probably didn't hear the songs on *New Life* more than once [before recording them]. Or maybe not even at all until we got in the studio. It was like plug up, start and go to work, and leave. *New Life* was like a blur," says McCorkle.

The title cut opened the album, once again employing the now signature sound of Jerry Eubank's flute, Toy Caldwell's uncommon guitar sound, and Doug Gray's familiar vocal treatment. The swing-propelled "Another Cruel Love" was a standout. "24 Hours At A Time" was a tune Toy penned while sitting in the back of the van crisscrossing the country. The song had been a favorite in concert and transferred well to the record.

Ever expanding the Tucker sound, Toy had decided that "Blue Ridge Mountain Sky" would sound good with a little banjo on it. He asked if anyone in the band could play banjo. McCorkle volunteered and then sat himself in a room for two hours and *learned* the banjo.

A New Life didn't yield any real hit singles, although the material was very well received in concert. The album itself was declared a success when it slowly made its way up the album chart to #37. It eventually was certified gold as well.

The Tuckers enjoyed the satisfaction of another hit album, but they concentrated even more on their live gigs. They were committed to taking Marshall Tucker to the people. George McCorkle views Tucker's road experience as an extension of their rural roots. "South Carolina boys raised in a small town," he reflects. "All we knew was a work ethic. We didn't know anything else. We just knew how you made a living is you worked like a dog. So we translated that into music and to our touring. We didn't consciously do it. We just realized later in life that we did."

Doug Gray simplifies the concept even further. "They thought we were out there working 365 days a year cause we were trying to prove ourself," he states. "We were working 365 days a year primarily because people wanted to see us, you know? These people wanted to hear us, so there we were."

The powers that be at Capricorn decided, perhaps prematurely, that Tucker's concert success indicated the time was ripe for a Marshall Tucker double album. *Where We All Belong* consisted of two distinct offerings. The first album contained live material that had been recorded at one of the band's Milwaukee concerts. It represented the first time the group was recorded live. The other album, which contained new studio material, was recorded on 24 track and offered a more countrified Tucker, with western swing figuring prominently on some of the cuts. "This Old Cowboy," which opens the album, is a song that the band members said was almost autobiographical for Toy.

Tucker friend Charlie Daniels had been brought in to play fiddle on the studio album. The band later laughed about the fact that for the longest time their fans believed Daniels was a member of The Marshall Tucker Band. Daniels appeared in concert with Tucker whenever the opportunity arose to include the now familiar sound of his fiddle in the live presentation of Marshall Tucker classics. "It sort of got to be a tradition that Charlie started jamming a lot on stage with them, and so we called Charlie in to play on the album," recalls Paul Hornsby. "He was a part of 'em, I mean as far as the studio end, and we had to have him."

The traditional country ballad "Try One More Time" is included on the album, as well as an original Toy composition, "Low Down Ways." A new tune titled "Where A

Country Boy Belongs" features some attractive slide playing by guest artist Elvin Bishop. "In My Own Way" is a showcase for Toy's pedal steel playing. Toy and Tommy co-wrote "Now She's Gone," and Doug Gray contributed a stellar blues vocal with "Try One More Time."

The live part of the album, recorded at The Performing Arts Center in Milwaukee, Wisconsin, opens with "Ramblin'." Gray had a particular affinity for that song: "The song's a great song. It kind of fit me more than it did anybody else cause I was the crazy guy that was ramblin'. Everything that happened to rock and roll bands was happening to us, except we have kept a splashy little sparkling white image. All the nastiness that we did, we never pushed it far enough to where we couldn't step back. We always knew when it was time to stop."

To further illustrate Marshall Tucker's command of its music, "Ramblin'" leads right into a fourteen-minute version of "24 Hours At A Time." B.B. King is paid tribute with "Everyday I Have The Blues," and the album closes with the usual Tucker show opener, "Take The Highway."

Because *Where We All Belong* is a double album, it was a little more expensive than the new-to-Tucker fans wanted to pay, and it failed to make the Top 40. Eventually, however, it was certified gold. In the meantime, the band continued to tour nonstop.

In 1974 The Charlie Daniels Band released *Way Down Yonder* and took to the road in support of Marshall Tucker. Being on the Tucker tour was great exposure for Charlie. The Tucker fans were crazy about him when he'd appear onstage with the band to contribute the sizzling intonations of his country fiddle. "We'd come out and do our show," Charlie remembers. "Then I'd come out and sit in with them on their show, play fiddle with them. A lot of times we'd end the night up with almost everybody on stage."

The family atmosphere of the Southern Rock bands held intact. They all drew together, determined to help one another when the occasion arose. One of the players, Paul Hornsby, was about to figure into the history of another Capricorn band.

An appearance at Grant's Lounge hadn't always resulted in recording contracts for the acts that played there, but the chances of having Phil Walden get down to have a listen were increased when a gig in Capricorn's hometown was booked. Such was the case with a new band out of Florida. Grinderswitch took its name from a

Tennessee railroad settlement. The band had been formed when Allman Brothers Band roadie and bass player Joe Dan Petty got together with guitarist Dru Lombar, rhythm guitarist Larry Howard, and drummer Rick Barnett to play some bluesy country rock. Joe Dan was popular in the Macon community. The ears of the local musicians perked up when they heard what Petty and his new band had to offer.

The members of Grinderswitch knew what it took to get people's attention. They were no strangers to the music industry. Joe Dan, of course, had watched The Allman Brothers Band stun its audiences with innovation and panache.

Dru Lombar felt he knew how to whisk an audience away from his own experience listening to radio, back in the days when Elvis was first pronounced king. "They were playing Elvis and all that kind of stuff," remembers Lombar. "But they were also playing Four Prep, Four Lad, clean-cut, all-American stuff that had no soul whatsoever. When we started hearing this black stuff and this rockin' stuff, man, we went, 'Oooh, energy.' We picked up on it and that became ingrained into all our beings. When we finally figured out what we wanted to be, that's what we did, and it came out in everybody's music."

Lombar and Howard wrote most of Grinderswitch's initial original material, and the band quickly realized that they had something special. A trip down to Jacksonville to play at one of that city's many clubs proved frustrating, however, when the band realized that it had only five long songs to play. The band returned to Houston County, Georgia and took up residence on a farm where the guys wrote and rehearsed for about eight months. Then they were ready.

Paul Hornsby demonstrated his faith in the band by helping the new entity put together a demo tape for Phil Walden. Soon Walden was down at Grant's, looking the band over to see what live appeal it might have. He wasn't disappointed. He signed Grinderswitch to one of his famous recording, management, and booking contracts. "Like him, hate him, whatever...," muses Lombar. "[Phil Walden] was slick, but he had the vision and knew how to pull it off. Without him, none of us would have gotten out of the cities we lived in. He provided the launching pad for everybody. I'm not going to say it was the greatest business deal in the world to be part of, but it was a place where if you had it together and you wanted to go out and show your stuff to the world, there it was. And he provided that stage."

Honest To Goodness was released as Grinderswitch's first album in June, 1974. The album was enthusiastically received by the rock press, who had by now been conditioned to pay attention to anything new coming out of Capricorn. "A tight, self-confident approach, tingling guitar licks, painfully intense vocals and swiftly-flowing musical undercurrents are the highlights of tunes like the chugging "Catch A Train," "Can't Keep A Good Man Down," and "Kiss the Blues Good-bye," on which Richard Betts matches guitar wits with Grinderswitch's Dru Lombar," wrote Ellen Mandell in *Good Times*.

Honest To Goodness is full of exceptional songs. Lombar's "Homebound" and "Roll On Gambler" were crowd favorites when performed in concert. Petty's "Eight Miles to Memphis" was a fast-paced number reminiscent of his former employers, The Allman Brothers.

Because of Petty's association and the fact that Grinderswitch was out of Macon and Capricorn, Grinderswitch was compared to the Allmans probably more than was appropriate. The band didn't mind, though. "We all sounded like that," says Lombar. "We all had that same format of jamming, long periods of time on stage. It was all Southern music. I was honored that somebody would compare us to some-body that great. [The Allmans] were very supportive of everything. They gave us equipment; they helped us get great dates. Everything I'm doing today I owe to those guys."

According to the members of Grinderswitch, the focal point of their music was to entertain. They weren't interested in being a political forum, as many other artists of their time were now becoming. "It's not our job to get up on the soapbox," asserts Lombar. "I think our jobs as musicians is just to play good music. We tried to write songs that had some depth to 'em, but we weren't trying to save the world. We weren't trying to change any political structure. I guess being in the South, you're far removed from that, and you feel like you don't have control in that arena anyway, you know? So why even bother? Everybody else was trying to save everything, so I figured it'd get done."

In the time between the recording and the release of the album, Grinderswitch took to the road, gaining experience as a performing band. The group's first tour was with The Allman Brothers Band. "We came from nothing to all of a sudden we were out there with the Allman Brothers playing for 10,000 and 20,000 people, man," recalls Lombar. "Overwhelming, I got to say. You know, we were like huhuhuh. . . ."

Not all the bands Grinderswitch played with were as musically similar as the Allmans, and some of the dates were less than enjoyable, especially a gig with Rush. "They weren't there to see no Southern Rockers," recalls Lombar, reflecting on that show's audience. "They were there to see Rush. Rush in Dayton. Boy, the people hated us."

Grinderswitch, like other Capricorn and Southern bands, played more up North and in the Midwest than around its local base. The audiences were hungry for the group's sound and turned out in great numbers whenever sons of the South appeared. "You'd go to New York City, and they'd go berserk," Lombar remembers. "Anywhere in New York State or anywhere out in the Midwest, they'd go berserk. Just nuts, totally nuts. Down South it's like, 'Oh yeah, I know those guys. . . .' The ole' prophet hath no honor in his hometown syndrome."

The hometowns of Southern Rock were primarily Macon and Jacksonville by this time. It is strange to think that the music of Blackfoot, a band known for epitomizing the Southern Rock sound in some circles, didn't come to fruition until the group moved from Jacksonville to New Jersey in an attempt to grab the brass ring. While retaining their allegiance to their Southern roots, the musicians in the four-piece band felt it necessary to leave Florida to jumpstart their career. Their hearts, as with their musical contemporaries, remained in Dixie.

Rickey Medlocke, Blackfoot's founder, was born to rock and roll. With a childhood steeped in the music of the Mississippi Delta Blues, Medlocke grew up loving music. Shorty Medlocke, his grandfather, who had legally adopted Rickey when he was an infant, had reared him to appreciate blues, bluegrass, and just about every other kind of music that entered their realm.

"My dad had a lot of bands," recalls Medlocke. "He was in and out of Nashville all the time. [He] was on a TV show out of Jacksonville, a local show called 'The Toby Dowdy Show.' When I was three years old, I took up playing banjo and joined him on that show. It was a father and son kind of thing. It was kind of a novelty thing, this little kid playing banjo on a country music show. I played 'til I was eight years old. The show lasted for five years. I took up playing guitar when I was like five.

"Now I look back on it as probably my father, Shorty, was the biggest major influence on my life. Not only was he a parent, but he was like my real buddy, a real best friend and mentor. He was a master at the five-string banjo and actually was a master at a lot of instruments, period. He played banjo, guitar, dobro, harmonica, the upright bass; he played the fiddle. He played 'em all. I looked up to him so much as far as a musician goes. To this day he's still here with me in spirit and still a big influence."

When Medlocke became a teenager, he expanded his music to include rock and roll. He listened to Jimi Hendrix, Eric Clapton, ZZ Top's Billy Gibbons, and Elvis. "I love music," laughs Medlocke. "I eat it, sleep it, drink it, breathe it. I love all types of music. I listen to everything from Bach, Mozart, Beethoven, all the way to black blues, all the way from the heaviest of rock to the softest of country. I'm a fanatic for flamenco guitar, classical guitar music. I listen to it all."

Medlocke knew what he wanted to do with his life since the age of seven when he saw Elvis perform in concert. "He made it rock, and he was very innovative," Rickey says. "What an imagination. I'm part Native American, so I'm a very spiritual person in the first place. I believe this guy was not from this plane and he was only here for awhile. I believe that's the way it was meant to be, to give us something we would remember forever and still play today. Music, basically was the essence, from the time I saw Elvis Presley. That's all I wanted to do."

Medlocke played with a variety of cover bands throughout his teenage years, including The Hot Water Blues Band (with Medlocke on bass), The Rocking Aces (with Medlocke on guitar), Candied Apple (with Medlocke on drums), Miracle Sounds (with Medlocke providing vocals), and Sunday Funnies.

With his boyhood friends, bass player Greg T. Walker and keyboard player Ronnie Sciabarasi, Rickey Medlocke decided to form a "serious" band. They found a guitar player down at The Comic Book Club named Charlie Hargrett and soon were calling themselves Fresh Garbage. This time around Medlocke played drums. Fresh Garbage played wherever they could find a gig. They especially favored The Comic Book Club, which was also hosting such bands as Hour Glass and One Percent at that time.

In 1969 Medlocke, Walker, and Hargrett joined with two musicians from a band named Tangerine: Medlocke's old friend drummer Jakson Spires and keyboard player Dewitt Gibbs. They called the band Hammer. While performing as the house band at a club called Dubbs in Gainesville, Florida, the band was approached by Nancy O'Connor of Hollybrook Records, a subsidiary of Epic. O'Connor thought the band had something special, and soon they were on their way to New York City to cut a demo for the label.

Nothing original was put on tape. In fact the band members were asked to try their hand at "Knock Three Times." Although that song became a hit for a pop group named Tony Orlando and Dawn, it wasn't the direction Hammer wanted its music to take.

About this time the musicians decided to rename their band and start over. They thought hard over what they should call themselves. "Finally Jakie came in one day and said, 'Hey, I been thinking about it,'" remembers Medlocke. "Since several guys in the band are part Native American, let's try using the name Blackfoot.' Everybody thought, 'Hey, you know what? That's kind of a cool thing to do. Let's go with it.' So, thus was born Blackfoot."

Blackfoot relocated from Greenwich Village to New Jersey. The guys stayed at The Royal Hotel, a hovel that seemed to be home to every type of itinerant musician and vagabond. Dewitt Gibbs decided to return to Florida. Blackfoot was suddenly a four-piece. Even so, the band became quite popular and soon was playing more gigs than the guys had anticipated. The band members felt they had something different to offer and were gratified that the bars and clubs along the Eastern circuit agreed.

Nancy O'Connor had replaced Ira Sokoloff as Blackfoot's manager. Soon personal problems concerning O'Connor and members of the band cast a cloud over the group. It wasn't fun anymore. Most of Blackfoot's gigs had been at colleges, and when the schools let out for the summer, more than half of the band's regular dates were suspended until the fall. At this time the members of Blackfoot were living with a band named Yiege. There was a lot of tension in the close quarters, especially without dates to play. Blackfoot's members decided to go their separate ways for awhile.

Medlocke, however, had no desire to leave the music business. He called up his friend Allen Collins looking for work with Collins's band, Lynyrd Skynyrd. Medlocke was desperate to get out of New Jersey and didn't particularly care if the job was as a musician or as a roadie. Collins was happy to hear from Medlocke and asked if he still played drums. Although Medlocke hadn't played drums in quite a while, he confirmed that he did. Collins wanted Medlocke to call Ronnie Van Zant and talk to him about employment. "So I called Ronnie up, and Ronnie says, 'What are you doing, man?' I says, 'Well, I'm needing a gig, you know? I just called Allen, and I told him I'd do anything, like load equipment or set up the equipment or drive the truck or whatever.' He goes, 'You still hammer around on the drums a little bit?' I said, 'Heck, yeah, man.' He goes 'Well, I'll tell you what. We need a drummer.'"

Medlocke jumped at the opportunity. Two weeks later he was laying down tracks with Skynyrd at Muscle Shoals for what later became *Lynyrd Skynyrd's First . . . and Last*. Medlocke even contributed two songs he'd written to the tapes, "The Seasons" and "White Dove." He loved his brief time with Skynyrd, but he decided that he didn't want to spend his career behind a set of drums. There was no room in Skynyrd for another guitar player, so it was time for him to move on.

By August, 1972, Medlocke had patched things up with Spires and Hargrett. Together with bass player Lenny Stadler, the three started jamming in clubs throughout North Carolina. Blackfoot was asked to open throughout the Southeast for such bands as Black Oak Arkansas, Poco, and Edgar and Johnny Winter.

In September, Stadler became ill. When a spot was discovered on his lung, he was scheduled for exploratory surgery. After an X-ray was taken minutes before the surgery, doctors determined that the suspected tumor had disappeared. Stadler quit the band and joined a gospel group called The Sammy Hall Singers. He eventually became a United Methodist minister.

By October, 1973, Greg Walker returned to the fold, and Blackfoot was once more operational. The band members returned to New Jersey where they sold out nearly every club they played. When Rickey Medlocke was sidelined as a singer during the summer due to nodes on his vocal cords, a singer named Patrick Jude came in to front the band. By the fall, Medlocke could no longer stand not singing and resumed his position as frontman. It was time to think about recording. Medlocke then approached Muscle Shoals' Jimmy Johnson to see if Johnson might help the band obtain a recording contract with a major label. Johnson was impressed when he heard Blackfoot. He produced several tracks, predominantly compositions by Medlocke and Spires.

In 1974 Island Records decided to release the tapes as an album. Blackfoot made its record debut with *No Reservations*. The record wasn't a priority with Island and received almost no promotion. Discouraged, the band members returned to the road. They extended their circuit to Texas, Virginia, Tennessee, and the Midwest and continued to be well received.

Gregg Allman decided to tour in support of his solo album in February, 1974. No sooner had the announcement been made than rumors that Gregg had left The Allman Brothers Band began to fly fast and furious. But this wasn't the case at this point in time. Gregg wanted to demonstrate the full range of his musical involvement. It was that simple.

Gregg put together a band consisting of Jaimoe, Leavell, Stewart, Talton, Boyer, and a bass player named David Brown. Gregg also brought in Randall Bramlett on guitar. Gregg went all out, adding a small string section, some horns, and three female backup vocalists.

In addition Gregg hired a mechanic named John "Scooter" Herring to accompany him on the road and provide whatever Gregg needed to get him through the tour. Herring was deeply involved with some major drug action around Macon, but his presence suited Gregg's purposes. He joined the tour as Gregg's personal valet.

Gregg and the band played to large crowds, and the tour was successful. As to the rumors of the demise of The Allman Brothers Band, after Gregg played for more than two hours in Cincinnati during an April 25 concert, the entire band joined him on stage for a ninety-minute encore.

The Allman Brothers Band hit the road as a unit for a multi-city summer tour at the end of May. The guys were joined on the road by The Marshall Tucker Band and Wet Willie. The tour was like old home week, and all of the band members enjoyed it.

The Allman Brothers Band's second date was in Atlanta for the Georgia Jam. Also on the bill were Marshall Tucker, Lynyrd Skynyrd, and Grinderswitch. Almost 62,000 fans descended on Fulton County Stadium. The day didn't get off to a very good start for the Allmans. A Southern rainstorm began as Marshall Tucker played "Can't You See." The rain caused the show to come to a temporary halt, although the Brothers' crew tried hard to work around it. The fans were forced to wait nearly four hours in between the time Marshall Tucker left the stage and The Allman Brothers Band came on.

Fan Stan Warren remembers what happened next. "From our vantage point, we were able to watch all the efforts by the stage crew," recalls Warren. "We were ecstatic when we saw the Allman Brothers finally climb up on stage, as we were really tired of waiting. They played either three or four songs, then stopped for a quick intermission. Gregg Allman was so wasted from waiting to go on stage that he could not go on and play. Two stage hands, supporting him from both sides, tried to sober him up by walking him around backstage, right in front of us. At times it looked like they were dragging him around, as his feet refused to keep up with them." The truth of the matter was that Gregg, Jaimoe, and Lamar had apparently been dosed with a strong hallucinogen. All three musicians recovered sufficiently enough to continue the show.

Concert disasters aside, the accolades continued for the band. *Playboy* magazine's annual readers poll named The Allman Brothers Band "Most Popular Rock Band." Duane Allman was named to the "*Playboy* Jazz and Pop Hall of Fame."

The creative juices of the band members continued to flow. Dickey Betts decided that he, too, would like his own project. Capricorn backed Dickey's idea of a country-tinged solo project that he titled *Highway Call*. He called on eminent bluegrass fiddler Vassar Clements, Conway Twitty's pedal steel player John Hughes, and Chuck Leavell to complement his guitar. A bluegrass group called The Poindexters contributed, as well as a gospel vocal group called The Rambos.

The album opens with "Long Time Gone," a reflection of Dickey's road-weariness. The album reveals Dickey's affinity for all things natural and mystical through "Rain" and "Let Nature Sing." Side B is entirely instrumental, with wonderful interchanges between Dickey and Clements.

Dickey's first solo project was released in August, 1974. Capricorn's double album *Duane Allman: An Anthology Volume II* was also released that month. Some people speculated that Dickey might resent being once again closely moored to Duane's artistry. Dickey's own album, however, was a strong entry into the guitar player sweepstakes. He needn't have worried. *Highway Call* stood on its own.

Dickey took his act out on the road, too, asking Clements and Muscle Shoals' Spooner Oldham to accompany him. Dickey tried something different. He wanted to present a show that would illustrate the history of American music. As weary of it all as he might have been, he wanted to play his music and give his fans their money's worth.

Through the efforts of all of Capricorn's hard-working artists, the label was on a roll. When Phil Walden saw how successful *Laid Back* had become, he issued a two-record set from Gregg Allman's tour in support of that album. Recorded at Carnegie

Hall and The Capitol Theater, *The Gregg Allman Tour* was released on the heels of *Highway Call.*

Gregg and Dickey's solo efforts were doing well, but The Allman Brothers Band as a cooperative entity wasn't. The band members rarely played together and hadn't recorded an album in nearly two years. It was time to see if they could put their personal difficulties aside and make their particular brand of magic again.

The Brothers returned to the Capricorn Studio to prepare for their next recording. They managed to lay down a sweet reworking of Muddy Waters's "Can't Lose What You Never Had," and it seemed like they would be able to pull it all off. But even the return to music didn't help the internal strife and fragmentation of The Allman Brothers Band. The Brothers had serious problems with drugs and alcohol, as well as a general apathy toward the group and the music.

The members of the band periodically wandered into the studio. Johnny Sandlin tried to get them to lay down instrumental tracts, but the project wasn't coming together. Gregg took off for California, where he ended up becoming involved in a tempestuous relationship with Cher. Only Leavell, Williams, and Jaimoe seemed to be interested in making a record. Sandlin was pulling out his hair. He finally went out to California himself to lay down what little he could with Gregg. The session left much to be desired, and the project came to a halt.

Around this time the Brothers also started to believe that their business dealings with Phil Walden were unfavorable to the band. Questions regarding royalties, payments, and back taxes were raised and didn't seem to be addressed in a satisfactory manner back at The Brothers' business office. Plans to deal with the issue, however, were put on hold.

Gregg finally returned from his extended trip West, having married, separated, and reunited with Cher. He didn't seem interested in resuming the recording session but agreed to give it a go. Although the band returned to the task at hand, the result was less than exciting or satisfying.

CHAPTER 12

The South's Gonna Do It Again

1975

Lynyrd Skynyrd's soldout tour of the United States and Canada was extended when more dates were added in Europe in support of Queen, Humble Pie, and Golden Earring. The band members played to a full house in late December at London's Rainbow on their first visit to England. They were scheduled to open for Golden Earring, but the promoter put them at the top of the bill after he saw what they could do. *Sounds* magazine summed up the change of plans as, "Supporting ain't their style, they're too damn good for it."

In England Ronnie Van Zant was compared to a barefooted Paul Kossoff. Ronnie no doubt enjoyed the comparison to the Free guitarist. But it wasn't all compliments and free sailing. When he talked to the British press, he was tired and most often in the company of a whiskey bottle. The band members gave their performances everything they had, though. An appearance at the Oxford Theatre even had to be canceled one night when Ronnie's throat was just too sore for him to sing. Skynyrd plugged away, playing loud and hard.

The band returned to the United States to play nearly nonstop dates from February through late December. Skynyrd appeared in nearly every state. Traveling from town to town was brutal. The band members started to get on each other's nerves as they all struggled to make the best of each appearance. The crew unceremoniously dubbed the outing "The Torture Tour."

The band members were on edge. The constant in-fighting and the craziness of being on the road week after week caused Ed King and Bob Burns to abandon the Skynyrd ship. Burns later claimed, "I just had to leave for my own sake. The touring, the recording, the constant motion was too much."[13] The tour was difficult for everybody. "We just never knew we were going to be working that hard," says Billy Powell. "I don't think we've worked that hard since. That went on so long. And we started getting at each other's throats."

Life on the road was one thing, but it was important to the band that the music be top-notch. "I especially felt for Ronnie, the vocalist, you know?" remembers Leon Wilkeson of that tour. "How he was able to stand that strain? I mean, you can't go to a music store and buy a new throat, you know what I mean?"

Lynyrd Skynyrd soon became known internationally as much for its offstage hedonistic lifestyle as for its gritty, down-home raunchy rock and roll. The tour, however, was successful musically. *Record World* reviewed the band's New York City gig at Avery Fisher Hall as a "power-packed, albeit short, set of some of the finest rock and blues to come across the Mason-Dixon line since The Allman Brothers took the big plunge and headed up to Yankee territory."

Lynyrd Skynyrd wasn't afraid to stand by its Southern roots, no matter where the group played. In the April 25, 1975, issue of *Performance*, the magazine separated the Skynyrd musicians from the Southern Rock term they felt they'd been saddled with. Michael Point wrote, "Their rock & roll, with punchy, three-guitar licks and Ronnie Van Zant's strong and surly vocals, makes Skynyrd probably the only Southern band capable of retaining the interest of say, a New Yorker strong on Bad Company."

That same spring, Alabama Governor George Wallace declared the members of Lynyrd Skynyrd Honorary Lieutenant Colonels in the Alabama State Militia. There was talk about doing a benefit for the controversial governor, and a brief public debate ensued regarding what this meant to the members of Lynyrd Skynyrd. Even the outspoken Ronnie Van Zant was vague about the issue. "Of course I don't agree with everything the man says," Ronnie told a journalist. "I don't like what he says about Colored people. Aw shit, I don't know anything about politics anyway."[14] Today, members of the band say that they don't know remember if they seriously considered doing any such benefits. Regardless, no benefits materialized.

With the success of the group's latest tour, Skynyrd's tenure as a supporting act was over. Lynyrd Skynyrd was simply too powerful a band to follow. As Billy Powell points out, "Who's gonna want to get up on stage after 'Freebird,' you know?"

"Freebird" was released as a single, and the band realized more success when the song reached the Top 20. The crowds clamored for its performance from the first notes of Skynyrd's set. "'Freebird' is Skynyrd's automatic encore, a tribute to the late Duane Allman and the late Berry Oakley," wrote celebrated rock critic Robert Christgau. "It combines an assertively banal ramblin' man lyric with a non-virtuoso rave-up in which all three guitars soar in effortless kinetic interplay. A perfect example of techno-pastoral counter-culture transcendence. It's central image: male freebirds like Duane and Berry flying off on their motorcycles."[15] Some people got it; others didn't. But the appeal of "Freebird" couldn't be ignored.

In spite of all the hard living, Ronnie Van Zant, Gary Rossington, and Allen Collins continued to be prolific songwriters. Even though they all continued to celebrate their new lifestyle offstage, Ronnie's lyrical efforts turned more introspective and socially conscious. His songwriting continued to develop and give voice to what was on his always active mind. "If you really sit down and concentrate, and listen close to, lyrically, what the man had to say, you can get very acquainted with him," says Leon Wilkeson. "He spoke straight from the heart. He wrote about true life experience and real people that he would just change the names."

"[Ronnie] didn't play piano or guitar or anything," says Judy Van Zant Jenness. "So he didn't sit down and do that part of it. But I think he knew where he was going with the song before he started putting the music to it. And he was way ahead of his time. He was writing about gun control and environmental issues and drugs, you know, all that stuff, years and years and years ago, before people even started talking about that kind of stuff."

Ronnie worked well as a lyricist, and Allen, Gary, and Ed King set his words to some incredibly inspired music. The guitars, piano, and backbeat fiercely enveloped the words of each song. The Skynyrd sound was equal parts lyrics and music. Every instrument was indispensable.

On May 20, 1975, *Rolling Stone* reported that Gary had broken the ring finger on his left hand when he slammed a door on it. Nevertheless, the band rocked as hard as ever on June 20 at the Capital Center in Washington, DC. *The Washington Post* reported that "when one guitarist gets tired or runs out of ideas, another is ready to carry on."[16]

Many incidents and accidents weren't so innocent, but the band played on. Skynyrd's fans were becoming just as rowdy as the band. On July 6, 1975, at a home-town concert at Jacksonville's Coliseum, Ronnie's throat started to bleed, and the band announced that the show was over. Five hundred people rioted, resulting in the arrest of sixteen Skynyrd fans.

In between live appearances, the band recorded *Nuthin' Fancy*. New drummer Artimus Pyle was introduced. Pyle was a welcome addition to Lynyrd Skynyrd. Thomas Delmar Pyle was born on July 15, 1948, in Louisville, Kentucky. Artimus was a nickname acquired later in college. Music was always a part of the Pyle household. Pyle's grandmother loved to listen to country music on the radio, and his father often conducted local bands. Pyle was given a job running a bulldozer for his grandfather's road building company when he was eight. "It's amazing when you're sitting on one of these big bulldozers," he says. "You hear all these rhythms. And you play along with them. I found myself kind of tapping along with them." He also found rhythm in the horses he loved to ride. Pyle was soon pounding on pots, pans, and his mother's Quaker Oats boxes. He was given a pair of bongo drums for his ninth birthday and continued to participate in a variety of musical activities, including choir, chorus, and boys ensemble. For his twelfth birthday, his father gave him a set of red sparkle Slinglands with a calf skin head, and he became part of his school's concert band.

Although Pyle enjoyed playing the drums, he didn't think too much about a career in music. He joined the Marine Corps after he graduated from high school; he did very well in the military and was named Best Honor Recruit in 1968. When his father was killed in a midair plane collision in Albuquerque, New Mexico, Pyle was given an early release from the Marines. He soon enrolled in Ohio State University. He eventually found his way back to the drums and returned to the South to live, taking up residence in Spartanburg, South Carolina.

Through past relationships with some of the members of Marshall Tucker, who were childhood friends of his first wife, Patricia, Pyle was introduced to Charlie Daniels. Some session work materialized as a result of the meeting, and Pyle's reputation as a resourceful drummer grew. When Bob Burns contemplated leaving Skynyrd, Pyle's friends recommended him for the job.

"When Ronnie Van Zant got the okay from Marshall Tucker and Charlie Daniels, hell, he hired me almost without hearing me," remembers Pyle. "He set up an audition for me with Ed King and Leon in Atlanta, but he didn't even show up.

He said, 'Hire the guy.' He gave me a paper sack in Nashville. He gave me a paper sack with $5,000 cash in it."

Pyle's first gig with the band was a benefit for Jacksonville's Food Bank held at Sgt. Pepper's Club in October, 1974, before Burns officially left the band. When Burns finally did leave Skynyrd in December, Pyle took over as Skynyrd's new drummer. The beat went on.

Also appearing on *Nuthin' Fancy* was a female trio consisting of Cassie Gaines, Jo Jo Billingsley, and Leslie Hawkins. The young women were dubbed "The Honkettes." They brought an additional sassiness to the music on the album.

Al Kooper once again came on board to produce. His production skills had well benefited the band in the past. "If we get off a good one this time, we're on easy street and cruisin'," claimed Ronnie. "We really want this one bad." In the end, though, Kooper claims that a lack of outstanding material and the mere thirty days of recording with almost no preparation made *Nuthin' Fancy* a classic of how not to make a record. Regardless of those limitations, Kooper feels the album turned out to be a good one. The members of the band were pleased with the recording. "It was the best time I ever had in a studio," claimed Allen Collins.[17]

The band had been relegated to a two-guitar front with the loss of original guitarist Ed King, and *Nuthin' Fancy* didn't quite live up to past albums. As *Sounds* magazine put it, "All in all a rather disappointing album. Disappointing because, rightly or wrongly, you expect a band like Skynyrd to wipe the floor with you every time." Still, the album contained some of the purest Skynyrd songs that the band had released to date. Skynyrd's country roots were honored with "I'm A Country Boy," King and Van Zant's "Railroad Song," and Jimmy Reed's "Big Lights, Big City." "Made in the Shade" tipped its hat to classic blues, and "Whiskey Rock A Roller" was classic Southern Rock. Another track on the album, "Am I Losin'," is one of Ronnie Van Zant's most poignant songs. As *Pop Top* magazine noted, "'Am I Losin' is an unusually gentle, plaintive ballad that comes right to the threshold of incandescence."[18]

The album gave the band the major radio hit "Saturday Night Special." The band had recorded the song before entering the studio to do *Nuthin' Fancy* for use in Burt Reynolds's movie "The Longest Yard." Ronnie had a message regarding handguns he wanted to relay. He'd been around guns all his life, and he realized all too well the irresponsibility that gun ownership could sometimes evoke. He wasn't, however, anti-gun. "[Ronnie] wasn't politically motivated, you know. He didn't get into these things," says Judy Van Zant Jenness. "He just wrote about it in songs. He didn't go out and try to cram it down somebody's throat. We had guns in our house. He was a hunter; he had rifles. He actually bought me a little .38 Special cause we lived out in a secluded area and he wanted me to have a gun for protection. He'd actually take me out, and we'd do target practice."

Evidently everyone wasn't disappointed. The album went to #9 on the charts. Soon after *Nuthin' Fancy* was released, another tour of the United Kingdom was arranged and Lynyrd Skynyrd was back on the road.

The Atlanta Rhythm Section continued to tour, but the band members also took the time to go back into the studio to record new product. Their next two albums, *Dog Days* in 1975 and a live album titled *Red Tape* did okay, but the sales were still a far cry from what Buie and the boys had hoped for.

Polydor had been patient, knowing that The Atlanta Rhythm Section wanted a hit record just as much as the record company. But only so much financial support was available, and if the group couldn't cut it, there were plenty of other hungry bands that wanted to try. The Atlanta Rhythm Section needed a hit. The band was told that it had forty-five days to record and deliver its next album to Polydor. The studio players returned to the studio to see what they could do.

Wet Willie was still selling records off the success of *Keep On Smilin'*. The Tom Dowd-produced *Dixie Rock* was released in 1974 but failed to make a substantial impression. Wet Willie continued to sell from its catalog but was unable to make any further breakthrough to the charts.

Wet Willie toured like crazy. The group often appeared with Lynyrd Skynyrd, the Allmans, and Marshall Tucker. Wet Willie came off the road long enough to record another album, but 1975's *The Wetter the Better* didn't garner much attention. The band's recorded popularity seemed unable to match what they'd been experiencing on the road.

Marshall Tucker also came off the road to record a new album. The band members had been enjoying success both in front of live audiences and through their records. They were ready to lay down something exceptional by the spring/summer of 1975. *Searchin' For A Rainbow* proved to be the band's greatest recorded success.

George McCorkle had written a song that he hoped to have included on a new Charlie Daniels album. Daniels had mentioned that he wanted to title his next album *Fire On The Mountain* during one of the band's long bus trips. Although McCorkle sat down to quickly pound out a title track that he felt Daniels might use, Charlie preferred to use his own material. He appreciated McCorkle's effort, but he passed on using it for his new record. "Charlie never did like to do other people's material," says Paul Hornsby. "Larry Gatlin summarized that one day. He said, talking about doing other people, 'I'd rather take *my* kids to the fair, you know?'"

The members of Marshall Tucker ended up including McCorkle's "Fire On The Mountain" on their own new album. "The whole thing is nothin' but experiences," muses McCorkle. "It's all it is. About a guy that's just leaving Carolina. Basically it's about me. All the things I saw. At the end of the song, everybody in the music business gets gunned down. It's just life's experiences."

Dickey Betts had come into the studio to contribute a guitar solo to the easy-to-listen-to title cut, Toy Caldwell's "Searchin' For A Rainbow." "Bob Away My Blues," another country swing song, was included as a nod to one of the band's favorite leisure time activities. "Walkin' and Talkin'" features Jerry Eubanks on a sorrowful saxophone. "Virginia," a gentle tribute to Toy and Tommy's mother, was included, as well as a rousing live version of "Can't You See" from the Milwaukee concert.

Marshall Tucker was delighted when the album shot up the charts to land at #15. This was the first of their albums to be certified platinum. The single of "Fire On the Mountain" was Marshall Tucker's first Top 40 hit.

Blackfoot was looking for a hit record, too. In 1975, the band moved back to Florida. Rickey Medlocke had a lung removed as a child, and the cold northern winters were beginning to affect his health. By this time, Island Records had sold the band's contract to Epic.

When Jimmy Johnson was called upon to produce a new Blackfoot album, he brought along David Hood to work with him. *Flyin' High* was released late that year. Again, with a minimum of promotion, few people heard the album, and it went nowhere. Although the album stiffed, Blackfoot was able to continue to play large venues with the likes of Detroit madman rocker Ted Nugent, the ever flamboyant rock and roll group Kiss, and pop/rock's flavor-of-the-day, the talented Peter Frampton.

Charlie Daniels, like others of the genre, wasn't clear on the exact state of Southern Rock by 1975, but he did know that people seemed to be showing a lot of interest in the South and the way Southerners viewed the world around them. Lynyrd Skynyrd had been successful with its Southern anthem "Sweet Home Alabama" in 1973, much to the surprise of everyone involved with the recording. Charlie detected a bit of a trend when his own Southern-based anthem "Uneasy Rider" hit the charts.

Charlie also made an appearance on Marshall Tucker's *A New Life* album that year. "It sort of got to be a tradition that Charlie started jamming a lot on stage with [Marshall Tucker]," recalls Paul Hornsby. "So we called Charlie in to play on the album. He played on every one they ever did from then on."

Charlie was in the Capricorn Studios at the onset of Marshall Tucker's recording of *Where We All Belong*. While Charlie was involved in the Tucker session, the time came for him to turn his thoughts to his own next album. He liked the creative atmosphere at the Capricorn Studio and thought that Hornsby would be exciting as a producer. "[Charlie] was not a hit act at the time," recalls Hornsby. "Charlie came in and was guest-shotting on the Tuckers' album, and so we immediately decided we'd start working together. We did the Tucker album, and then I immediately started with Charlie Daniels's album."

Fire On the Mountain was released in 1975. Charlie had been thinking about the material he was going to include for awhile, and his choices were right on. Two songs on the album were released as singles and hit the charts. "The South's Gonna Do It Again" pays homage to the Southern acts that The Charlie Daniels Band had been opening for and supporting. "It was the tribute to Southern music," says Charlie. Charlie's fans enjoyed the recognition paid to their other favorite bands. "Long Haired Country Boy" seemed to bridge the gap between long-hairs and rednecks in a fun but assertive manner. It was obvious that the audience related to the individualism expressed in the lyrics when The Charlie Daniels Band performed the song in concert. The song addressed a sentiment that they could appreciate and support. The fans' appreciation was loud and enthusiastic.

The singles received a lot of airplay, and the album was a hit. "He just took off," says Paul Hornsby. "'The South's Gonna Do It Again' was the first single pulled off that album. It was a hit, Top 40 single. The album was a gold album right off. Charlie's on his way, you know?"

Charlie Daniels continued to open for such acts as Marshall Tucker, The Allman Brothers Band, and Lynyrd Skynyrd, exposing his engaging and now hit music to as many people as he could. The fans treated a Charlie Daniels Band appearance as if it were the icing on the cake. The band paid tribute to Southern Rock by offering their own unique blend of country, jazz, rhythm and blues, gospel, and rock and roll.

"When I first went to see him play, their original stuff sounded like The Allman Brothers," remembers Paul Hornsby. "I mean, it was obvious who their heroes were. Well, then they came back out for an encore, and Charlie brought his fiddle with him. This is at the end of the show. He went to sawing on this fiddle, and the crowd went nuts. He did two or three fiddle songs, and then they called it a night. That's the way I think of Charlie Daniels [now], as holding that fiddle in his hand. That was just a novelty thing he'd pulled out at the end of the show."

Something other than hit records came out of the recording of *Fire On the Mountain*. Charlie had decided that like the other Southern Rock acts, a lot of what makes him unique is in-concert performances. He wanted to capture some of that for the album. In particular, Charlie wanted to place "Orange Blossom Special" and his own "No Place To Go" as live cuts on the record. He felt that he could surely draw a recording-size crowd in Nashville and booked the War Memorial Auditorium for what he called "The Volunteer Jam." Tennessee, after all, was the Volunteer State.

When the members of The Charlie Daniels Band took the stage on October 4, 1974, they experienced everything they needed to make those two songs come alive. The cuts turned out to be distinctive additions to an already exceptional album. After those songs were in the can, the band was joined onstage by some friends who happened to be in town. Dickey Betts and Marshall Tucker's Paul Riddle and Jerry Eubanks walked out and proceeded to jam with Charlie and his band. Little did any one know that a tradition would be born that night: Charlie would make his Volunteer Jam an annual event.

In 1975, The Charlie Daniels Band released *Nightrider*. The album was the group's last for Kama Sutra, but it produced a large size hit when the rock-edged instrumental "Texas" was released as a single. Everyone involved with the song was surprised when "Texas" hit the Country Top 40 rather than the pop/rock charts.

It was evident on *Nightrider* that Charlie was starting to hit a groove with the band he'd put together: Joel "Taz" DiGregorio on piano, Charlie Hayward on bass, Tom

Crain on guitar, and Fred Edwards and Don Murray on drums and percussion. Charlie Daniels and his band were a tight, productive musical unit that was wildly popular with its audience. The band planned on being around for a long time.

Some of the Southern Rock acts were doing well, while others were struggling. But infusing the genre with new acts could only serve to draw attention to the genre as a whole. In 1974 Alan Walden decided to sign a band from Tampa called The Outlaws. The group was fronted by Hughie Thomasson and Billy Jones, two musicians who had been listening intently to The Allman Brothers Band for the past few years. The Outlaws had established a solid regional following, and Phil Walden liked both their original melodies and their harmonies. The Eagles had been coming on strong and were a viable entity within the music business by this time. Those involved with The Outlaws felt that perhaps the band could be the Southern challengers to that sound, as well as present their own hybrid of musical appeal.

Hughie Thomasson had grown up in a musical family. "My folks played a lot of gospel music when I was young," he remembers. "Mama said, 'Get the guitars. You're gonna play. Your sisters are singing.'" By the time Thomasson was twelve, he'd replaced the lead guitar player in a band called Dave and the Diamonds. Throughout his teens he played with Dave and the Diamonds, Rogue, and Four Letter Words.

In 1968 Thomasson began playing with a group known as The Outlaws that was led by Frank Guidry. The band included Herbie Pino and Dave Dix (of The Diamonds). Thomasson had become good friends with Billy Jones, a drummer he sometimes played with. When it became known that The Outlaws were looking for a full-time guitarist and drummer, Thomasson and Jones auditioned and got the jobs. Two weeks later Guidry decided to join his family business and broke up the band.

Thomasson and Jones gathered a few of their friends to form a new band. When Thomasson asked Guidry if he could keep the name The Outlaws, Guidry readily agreed. Henry Paul, a Tampa folk singer, had been playing locally with a country rock band called Sienna. Paul was brought in on guitar. Frank O'Keefe came onboard to play bass. Thomasson liked the double lead guitar that the Allmans employed and convinced Billy Jones to switch from drums to guitar. Monte Yoho was brought in on drums.

All of the band members started writing songs. Their original compositions were well received as they played clubs and outdoor gatherings whenever they could get themselves placed on a bill. Charlie Brusco and Alan Walden entered the picture as managers, and The Outlaws started to receive additional exposure. Word of mouth about the band became so positive that several labels came around to check out the group. Walden considered striking a deal with his brother Phil's label, but for some reason decided against it. While there was substantial interest in the band, none of the major labels offered a firm commitment.

In 1974 Clive Davis established a new record label he called Arista. Davis was hungry for exceptional artists with broad appeal. Alan Walden felt Davis might be interested in his band and secured a commitment from Davis to catch The Outlaws' act.

The Outlaws arranged to open for Lynyrd Skynyrd for this most important showcase. Davis flew in to Columbia, Georgia, to see the show. He immediately recognized the band's potential and signed The Outlaws as Arista's first act.

The members of The Outlaws entered the Electra/Asylum Studio in Los Angeles to record their first album, armed with ten original songs. Paul A. Rothchild, producer of such artists as guitarist/harp player Paul Butterfield's Butterfield Blues Band, The Doors, folk singer Tim Buckley, and Janis Joplin, had been called in to work with the band. J.D. Souther, who had worked with Linda Ronstadt, Jackson Browne, and The Eagles, came to the studio to lend his vocal support to "It Follows From Your Heart." The songs were solid, and the production was direct and full. The result was 1975's *The Outlaws*. Both the band and Arista had a hit on their hands for their first effort.

The Outlaws' album had been anticipated with a certain degree of excitement within the record industry because everyone was anxious to see what Clive Davis's debut act could do. It was a simple little song by Hughie Thomasson and Monte Yoho, however, that grabbed everyone's attention when it was released as a single.

"I think we were playing a club in Athens, Georgia," recalls Thomasson. "Staying at the Days Inn, I do believe. Monte came running into my hotel room and says, 'I got it . . . got it!' I thought something was wrong with him. You know, 'What's the matter with you?' He says, 'No, no, I got it!' I says, 'What?' He says, 'There Goes Another Love Song!' I said, 'I like that.' Monte came up with that line, and I wrote the rest of the song and that's how that came to be." "There Goes Another Love Song" was a huge hit for the new band.

Another standout on the album was "Green Grass and High Tides." "[That was written] in St. Augustine, Florida," recalls Thomasson. "I was there for the weekend at a friend's house. We were up there hanging out, being kids. I didn't take the guitar with me for some reason, and there wasn't a guitar anywhere around. Everybody else had gone to bed, and I couldn't sleep. So I was sitting up in the big lounge chair and got a pencil and paper and wrote the words to "Green Grass and High Tide." Wrote the music probably three or four days later, and then it evolved over a period of time. It went from being three minutes up to nine minutes on the record. Eventually nineteen minutes on the live record, and it just kept growing and growing and growing. All the guitar work that was going on, we kept finding more things to play. It was fun playing it, and it was something that nobody did. Nobody played really long songs [commercially] you know, but we didn't care."

Radio ate up *The Outlaws*, and it quickly climbed the *Billboard* Album chart, reaching #13. "The [listeners] liked what they heard and demanded that they hear it," says Thomasson. Listener requests kept the album active and The Outlaws on the radio.

Arista followed up "There Goes Another Love Song" with the release of "Green Grass and High Tides." "We were fortunate that some people liked our music," recalls Thomasson. "[They] liked ["There Goes Another Love Song"] and 'Green Grass and Hide Tides' just as well. We were very thankful, very grateful, to be able to do a record just to begin with. To have it take off and do as well as it did, our first record, was really, really incredible." The Outlaws were well on their way.

While The Outlaws climbed the charts, The Allman Brothers Band seemed to be faltering. It was evident that the band's entity as a brotherhood was facing serious difficulties when the Brothers released *Win, Lose or Draw* in August, 1975.

The first song recorded, "Can't Lose What You Never Had," is true to the Brothers' sound. The quality of the musical performances after that are sorely lacking. "High Falls" might be one of Dickey Betts's best instrumentals. Unfortunately, his hesitations and impulsive turns in this recording hamper its effectiveness.

Most of the songs are as good as ever, but the vocals and instrumentation are insufficient and pedestrian. The "band" heard on each track differs. The musicians were composed of whoever happened to be available in the studio when the tracks were being laid down, catch as catch can. Johnny Sandlin and Bill Stewart had even been called on at one point to contribute to the percussion.

The end result is disjointed and inferior to anything The Brothers had ever put on tape. Even so, because of the band's stature in the rock community, the album received mixed reviews. Most of those involved in the production of the album were mildly surprised when it eventually went gold.

When the band toured in support of the album, Chuck Leavell grabbed hold of the concert reins to draw attention away from the fatigued founding members. His performances were energetic and on target. Still, Leavell's ebullience only emphasized what the fans now seemed to realize: The Allman Brothers Band had temporary lost its soul.

On October 6, 1975, the band appeared at The Omni in Atlanta, where they were introduced by Phil Walden's friend, Georgia governor and presidential candidate Jimmy Carter. Carter wanted to appeal to a young, hip audience, but his interest in rock and roll was real. "I used to be obsessed with classical music when I was a midshipman and when I was in the Navy," Carter claimed. "Then I started listening to Bob Dylan's music primarily because of my sons, but I got to like it and I used to spend three or four hours a day listening to Paul Simon, Bob Dylan and The Allman Brothers. At home I'd study government reorganization or budgeting techniques while I listened to rock."[19] Carter's wife, Rosalyn, said that his listening to the music as loud as it would go drove her up a wall.

The Allman Brothers' tour was rife with problems. Personal relationship troubles plagued the band, and Jaimoe's back was causing him serious discomfort. Phil Walden had arranged a series of benefit concerts to raise money for Jimmy Carter, and called on The Allman Brothers, Marshall Tucker, and Charlie Daniels to headline. The Brothers did manage to pull off their part. More than $150,000 was raised for Carter's campaign. Carter was grateful to Walden and the rockers who had played for him.

Lynyrd Skynyrd rehearsing at Hell House, ca. 1976. (Left to right) Allen Collins, Ronnie Van Zant, Gary Rossington, Artimus Pyle, Leon Wilkeson's back. Credit: Judy Van Zant Jenness Collection.

CHAPTER 13

A Long, Hard Ride

1 9 7 6

Lynyrd Skynyrd's next album, *Gimme Back My Bullets*, was released in 1976. The bullets referred to weren't those shot out of a gun, but rather the type *Billboard* magazine awards for successful, rising records. Ronnie Van Zant knew that the band was suffering post-traumatic stress, and he was ready to do whatever it took to get his dream back on track. All of the stress between Al Kooper and the band members resulted in a mutual decision to seek someone else to produce the group's next album. The Allman Brothers Band producer Tom Dowd was called in to pick up where Kooper had left off.

Gimme Back My Bullets reaped several rewards for the band. Once again a Skynyrd album climbed into the Top 20, and the effort resulted in the band's fourth gold record. The bullets were returned.

Skynyrd was invited to play at the celebrated Knebworth Festival in England as one of the opening acts for the members' boyhood heroes, The Rolling Stones. They would share the bill with Creedence Clearwater Revival; Hot Tuna, the offshoot band of Jefferson Airplane's Jorma Kaukonen and Jack Casady; the eclectic pop rocker Todd Rundgren; and newcomers The Don Harrison Band. Although there was an English drought and more than 250,000 people in attendance that day, nobody overdosed and nobody was hurt. The crowd was there for the music.

Artimus Pyle later stated that Lynyrd Skynyrd blew The Stones off the stage that day. His bandmates agreed with him. When you watch the crowd reaction during the concert in *Freebird: The Movie*, the band's assessment isn't far from wrong and could well be accurate. Leon Wilkeson remembers the performance fondly, except for the part where he says "my cord was too short." Allen Collins made quite a visual impact that day. "Allen would jump seven feet in the air," remembers Pyle. "He looked like a big daddy long legs. And that energy that he possessed on stage and that raunchy guitar playing. Those long fingers, you know? That boy was born to play guitar."

Billy Powell says that while it is true that Skynyrd was extremely hot that day, the fact that The Stones made the crowd wait so long didn't help the band's appeal. "[The crowd] was drunk, or stoned, or tired; you know, tired of waiting," claims Powell. "The enthusiasm wasn't anything like it was when we were up there."

Lynyrd Skynyrd had almost as much fun backstage that day. Paul and Linda McCartney, rocker Rod Stewart, actor Jack Nicholson, The Stones, Jon Anderson of Yes, Eric Clapton, keyboard player Billy Preston, rock group 10cc, and many other celebrated rock stars all hung out. The atmosphere was very much like an insiders' party. The Knebworth gig was certainly good for Skynyrd's glowing reputation as a musical force to reckon with.

Lynyrd Skynyrd also had a lot of fun roaming through Europe as it continued to be offered dates overseas. Artimus Pyle remembers that some of the band members and crew were thrilled to visit so many exciting places. "Paris, London, New York, everywhere . . ." he recalls. "Dean and I would get out and walk. We would walk and walk until we dropped and then we'd just fall into a cab and give 'em the matchbook to take us back. You know, if we didn't speak the language, we'd just give the driver a matchbook. And he'd take us back to the hotel."

The band continued to live large—sometimes too large. Gary Rossington injured his hand in a car crash right before the band began efforts for its next album. Gary's injury didn't slow Skynyrd down. The band members decided to buy a building that they could use for rehearsing and recording. They moved into Riverside Studios.

Skynyrd was in a bit of a bind after Ed King left the band. Honkette Cassie Gaines suggested to Allen Collins that he and the boys might want to have a listen to her brother Steve when they played Kansas City, which wasn't far from Steve's small farm near West Seneca, Oklahoma.

Cassie Gaines had been one of Skynyrd's Honkettes since 1976. She had a good deal of show business experience. Although Cassie had been to college and earned a degree in physical education, singing was her first love. She'd relocated east from

Oklahoma to appear in the Broadway production of *Hair* before eventually hooking up with Skynyrd.

Lynyrd Skynyrd had become comfortable with its three-guitar sound and was looking for a guitar player that might be able to replace King. Cassie knew that her brother Steve was an exceptional guitar player. She was happy to arrange the audition.

Steve Gaines was born on September 14, 1949, in Miami, Oklahoma. He became interested in playing the guitar after attending a Beatles concert in Kansas City. Steve's father opened up a teen canteen so the kids in the neighborhood would have a place to hear music and his children would have a place to perform it. Steve's first band, The Ravens, went so far as to record at Memphis's famed Sun Recording Studio. Steve also enjoyed stints with regional bands Crawdad, RIO Smokehouse, and Rusty Day and Detroit. While working in Detroit, Steve cut some tracks with producer John Ryan. These later surface as a Steve Gaines solo album titled *One In The Sun*.

After Skynyrd's Kansas City soundcheck, Steve met the band. It was agreed he could jam with them on one song, solely on Cassie's recommendation. Kevin Elson, Skynyrd's soundman, was directed to use discretion when Steve took the stage. "The band said to me, 'Look, this is Cassie's brother,'" Elson recalled. "'We're just going to let him play. If it's good, fine. If it's not, turn him off.'"[20]

Steve plugged in his small Fender Twin reverb amp. The sound was so low the band members could hardly hear him. But as Steve tore into "T For Texas," putting a slide on it just to be different, what they could hear, they liked.

Only a month later, Steve was a member of Lynyrd Skynyrd and a participant in the group's next album, a live recording. His soulful gold-top Les Paul and raunchy Stratocaster were welcome additions to the other two guitarists. "Stevie Gaines actually had a pretty unique style," says Rodney Mills. "He had a certain style of playing slide guitar which was totally different from Gary Rossington's."

Although Steve Gaines was very special, he'd been hired to replace Ed King. A lot of the Skynyrd sound had to do with what King brought to the band. "To a certain extent, Stevie was a very fast player and Ed King was a very fast player," muses Mills. "They weren't wanting, on some of the songs that Steve was playing Ed King's parts, to go in there and change them. Stevie picked up on that. That's kind of the way it should be because some of that stuff is signature."

The new Lynyrd Skynyrd album was called *One More From The Road*. It was a double live recording made during a three-night stand at the famous Fox Theater in Atlanta in an effort, primarily made by Atlanta promoter Alex Cooley, to raise money to save the deteriorating art deco landmark. Skynyrd was happy to be playing again in the heart of Dixie, and the show demonstrated this sentiment. The band members looked at the show as an opportunity to thank their Atlanta fans for their continued support. The band also wanted to thank Cooley because he had been, and continues to be, a champion of Southern Rock. Many of the Southern Rock bands had been booked into Cooley's venues at the start of their careers. Fan Steve Powell remembers the impact the band's "Southerness" had during the concert. "The most vivid thing I remember was during 'Sweet Home Alabama' when Ronnie says, 'Southern man don't need him around anyhow' the huge Confederate flag unfurled. The crowd went absolutely nuts. The roar from the crowd was so loud it literally drowned out the music from the stage."

Although Skynyrd fans welcomed Steve Gaines into the fold, Ed King continued to be missed. "[Ed] was such an important part of the development of that band," claims Skynyrd friend and .38 Special guitarist Jeff Carlisi. "From playing all the bass parts on the first record, you know, before Leon [Wilkeson] came in there, and to having the original idea for 'Sweet Home Alabama.' He was so important, such an integral part."

The fans would have to wait for the return of Ed King, but in the meantime they were very curious about the man who had been hired to replace him. King himself

later said that Steve Gaines "was brilliant." King didn't really feel the competition because, he says, "I couldn't play his parts, and he couldn't play mine." Each would forge his own legacy within the band.

One More was an instant success, hitting #9 on the charts. The result was the band's first platinum album. The new, live, version of "Freebird" climbed the chart.

(Left to right) Toy Caldwell, Presidential candidate Governor Jimmy Carter, George McCorkle. Credit: The Collection of George McCorkle.

Immediately following the recording of *One More From The Road*, Skynyrd was asked to participate in a benefit concert for President Jimmy Carter at Florida's Gator Bowl. Marshall Tucker and Wet Willie shared the bill, along with a handful of other acts. The members of Lynyrd Skynyrd had been looking forward to the benefit, but at the last minute they were unable to perform together. Ronnie Van Zant's vocal strain from recording the shows at the Fox made it impossible for him to sing. The rest of Skynyrd jammed with the other groups, but Lynyrd Skynyrd as an entity didn't appear.

"Ronnie just could not sing," remembers Artimus Pyle. "His voice was gone. And then everybody that played that day, Wet Willie and all the other bands, they all got a signed picture of the president and we didn't. I felt real bad about that. [Because] we did play."

Marshall Tucker was well received at the benefit. The guys received quite a few requests to play special dates and venues. They even had the opportunity to promote their new album through a guest appearance by Toy Caldwell, George McCorkle, and Paul Riddle on "The Hollywood Squares" television game show.

The band was excited about its 1976 album, *Long Hard Ride*. "Long Hard Ride," the name of the title cut and the opening track, is something that the Tucker boys had never before attempted to put on vinyl. The band was known for its varied and exceptional musical abilities, but most of those abilities had been bolstered by the lyrical content of the songs. Toy's "Long Hard Ride" is an instrumental.

The Marshall Tucker Band, ca. 1976. (Left to right) Jerry Eubanks, Toy Caldwell, Paul Riddle, George McCorkle, Franklin Wilkie, Doug Gray. Credit: Doug Gray/Michael B. Smith.

The song also features the bluegrass talents of The Nitty Gritty Dirt Band's John McEwen on banjo and Charlie Daniels on fiddle. George McCorkle even played bullwhip on the song. "That was the first time ever seeing somebody put something in a song that wasn't recorded when it went down," says McCorkle. "It was overdub in its way, but we placed it in the song where we wanted it. Pretty unique, for that time, for that era."

Marshall Tucker shot a music video, something that wasn't a common occurrence in 1976. The band members appeared in period costume, performing their own "cowboy" stunts. The video drew attention to the song, and the production of it was certainly money well spent.

"Long Hard Ride" brought about something that the band never really considered and certainly never discussed: a Grammy nomination. The song was in contention for "Best Country Instrumental." Although "Country Instrumental" probably wasn't the category the band would have preferred, the nod was certainly an honor. "Me and Doug both went to the Grammys that night," laughs McCorkle. "I had to buy a suit to go. I didn't own one. Matter of fact, Phil Walden bought it for me. We didn't know much about that side of the business. We were just players." The Grammy went to Chet Atkins.

Despite the instrumental recognition, *Long Hard Ride* did feature good lyrics. McCorkle's ballad "Holding On to You" particularly stood out, as did the ballad "Am I the Kind of Man." This song was particularly important to Toy Caldwell.

The Marshall Tucker Band with gold album, ca. 1976.
Credit: Doug Gray/Michael B. Smith.

"Those are Toy's words," says his wife, Abbie, "and the way he believed." Toy's country-based "Property Line" and the blues reflected in "Walkin' the Streets Alone," "Windy City Blues," "You Say You Love Me," and Tommy Caldwell's "You Don't Live Forever" rounded out the album.

Long Hard Ride was a success. It reached #32 on the charts and earned the band another gold record. McCorkle remembers the headiness of those days. "The band was just like somebody lit a fire under us," he recalls. "It was incredible. I never did understand it cause we never changed the way we played. We never changed anything. We were just doing exactly what we did."

The members of Wet Willie had enjoyed some commercial success and continued to do what they did to remain a concert favorite. To some members of the group, however, it seemed time to move on to other projects. In 1976, Rick Hirsch decided to join Gregg Allman on his solo effort and move to Los Angeles. John Anthony and Lewis Ross also left the band to pursue other interests.

The Halls brought in drummer T.K. Lively, guitarists Larry Berwald and Marshall Smith, and vocalist Mike Duke. The new band members had a new sound. Additionally, they felt it was time for a label change. The executives at Epic were Wet Willie fans, and the label contracted the band to do two albums. Wet Willie once again hit the charts with "Street Corner Serenade" and "Weekend."

Epic was also extremely interested in signing Charlie Daniels. He continued to have hit records and possessed an impressive fan base. *Saddle Tramp*, Charlie's last Capricorn record, featured some good songs, especially "Dixie On My Mind" and "Wichita Jail," but didn't really break out at that time.

The artist, in typical Charlie straightforward fashion, put Epic executives to the test when they flew in to Houston to talk with him. They promised that if Charlie were to sign with their label, they would always be accessible to him. One morning at 3 A.M., Charlie called Epic president Walter Yetnikoff at home. When Yetnikoff answered his call, Charlie informed the sleepy executive that he'd just signed himself an act.[21] Signing pop/rock acts out of Nashville wasn't usual at that time. Charlie Daniels's 1976 $3 million contract was certainly something new.

The Charlie Daniels Band continued to tour relentlessly, but since the guys were in it for the music, they didn't much care. They frequently crossed paths with another band whose members well knew life on the road: Lynyrd Skynyrd. The two bands spent a lot of time together, and the guys became good friends.

Charlie Daniels and Ronnie Van Zant developed a close relationship through their time together on the road. Some people were surprised by the friendship between the wild rocker and the affable country crossover. Not Charlie. "We all basically came up the same way," Charlie reflects. "It was easy to relate to those guys. It's like somebody you'd known all your life, basically. You run into people sometimes that were raised in the same type of surroundings that you were, and basically in the same way, and you feel like you know these people. You just hit it off, you know, and that's the way it was with Ronnie."

Ronnie had the greatest respect not only for Charlie's music, but for his ethics and common sense. "Now he used to call me the King of Dixie," Charlie laughs. "I was in, I think it was Utica, New York. It was my birthday. This is years and years ago. I was in the bar or a restaurant or something. Somebody came in and said, 'You have a call from Europe.' I said, 'Who the heck is calling me...?' I went to the phone; it was Ronnie.

I thought he called to wish me a happy birthday, but I don't think he knew it was my birthday. Maybe, I don't know. He said, 'How you doing?' I said, 'Fine.' He said, 'Charlie, I want to ask you something. Well, you know that big Dixie flag that we carry on the stage with us?' I said, 'Yeah.' He said, 'Well, last night it fell on the floor, and we took it out in the alley and burned it. Do you think it'd be all right if we went on stage without that flag? You're the King of Dixie, tell me.' And I said, 'Well, yeah, Ronnie, it's all right with me."

"[Ronnie and Charlie] were so close," remembers Artimus Pyle. "I have a vision in my mind of them right now, sitting in a hotel room, on the beds, facing each other, swapping hats. Charlie's hat came down over Ronnie's ears, and Ronnie's hat just sat on the top of Charlie's head like a Deputy Dawg [a cartoon character]." The two men would be friends until the end.

The veteran Southern Rockers were happy to include The Outlaws in their tours. New bands weren't a threat to them. They had all once been new to the game themselves.

The Outlaws were an extremely popular opening act and had no trouble finding bands to play with. "We did a lot of shows with Lynyrd Skynyrd, we opened for The Who [on the European leg of the *By the Numbers* tour], Rolling Stones [on the U.S. *Black and Blue* tour], Starship," remembers Hughie Thomasson. "We played shows with Molly Hatchet, Marshall Tucker, Charlie Daniels; just about anybody you can name, we played with. There were a lot of outdoor festival shows where there were lots of groups. That seemed to be the thing that couple of years. Lots of stadiums and stuff. We toured the world. We went to Europe, did a big pop festival with Little Feat. We toured with everyone."

The Outlaws were well received by the fans of the other groups. "They played a show in Boston at The Orpheum with the Steve Gibbons Band and Charlie Daniels," remembers fan Todd Remsburg. "Those guys blistered the stage on fire with their playing, and I'll never forget it. That night those boys left nothin' in reserve."

Although The Outlaws had recorded both its albums in Los Angeles with a producer directly linked to the "California Sound," the group by no means deserted its Southern roots. "We were only [in L.A.] to record," says Thomasson. "We went in, did our recording, and went home. We were there to play music and record records and so that was the most important thing to us. To do a good record, a great record. So we just went about our business, and when we were done we came home. Then

["There Goes Another Love Song"] took off, and we went back on the road and stayed there for about fifteen years."

When it came time for The Outlaws to come off the road long enough to record an album, Paul Rothchild was again recruited to produce. The band members returned to Los Angeles. They would initiate their recording at The Record Plant, but finish it at Criteria in Miami.

Arista released *Lady in Waiting* in 1976. While the songs were just as good as on the first album, nothing clicked in a big way with radio. But all wasn't negative for the band. "Green Grass and High Tides" was still being played on the radio, and "There Goes Another Love Song" was well on its way to becoming a classic.

The classic music of The Allman Brothers Band was interrupted again when a new twist on an old problem developed. The Federal Government had become involved in an investigation of corruption within the Macon police department. They soon uncovered some serious criminal behavior in regard to drug trafficking and distribution. Gregg's assistant Scooter Herring was mentioned as being one of those who was involved. Before long, Gregg Allman was implicated in the exploration of what was happening on Macon's drug scene.

Gregg's attorney was able to cut a deal with the authorities. Gregg wouldn't be prosecuted for his illegal association with Herring if he would openly discuss his involvement with those who were of concern to the grand jury. Gregg was ordered to appear at the trial through a warrant that the Federal Government issued.

For two days in January, 1976, Gregg was called on to give testimony to the grand jury. The case against Herring and the man he worked for was well set and was really neither hindered nor helped much by Gregg's testimony. Herring was convicted on narcotics distribution charges and sentenced initially to seventy-five years in prison.

Someone within The Allman Brothers Band organization posted Herring's bail. When Herring appealed his case, it was wrangled through the legal system for the next two years. The case included a variety of twists and turns that involved Herring's alliance with Gregg Allman and his very visible drug problem.

Herring's conviction was eventually overturned when alleged death threats against Gregg compromised the testimony given during the trial. After several appeals and reversals, as well as complicated legal maneuvering, Scooter Herring pled guilty to using a telephone to distribute narcotics and possession of cocaine. He was sentenced to serve thirty months at a Federal prison camp.

The other members of The Allman Brothers Band were furious with Gregg. They felt he'd betrayed a member of the brotherhood. Gregg might not have been given much of an opportunity to explain that he felt he'd been given no choice in the matter. The Allman Brothers Band wanted nothing to do with him.

Scooter Herring's trial wasn't the only hardship plaguing the band. The Allman Brothers Band as an entity found itself out of money. Years of high living had eaten away at whatever great amounts of money the guys had been able to earn. The band members employed a massive road crew that far eclipsed what they needed, and they traveled in a manner that took a huge bite out of their finances. Because they'd been making an awful lot of money, they felt that something was wrong in the management of their funds, royalty payments, and operating expenses. Dickey Betts and Gregg Allman asked their accountants to audit Capricorn Records.

The personal problems continued. Dickey was arrested and convicted for resisting arrest, destroying city property (after kicking two garbage cans) and disorderly conduct. He was fined and given a twelve-month suspended sentence.

A week later, Dickey's attorney filed a lawsuit to sever his ties with Capricorn Records. Dickey claimed he'd been underpaid in royalties and misrepresented in terms. Phil Walden countersued. Dickey and Capricorn reached an agreement by which he was free to sign with Arista as a solo artist with a buyout provided to Capricorn. Dickey would be allowed to audit Capricorn, but if a settlement couldn't be reached the issue would be submitted to binding arbitration.

The issue of Capricorn's continued relationship with the band wasn't addressed other than the record company's acknowledgment that the members of The Allman Brothers Band could appear on Dickey's solo efforts as long as they weren't billed as The Allman Brothers Band. It really didn't make much difference. With the other band members still angry with Gregg, there was no Allman Brothers Band.

Gregg turned his attention to his own solo record. Butch headed down to Tallahassee to enroll in Florida State University. Jaimoe, Chuck, Lamar, and a local Macon musician named Jimmy Nalls signed a contract with Capricorn to release an album by their new group, Sea Level. For the time being, the future of The Allman Brother Bands remained up in the air.

CHAPTER 14

You Got That Right

1977

It seemed like the money just rolled in for Lynyrd Skynyrd. The boys were in as much demand as ever, but it was a fact that they were just plain tired out. Years of touring and recording had taken their toll. The Skynyrds decided that the only way they could save their musical muse, to say nothing of their rock and

Steve Gaines and Dean Kilpatrick, 1977. Credit: Harriet Kilpatrick.

roll souls, was to deny the call of the road, stay home awhile, and recharge themselves. Although they played about fifty dates and did a mini-tour of both Japan and England during 1977, the band managed to steer clear of long road trips and all of the hoopla that accompanied them. Ronnie Van Zant fished; hung out at Whitey's Fish Camp; relaxed around his Brickyard Road home with his wife, Judy, and daughter, Melody; and let his creative mind wander.

Skynyrd was rewarded for the necessary hiatus by a triumphant return to the studio to record a new album. The new record contained exceptional songs from the magic satchel of Ronnie Van Zant, Gary Rossington, and Allen Collins, as well as those of newcomer and extraordinary songwriter Steve Gaines.

The recording process, however, had problems. The band members had been persuaded to record at Criteria Studios in Miami, where they would once again use the talents of producer Tom Dowd. As the album progressed, the band became more and more dissatisfied with the way the tracks sounded. The band's soundman, Kevin Elson, arranged to fly up to Atlanta with Artimus Pyle and some safeties of the multi-tracks. Elson wanted to talk with engineer Rodney Mills.

In the Studio, ca. 1977. Donnie Van Zant, Kevin Elson, Ronnie Van Zant. (Standing) Jeff Carlisi. Credit: Judy Van Zant Jenness Collection.

The guys decided that Studio One, where Skynyrd's first album had been recorded, might work better for the band's sound. Criteria just didn't seem to be conducive to what Skynyrd wanted to hear. The band also thought it would be a good idea to have Mills mix the remaining tracks should the rest of the album be recorded at Studio One.

"We love Tom Dowd," Mills remembers Ronnie telling him. "He's a wonderfully creative genius. The things he does with us as far as arrangements and things are just wonderful, but we don't want him to mix the record." Ronnie tried to explain to Dowd that he was pleased with the work Dowd had done, but he wanted other people involved as well. Dowd decided to end his participation in the project. Rodney Mills and Kevin Elson mixed and produced the rest of the tracks.

Despite the studio glitches, the band members were committed to the record. "Everybody realized the importance of that album," says Mills. "Everything was incorporated in Lynyrd Skynyrd, so I think that Skynyrd evolved on that album quite a bit. A new personality emerged out of that thing that I think made a real difference in their sound on that album." The album was titled *Street Survivors*. The cover art presented the band emerging from flames. The implication was that Lynyrd Skynyrd had survived the hell it had created for themselves and had emerged triumphant to rock and roll once again.

Those who heard the new album were impressed with the cohesiveness of the selected songs. Steve Gaines might have been new to the group, but he was allowed to fully participate and contribute some of his own compositions to the album. "I Know a Little" was an upbeat, rowdy boogie that displayed Gaines's lithesome guitar work admirably. He demonstrated his affinity for blues guitar with "Ain't No Good Life."

Although Gary Rossington and Allen Collins were certainly no slouches when it came to exceptional guitar wizardry, Gaines brought a new dimension to the already powerful multi-guitar assault Skynyrd was known for. His mesmerizing bridges and fret leaps revealed an artistry much advanced for the young man's physical years.

Gaines might have been an artiste, but he also knew how to have fun with his music. His duet with Ronnie on their co-written tune "You Got That Right" revealed a sparkle in Van Zant that had been underexposed in the past. Ronnie was good at smirking and delicately, if not pointedly, revealing the underbelly of the rock and roll beast, but rarely did he cut up on a record.

The first single pulled off the album was "That Smell." The song rages against self-destruction. It resolutely takes issue with the smell of death that had surrounded the band in the not-too-distant past.

"Steve Gaines's presence in the band pushed Allen and Gary," Mills remembers. "There were some magical moments during the cutting of that record. Gary must have come back to his solo section of that thing ["That Smell"] like two or three different times to get it the way he wanted it. Allen would come in and do a guitar solo . . . and everybody was like, 'Wow, that's really, really good.' Billy Powell played a couple of piano solos on things, and everybody just kind of looked at each other and said, 'Well, it just don't get any better than that.'"

Ronnie countered the seriousness of "That Smell" with a tribute to the band's groupies in "What's Your Name," which he co-wrote with Gary Rossington. "Georgia Peaches" is another lark, which Ronnie penned with Gaines. "One More Time" rounds it all out. The songs are well balanced, and the album flows evenly.

Ronnie's previously insolent lyrical approach to love found and lost was replaced by a poignant tribute to devotion and commitment in "I Never Dreamed." A lighter, softer side of Ronnie was definitely emerging. He still could make a point and remained committed to exposing social injustices and warning others off the road to ruin. Yet with age, he realized that any whiskey rock and roller worth his salt could also poke fun at himself. Skynyrd's dedication to partying with loose women in smoke-filled bars was represented on the album by Merle Haggard's "Honky Tonk Night Time Man."

Recording the album was an enjoyable and fulfilling experience for Lynyrd Skynyrd. The boys were ecstatic to learn that *Street Survivors* would ship gold when it was released on October 7. Within days of the album's release, the group embarked on the first leg of a worldwide tour to promote it. The initial dates of the tour went extremely well. The band members found that they'd lost no professional momentum by choosing to focus on their music and families rather than "the lifestyle" over the past months. One of Ronnie's dreams, to headline at Madison Square Garden, was about to come true. The date had been set.

The fans had seen some personnel changes in Skynyrd over the years, so the addition of Steve Gaines wasn't that big a surprise. What was a surprise was the role Steve took on stage. Ronnie had never shared lead vocals with anyone before. Not only was Steve being called upon to step into that position, but he was playing his own material with a guitar vengeance that hadn't been seen by Skynyrd fans in some time.

Skynyrd fan John Stucchi remembers the October 15th performance at Florida's Hollywood Sporatorium. "When Ronnie announced that they had a new member, the first thought that came to mind was, 'He's the new kid in town and is going to have to pay his dues,'" Stucchi recalls. "But when Ronnie cut him loose, you knew that Steve was no ordinary musician. Right away I could tell he had a big influence on the new music."

Leon Wilkeson remembers Steve commenting that his involvement with Skynyrd was kind of like a "Disneyland tale." Wilkeson says that Steve and Allen were indeed a "match made in heaven." Steve himself said, "This is like the start of what I want to do. This is the beginning. I hope that I can be good enough to keep on going. This is all I ever dreamed about, you know? Just doing this."[22]

Ronnie Van Zant was feeling good. He'd sworn off excessive alcohol intake, he'd been jogging two miles a day, and he was eating a high protein diet to get in shape for the road. Everything seemed to be coming together for a great tour. Tour manager Dean Kilpatrick was even ready to take his rightful position on the road after having been sidelined for awhile because of a nasty van accident, which had resulted in the loss of his spleen. By the time the first date of the tour rolled around on October 13, Lynyrd Skynyrd was ready to rock and roll.

The Atlanta Rhythm Section had been rocking, but the members couldn't help but sometimes wonder if anybody heard them. That situation was about to change because of a variety of reasons. The change might have been due to the band's extraordinary musicianship. The sexy vocals of Ronnie Hammond and the contemporary lyrics definitely played a role. The reason for the change could have been the fact that The Atlanta Rhythm Section had been on the road for so long people were starting to become familiar with their music.

Whatever it was, when "So In To You" was released as a single off 1977's *A Rock and Roll Alternative*, it hit the radio with a vengeance. The band was relieved, excited, and vindicated to see the record not only climb to #7 on the *Billboard* Singles chart, but go platinum as well. After years of hard work, The Atlanta Rhythm Section was finally receiving the recognition it deserved.

In January, 1977, the boys in Marshall Tucker were rewarded for their hard work with a special treat. The group had played a number of shows in support of presidential candidate Jimmy Carter the previous year. The band was thrilled to be asked to join Charlie Daniels, Sea Level, and the ever-popular Guy Lombardo as the musical entertainment for Carter's inauguration.

It was a night they would always remember. "I didn't really know what to think of it, you know?" says George McCorkle. "I thought it was just really unique the President was letting rock and roll bands play in Washington." Doug Gray felt the same way. "It still, to this day, doesn't seem like we were there, except I have memories of it, you know?" remembers Gray. "It happened so fast. We was 'The Peanut Band.'"

Marshall Tucker had traveled the rural highways and byways of South Carolina to an evening with the President of the United States. The Tucker boys never forgot their roots, though. Continuing to live in Spartanburg during those rare off times was important to them. "Every time we'd come off the road, I'd come back and touch reality," says Gray. "And reality is being able to go over to the neighborhood grocery store or the drug store—walk in and seeing people you went to high school with. Because they make you realize you're no big deal."

To further illustrate that they were just hometown boys, the members of The Marshall Tucker Band organized a benefit concert for the people of Spartanburg in June, 1977. Charlie Daniels, Jaimoe, and a popular hometown female musician named Marshall Chapman joined the Tuckers for a four-hour show. The show was a gift for the people of Spartanburg, who had been there for Marshall Tucker since the beginning. Almost $24,000 was raised for the Shriner's Hospital for Crippled Children.

Tommy Caldwell later told *Circus* magazine, "We're a people's band. We've got respect for an audience. If you forget the people, you're out on the street pitching pennies."[23] The Tuckers always paid tribute to their hometown. It became a Marshall Tucker tradition to send holiday greetings and erect a Christmas billboard in downtown Spartanburg.

Toy Caldwell. Credit: Doug Gray/Michael B. Smith.

Performing for people who were special to them was fun, but the recording career of Marshall Tucker continued to be rewarding as well. *Carolina Dreams*, Tucker's next album, contains the band's first Top 20 single. Both the band and their producer could sense that "Heard It In A Love Song" was going to be a hit for them from the first time they heard Toy play it. Even so, there had been some difficulty recording it. "It was kind of strange," recalls Gray. "I had bronchitis. I never could get that hoarseness out of my voice, so we just continued on to try and do it and then we steeled for that."

If "Heard It In A Love Song" had been problematic, Gray had been able to turn in a stellar vocal performance with the plaintive "I Should've Never Started Lovin' You." Some other, now classic Marshall Tucker songs sweeten the album: "Fly Like An Eagle," "Never Trust a Stranger," "Tell It To the Devil," and "Desert Skies."

In the spring of 1977, "Heard It In A Love Song" moved up to #14 on the *Billboard* Singles chart. By summer, it was all over the airwaves. The boys were ecstatic. They were also very tired. Years of giving their hearts, souls, and music to everyone who would have them was beginning to take its toll on the band. Substance abuse was a major problem in the music industry then as it is now. It was no different with The Marshall Tucker Band. The long and irregular hours, hotel rooms, and time spent away from their families wasn't something that they'd been raised to expect, but it was now their life. It had all finally gotten old. Tempers flared, musical directions differed, and fights and arguments broke out.

Tommy Caldwell, ever the peacemaker, did what he could. "[Tommy] was the guy that made everybody want to do the best they possibly could, even if they didn't feel like it," remembers Doug Gray. "When somebody would feel bad, he would be the one that felt it personal to take the slack up. [He'd] play that much harder and take the pressure off the person that wasn't feeling good." Even Tommy didn't seem to be able to fix whatever it was that was broken. Capricorn Records, through mismanagement or misadventure, was experiencing some difficult times itself. The need to tighten the corporate belt somehow resulted in Paul Hornsby being forced to hand over the production duty of The Marshall Tucker Band to Stewart Levine. Levine had previously produced raucous soul man Joe Cocker, the jazz-blues instrumentals of The Dixie Dregs, and the jazz-fusion band The Crusaders. "Stewart was a performer's dream," says Gray.

The band members had nothing against Levine, but they missed Hornsby's contribution to their sound. "I was real proud of Paul Hornsby because everything that he's done for us always turned into something that was successful," says Gray. "He had the same drive and ambition that I think the whole band did during that period of time." Losing Hornsby constituted a major change for The Marshall Tucker Band and certainly wasn't one they'd anticipated or planned.

Whether the move to Epic was planned or not, it was a change in direction for The Charlie Daniels Band. Three albums released during 1976 and 1977 period revealed more of Charlie's country roots than the rock edge that he demonstrated on stage. *Saddle Tramp* contains country radio favorite "Wichita Jail." *High Lonesome*'s "Billy the Kid" is one of those outlaw songs that become perennial favorites.

Midnight Wind, released in 1977, is dedicated to Duane Allman and Berry Oakley. "There's the guys that deserve

Backstage at the Volunteer Jam, 1977. Paul Hornsby (third from left), Charlie Daniels (third from right). Credit: Paul Hornsby/Charlie Daniels Band.

the title of "Father of Southern Music," says Charlie. "Duane and Berry. I think Duane was the driving force in the whole thing. I never knew him, but he spoke through his guitar and that's pretty doggone strong. Duane Allman's guitar playing is still classic, to this day. He's still the idol of an awful lot of kids out there wearing a slide on their ring finger." Even though the album is dedicated to the two rockers, as with Charlie's previous two albums, it had a definite country flavor. It was time for some kind of change.

The Outlaws was still an extremely hot touring band, and its two hit songs continued to be radio staples. It was time for another hit record, but first it was time for a couple of changes for the group members, too. Frank O'Keefe, as had Skynyrd's Ed King, found life on the road to be overwhelming. He left the band and was replaced by Harvey Dalton Arnold, a bassist from North Carolina. Banjo and pedal steel were added to The Outlaws' sound, proficiently supplied by Hughie Thomasson.

Bill Szymczyk, The Eagles' producer, was brought in for *Hurry Sundown*, The Outlaws' third album. "Clive Davis hooked us up with him," remembers Thomasson. "Partly because it would be a good combination cause of the way we sang, harmonies that we used and guitar playing. He thought that Bill Szymczyk would be the right guy. I must agree with him; he was. He was really great to work with, and I think we made a great record."

Comparisons to The Eagles didn't bother Thomasson. "Not at all," he says. "I always had this thing where I wanted to play like The Outlaws and sing like The Eagles. I love their harmony. That's one thing that we really learned a lot about from listening. In The Outlaws, we use the whole lineup. We use a whole lot of harmony."

"Hurry Sundown" is the standout song on the album, which was released in 1977. "I had the sound turned down on the TV one day," recalls writer Thomasson. "There was a western on, and there was a gypsy wagon. It just started me thinking about gypsies. The next thing you know, I wrote that song. That one came pretty quick and pretty easy."

With the exception of "Hearin' My Heart Talkin'," which was written by Walt Meskell and Tim Martin, all of the compositions on the album were once again Outlaw-inked. Szymczyk and The Outlaws were a winning combination. Although their recorded efforts had been well received, The Outlaws continued to be extremely popular as a live band. It was decided to recognize their concert achievements with a live album. Two concerts were scheduled to accommodate the recording.

Henry Paul had left the band by the time of these concerts. He'd decided to pursue a solo career and was signed by Atlantic Records to a four-album recording contract. He was replaced in The Outlaws by former Chambers Brother Freddie Salem, who contributed "I Hope You Don't Mind" to the set. David Dix rejoined the band on percussion.

The songs on *Bring It Back Alive* were recorded at The Aragon Ballroom in Chicago on September 9, 1977, and the Santa Monica Civic Auditorium on November 1, 1977. The album was eventually certified gold. The Outlaws remained a successful band.

.38 Special. (Left to right) Danny Chauncey, Larry Jungstrom (back), Jeff Carlisi, Donnie Van Zant, Max Carl. Credit: John Halpern/Charisma/Jeff Carlisi Collection.

The success of The Outlaws demonstrated to aspiring bands that, with talent, they, too, might break through to the big time. .38 Special was a new band that had experienced success second-hand, and the members now wanted to see if they could achieve it on their own. They had all the right tools and certainly a legacy of knowing what might work and what would not. Even though they were a untried group, they weren't new to "the biz."

"Even wanting to get into the music business was wanting to be like big brother to begin with," muses Donnie Van Zant. "I remember when [Lynyrd Skynyrd was] called the One Percent, and they used to rehearse right there in my mother and father's living room. I remember looking at Ronnie and going, 'Man, it looks like he's having a ball.'"

Making music looked like enough fun to make Donnie want to pursue a career in rock and roll, yet not necessarily follow directly in his brother's footsteps. Although Donnie admired Skynyrd's raw appeal, he envisioned a band centered around less confrontational songs with prettier melodies. Donnie and his friends had something a little different in mind.

Donnie Van Zant had been involved with several small bands throughout his teenage years. There had been the briefly notable Alice Marr, another called Sweet Rooster, and a couple of other groups whose names he can't even remember. Playing in bands was a regular thing with Ronnie Van Zant's little brother.

Donnie loved music but questioned whether he had what it took emotionally to try to put something special together and invest the years it would likely take to get a decent band off the ground. "I had been through so many bands breaking up and all that, as a teenager and [in] my young twenties that there came a time in my life where I really didn't know whether I wanted to be in the music business or go after something with a little more security," recalls Donnie. "I'd had an offer from a couple of railroad companies, called Seaboard Railroad, and I think the other one was called East Coast Railroad. So, I went to Ronnie, and I just hit him with a question. I said, 'Man, would you go with the security of this railroad here? I've been through so many bands breaking up and all that, that it just don't look like it's going to happen, you know?' He actually laughed at me and told me that I had music in my blood, whether I realized it or not. And that I would probably regret it the rest of my life if I really didn't try it one more time. So that's actually when I got .38 Special together with Don Barnes."

The new band played primarily original compositions featuring the vocals of Van Zant and Barnes. The lineup included Jeff Carlisi and Don Barnes on guitar, Ken Lyons on bass, and Jack Grondin and Steve Brookins on drums. Van Zant and Barnes were excellent songwriters. Their songs added depth and texture to the sound of the band.

Carlisi brought a lot to the band through his songwriting abilities. He was also extremely talented on guitar. He'd been influenced in his playing by guitar players who ran the gamut from B.B. King, to Eric Clapton, to Leslie West, to Allen Collins.

Carlisi had been in the band Sweet Rooster with Donnie Van Zant when both were teenagers. "Half of our show was playing 'Power of Love' and 'Down In Texas' and all the stuff from the Hour Glass record," recalls Carlisi. "At the same time we were doing stuff by a band called The Illinois Speed Press, a band that had Paul Cotton, who ended up in Poco." The Illinois Speed Press was extremely popular in North Florida. It had also been one of Ronnie Van Zant and Gary Rossington's favorite bands. "I remember Skynyrd did the whole [Speed Press] album one night," laughs Carlisi.

Carlisi relocated to Atlanta to attend Georgia Tech after graduating from high school. When the members of Skynyrd came to Atlanta to record their first album, they connected with their hometown friend and Carlisi sometimes jammed with them. Carlisi met Al Kooper through his association with the band.

During Carlisi's junior year in college, Kooper asked the young guitarist to play with him in The Blues Project. "I'm thinking, 'Yeah, maybe this is something I want to do,'" remembers Carlisi. "But I called Ronnie one night. I said, 'Ronnie, here's the deal. Al wants me to do this, and I don't know what to do. It's a great opportunity. Should I quit school and do this?' Ronnie was an extremely, extremely bright person. He obviously had a lot of street sense, but he didn't have a formal education. It didn't matter, he was a very, very wise person. He said, 'The answer is easy. You stay in school. You finish it. You got the rest of your life to do anything you want to do, and you'll be great at it, whatever you do. You don't want to make a decision like this for something that you don't know what's going to happen with it.' And I hung up and went back to school."

Donnie Van Zant and Jeff Barnes called Carlisi at a later date to tell him that they were putting together a "serious effort." They asked him to come onboard. After receiving his degree in architecture, Carlisi returned to Jacksonville and the new venture.

As with any band, a name had to be decided on. The group had been rehearsing in a old abandoned warehouse called The Alamo on the outskirts of Jacksonville in Euley, Florida. "We were out there rehearsing one night," recalls Donnie. "We heard these sirens and all that stuff going on. Before we could even get our guitars off to answer the front door, they'd knocked the door down. They were called constables out in that area. They came in with their guns pulled out and they were .38 Specials. They told us to go outside or these .38 Specials would do their talking for 'em. They scared us to death. But that made an impression on us."

The new band, now known as .38 Special, was ready to hit the clubs. And hit the clubs it did. The guys played at teen centers, The Comic Book Club, The Forest Inn—wherever they could get bookings. "We jumped in the back of a Ford van and had a little truck and went all around from Kansas to Michigan to wherever, playing clubs seven nights a week, four sets a night, doing the proverbial 'paying your dues,'" recalls Carlisi. "But I don't really remember it being paying dues. We just had a blast!"

Things started to change as the band got more experience. "We played honky-tonks probably for about five years," laughs Donnie Van Zant. "Ronnie came out and listened to us at this particular club in Jacksonville. I said, 'What do you think?' He says, 'Come back and see me in about five years.' And I says, 'Oh, well, thanks a lot!' But he held true to his word. It was about four years later, and I went back to him and said, 'Hey, man. We're pretty tired of this. We got something to offer you here.' So we played what we had, and he liked what he heard and introduced us to a few people. We then got introduced to Jerry Moss of A&M Records, and that's when it all started for us.'"

Peter Rudge, Skynyrd's manager, introduced the band to Moss. By the time *.38 Special*, the eponymous first album, was released in 1977, those involved with the group knew that it could be big. According to Carlisi, the album sold only about 20,000 copies, but it was a start. The album was, at least, an introduction to .38 Special's music.

The band had been opening for Lynyrd Skynyrd even before the release of *.38 Special*. The guys continued to play with Skynyrd after the new album had hit the bins. It was fun for Donnie Van Zant to be on the same bill with his brother, but the co-billing also presented a certain degree of competition. "You can appreciate and respect the other guys, but that competition is intense," says Carlisi. "I think it's probably more intense than professional sports. Ronnie used to tell us that. He'd say, 'Little brother, we're going to have to hurt you tonight.' I remember, it was probably 1975, we played in Myrtle Beach, and we opened for Skynyrd. I remember Ronnie came back after we played, cause we stuck around there, so when it was over he came back, tipped his hat, and said, 'Looks like y'all won tonight. . . . We'll see you tomorrow, though.'"

Donnie Van Zant might have felt the need to be competitive, but his heart wasn't really in it. "If there's anybody that should be in the Rock and Roll Hall of Fame, it should be the Lynyrd Skynyrd Band," says Donnie. "I think one of the main reasons why is Ronnie Van Zant."

The new Southern Rock bands had chosen to throw their lots in with other labels, but Phil Walden and Capricorn were still doing all right. Two of the label's breakout singles were climbing the charts. Marshall Tucker's "Heard It In A Love Song" and Elvin Bishop's "Fooled Around And Fell In Love" were both radio favorites. Even so,

Walden was having money problems of his own. All the legal hassles, high living, and artist unpredictability were affecting Capricorn's cash flow and investments.

Johnny Sandlin, one of Walden's in-house producers, had left the label after a dispute with the company over money he felt was owed him. Walden didn't need another lawsuit; he wanted to concentrate on releasing records.

Walden couldn't help but hope that a release from one of the members of The Allman Brothers Band might hit big. In the meantime, he released *Wipe the Windows, Check the Oil, Dollar Gas*, a two-album live set of The Allman Brothers Band. Neither Dowd nor Sandlin was there to give the album the usual cohesive sound, and the recording suffered greatly in their absence.

Dickey Betts put together a band with guitarist Dan Toler, singer Mickey Thomas, actor Don Johnson, and such talented players as Tom Broome, Topper Price, Donnie Sharbono, Jerry Thompson, and Kenny Tibbetts. Dickey had come up with the name Great Southern while waiting for a train load of Great Southern freight cars to roll by. He later implied the only reason he'd constructed a band was because the Brothers weren't together.

Dickey Betts and Great Southern, the group's first album, was released in 1977. Other than offering some nice vocals from Dickey, the album left a lot to be desired. The songs are fairly weak, with the exception of the rhythmic "Nothin' You Can Do" and a gentle and sweet "Bougainvillea."

Great Southern released *Atlanta's Burning Down* the following year. As well as the original members of Great Southern, Dickey had added David Toler on drums and Rook Goldflies on bass. Dickey enjoyed the band, and he continued to make good music. But it wasn't The Allman Brothers Band.

Gregg Allman's next solo effort didn't fare well either. *Playin' Up A Storm* was, in a word, overproduced. With the exception of "Sweet Feeling," little on the album shows Gregg at his finest. In fact, the album far from approaches Gregg's capabilities.

Sea Level, on the other hand, is a fine demonstration of the jazz compositions that Jaimoe, Chuck Leavell, and Lamar Williams had been aching to perform. The original songs are a bit underdeveloped and Leavell's vocals are somewhat weak, but the music is "in your face." The album delivers. Simon and Garfunkel's "Scarborough Fair" is a standout. Sea Level's presentation far exceeded the original bare bones the duo offered. At least one of The Allman Brother Band factions sounded pleased with their current carnation.

While Phil Walden waited to see what the solo efforts would do, Capricorn continued to have financial problems. He signed a $1.5 million distribution deal with PolyGram, which helped his company's finances at least a little. When Capricorn was able to release *And The Road Goes On Forever*, two discs' worth of previously released Allman Brothers Band material, the label's finances were buoyed a little more.

Gregg Allman and his wife, Cher, decided to record an album together. Johnny Sandlin was called in to produce *Two The Hard Way*. The fact of the matter is, even with two talents like Cher and Gregg, the record isn't very good. The album also demonstrated that there was little magic left in the marriage, and Cher and Gregg soon divorced. Gregg had been doing better with his drug problem, but now was an alcoholic. He decided that he'd had it with Los Angeles and returned to the South, hoping to reconcile with Dickey Betts and the other members of The Allman Brothers Band. Phil Walden and Gregg had a meeting with Dickey to discuss getting the band back together.

Dickey was recording *Atlanta's Burning Down* at the time of this meeting. Although he was involved with his new band, he indicated that if the rest of the Brothers were interested in getting back together, he might be, too. It was worth talking about.

The guys in the still defunct band had started to soften their position on the role Gregg had played in the Scooter Herring trial. Perhaps Gregg had felt that he had no choice to testify other than how he had. Perhaps they could get together and see what would happen. It was time to give The Allman Brothers Band another shot.

CHAPTER 15

Disaster in Mississippi

1977

The members of the Lynyrd Skynyrd band had been in good spirits when they boarded their 1947 Convair 240 airplane late in the afternoon on October 20, 1977. Their tour had gotten off to a great start. The new material from *Street Survivors* was being as well received as their older material.

The first four nights in Statesboro, Georgia; Miami; St. Petersburg; and Lakeland, Florida, had gone exceptionally well. The band had really rocked the previous night in Greenville, South Carolina. The fans had screamed and hollered until they had nothing left to give.

This tour had started off a lot less manic than the last one. There had been too many nights out the preceding year. The members of the band, and the crew, too, had eaten themselves alive with the glorious excesses of rock and roll and life on the road. Since leaving home a week ago, the boys had been doing their best to keep the drugs and alcohol to a minimum. Since cocaine, Quaaludes, and bottles and bottles of Jack Black, or whatever, hadn't been consumed on an hourly basis, the band was tight and Ronnie Van Zant was happy. The boys liked it when Ronnie was happy, but were surprised to realize that they were happy, too. Maybe this time would be different, and the tour would go off without a hitch. Maybe it would actually be fun.

Ronnie claimed that he and the band were just street people who wanted to take their music to the people for no other reason than to have it be enjoyed. That they were clear-headed, unhampered by drug-induced moodiness and paranoia and now in a position to enjoy it themselves, caused the band members to name their latest outing the "Tour of the Survivors."

The Skynyrd boys weren't happy with the airplane that had been chartered for the American leg of the tour. They'd been scheduled to lease Jerry Lee Lewis's plane, but the deal fell through at the last minute. The band members felt the replacement plane was inferior to what they'd been promised, yet the leasing company had tried to make it acceptable. "They painted Lynyrd Skynyrd on the nose of the plane," recalls Artimus Pyle. "How can you resist that?"

On the way from Lakeland, Florida, to Greenville, South Carolina, the airplane started to make some troubling noises. "The right engine backfired a lot," remembers Skynyrd sound technician Kenny Peden. "We watched it catch on fire . . . had a flame about six feet long out the engine."[24] Pilots John Gray and Walter McClary were asked about the fire. They assured everyone onboard that nothing was seriously wrong. Maybe not, but everyone was relieved when the plane landed in South Carolina without any major, or minor, incident.

The band members talked about buying a new Lear jet for themselves and a new tour bus for the crew. That way they wouldn't have to rely on antiquated transportation. For the time being, however, maybe it was wise to travel to their next venue, in Baton Rouge at Louisiana State University, in the daylight.

Some of the band members were anxious about using the replacement airplane at all. They asked Dean Kilpatrick and Ron Eckerman to obtain assurances from the pilots that the airplane was safe. Kilpatrick and Eckerman were surprised to find Gray and McClary gone when they knocked on the door of the pilots' room on the morning of October 20. A message had been left at the desk informing the road crew that the pilots had gone to the airport to work on the engine. The band and crew were to meet them there at the appointed departure time.

The band members were forced to wait quite a while when the customary limousines failed to arrive to take them to the airfield. The limos never did show up. The guys grew agitated while they waited in the hotel lobby, and they finally decided to forget the limos altogether and hire some alternate transportation. The band and crew piled cheek to jowl into five cabs and finally made it out to the airport.

Walter McClary met the band and crew at the airplane. He explained that there was a problem with the magneto in the right engine of the plane. McClary assured them that everything would be okay for the flight. A mechanic was scheduled to meet them in Baton Rouge to make repairs.

Kilpatrick and security manager Gene Odom expressed surprise that the pilots would take the plane up with a faulty part. Again they were assured that the airplane was safe. McClary told them that even if one engine failed, the airplane could fly safely on the other. The pilot would be endangering himself, as well as his passengers, if there was a real problem. Skynyrd's two representatives could only acquiesce to the pilot's greater knowledge of aviation and trust that he knew what he was talking about.

The band and crew boarded the plane and prepared to sit back and try to relax during the trip to Baton Rouge. Some of them played poker, while others strummed their guitars or chatted quietly. Ronnie Van Zant had worked hard the night before and was still tired. After the plane was up in the air, he decided to curl up on the floor in the area right behind the cockpit and snooze. Steve Gaines and his sister, Cassie, sat talking across from Ronnie. Dean Kilpatrick sat beside them. Always committed to the details and the band, he was no doubt wondering what had happened to the limousines.

The airplane started to struggle during the last leg of the flight. Trying to compensate for the incapacitated right-engine magneto, the pilots employed a procedure called "autorich," whereby one engine is given more gas than normal. Gray and McClary were somehow unaware that they were causing an exceptionally rich fuel mix that would cause excess fuel consumption. They attempted to switch to alternate fuel tanks but found that the tanks were empty. McClary radioed Houston Air Control that the plane was having fuel problems.

John Gray emerged from the cockpit shaking and barely able to speak. He informed his passengers that McClary was going to try to set the airplane down in a field. He instructed them all to put their heads between their legs and "hold on tight." "Everyone was instructed to strap into their seats . . . which they did," Peden remembers. "They were fairly calm from what I could tell. Of course they were worried, scared, but they weren't panicking."

No one could have held on tight enough. Within minutes the plane had disappeared from Houston radar. Around 7 P.M. on the evening of October 20, rural residents of Amite County, Mississippi, heard a low-flying airplane and then a terrible, metal-crushing thud. The plane had slammed into swampland. It hit the ground so hard that luggage and clothing were later found buried deep in the mud. The forward section of the plane, where Ronnie, Steve, Cassie, and Dean had been sitting, broke away upon impact.

As soon as Artimus Pyle realized what had happened, he quickly surveyed the gravity of the situation and took off through the muck and mire to get help. "My friends were bleeding and dying," remembers Pyle. "I didn't think about it; I just took off running." Pyle, who himself had a serious chest injury, didn't stop running until he came upon a farmhouse. "Here I came, covered with blood, looking like Charlie Manson," says Pyle. He was greeted with a blast from a shotgun. The shot peppered his shoulder. When he was finally able to holler the words "plane crash," the farmer understood. "He said, 'Is that what that was?'" recalls Pyle.

The people who lived closest to the site of the impact arrived by tractors and four-wheel trucks within forty-five minutes to do what they could to help the survivors. The tractors pulled away pieces of the plane to free the passengers who had been trapped inside, some piled on top of each other in the middle of the plane. Injured band and crew members were carefully picked up and carried in the arms of the good folks of Amite Country across the creek, where they were placed in vehicles that rushed them to the nearest hospital.

By the time rescue workers reached the crash site, they found Ronnie Van Zant, Steve and Cassie Gaines, Dean Kilpatrick, John Gray, and Walter McClary dead. They'd been killed on impact. Six other members of the Lynyrd Skynyrd organization had been critically injured. Almost everyone onboard had been seriously hurt.

The people of the nearby city of McComb moved quickly over the wreckage to do what they could. The surviving passengers stayed where they were, dazed and confused. Billy Powell sat quietly on what remained of the wing. His nose had been nearly severed.

Among the passengers rushed to the hospital, Gary Rossington, Allen Collins, Billy Powell, Leon Wilkeson, Leslie Hawkins, Gene Odom, and Kevin Elson were the most seriously hurt. Most of Gary's bones were broken. His damaged leg later required a brace. Allen had a large piece of metal stuck in his arm that would necessitate a bone graft upon its removal. Leon had severe internal injuries and a broken arm. Billy had the nose injury and a deep gash in his forehead. Kevin's leg was so crushed that it was nearly severed, and Leslie Hawkins suffered a broken neck and serious facial lacerations. Gene Odom was the only one of the survivors who was burned, but nobody knew from what. Odom's left arm and face required months and months of extensive treatment.

Aboard the plane that day in addition to the band and The Honkettes was Skynyrd's crew, which consisted of James Brace, Ron Eckerman, Kevin Elson, Mark Frank, Mark Howard, Clayton Johnson, Don Kretzschman, Steve Lawler, Gene Odom, Craig Reed, Paul Welch, and television crewman Bill Sykes. The degree of injuries varied from broken bones and contusions, to the very serious wounds of Kevin Elson and Gene Odom. The entire crew experienced traumatic physical and/or emotional injuries. The entity that had been Lynyrd Skynyrd was devastated.

There were many distressing injuries to the passengers aboard that airplane, but the most traumatic information the surviving band and crew received that night was that Ronnie, Steve, Cassie, and Dean had died. On that ghastly night in a Mississippi swamp, the musical essence of Lynyrd Skynyrd had been silenced.

The Van Zant family was emotionally devastated by the loss of Ronnie. "Actually I remember hearing that [Ronnie] was killed, and that's about it . . . you know, seeing the reaction my mom took. It's all a blur," says Johnny Van Zant, Ronnie's youngest brother. "My brother Donnie, you know, we made a pack then, that we were going to stick together and carry on what [Ronnie] started."

Ronnie Van Zant's funeral was an emotional experience for all who attended. One hundred and fifty of his close friends and family attended the service in Orange Park, Florida. His favorite fishing pole and Texas Hatters black hat had been laid in the casket beside him. Merle Haggard's "I Take A Lot of Pride In What I Am" and David Allen Coe's "Another Pretty Country Song" were played before Charlie Daniels sang a haunting "Amazing Grace." It was almost impossible for Ronnie's friends and family to believe that he was really gone.

CHAPTER 16

Recovery and Enlightened Rogues

1978

MCA acknowledged a request that Steve Gaines's widow, Theresa, had made by briefly withdrawing *Street Survivors* to replace the album cover's photo of the fire-engulfed band with something less disturbing. Taken from the same photo session, the new cover shot was a simple photo of the band. The album quickly reached #5 on the charts, as well as attained platinum status. Soon "What's Your Name" was #13 on the *Billboard* Singles chart. "You Got That Right" also charted high.

MCA released the tragically titled *Skynyrd's First . . . And Last*, a compilation album featuring songs that Skynyrd had recorded during the Muscle Shoals session before hitting it big. The "new" album went platinum, brought some comfort to Skynyrd fans, and perpetuated the Skynyrd myth. But *Skynyrd's First . . . And Last* wasn't the end of Lynyrd Skynyrd's story.

The survivors of the crash attempted to salvage their lives, both physically and mentally. Some band and crew members took years to physically recover from their injuries. "Everybody in the band that survived was real bitter," recalls Billy Powell. "We were blaming God and everything, for destroying our careers. We were really very bitter, and that was probably the heaviest drug use of our lives back then. We were just all getting drunk all the time and doing downers and stuff."

Chuck Flowers, one of the early roadies, had been fired from the band over a minor infraction of the rules right before the plane crash. Flowers's guilt at not being with his old friends during that catastrophic event overwhelmed him. Using a rifle Ronnie Van Zant had given him as a gift years before, Flowers shot himself in the head.

The loss of the members of the band who had died in the crash continued to be felt deeply by each and every person whose lives they touched. It was a grief that never went away. It seemed the names Ronnie, Steve, Cassie, and Dean were on someone's lips every day.

Although the loss hurt enormously, some of these individuals had uneasily anticipated the tragedy. "I knew something bad was going to happen to the band when I left it," says Ed King. "When my mother called to tell me about the crash, I knew Ronnie was dead. He always said he was going to die before thirty, and I believed him. I wasn't surprised at all."

It was Steve Gaines, in the third guitar spot, who was on board the airplane instead of King. "I was so fortunate not to be there," he says. "Steve Gaines and I had the exact same birthday. I didn't know that until I visited his grave and saw the date on his headstone. They've told me about the crash, what they went through. Those guys have a common bond that can never be broken. They experienced indescribable horror that will be with them for the rest of their lives."

Cassie Gaines is greatly missed as well. "[Cassie] could make a Holiday Inn hotel room, in five minutes, with a couple of sticks of incense and a scarf or shawl here or there, she could make it seem like home," says Artimus Pyle. "You'd walk in her room, and you'd think, 'Wow.' It felt like you were in somebody's house. She'd rearrange the room. Cassie and Steve and Dean and Allen and Ronnie . . . not having them around, there's a pretty big hole there."

Even though the band was no longer touring, road manager Dean Kilpatrick was missed tremendously by the surviving members of the group. "Dean was the most dedicated guy you can imagine," recalls Ed King. "He'd do anything for you and was always there if you needed someone to talk to."

"In Japan, Ronnie told me that he would not live to see thirty," recalls Artimus Pyle. "And he would go out with his boots on. [After Dean's van accident] Dean told me that he would not live out that year. I remember saying to myself, 'Well, Dean knew his destiny.' He lived, breathed, and ate Lynyrd Skynyrd. And I loved Dean. . . . I loved Dean very much."

Although the members of The Atlanta Rhythm Section were deeply shocked and saddened by the loss of their friends in Skynyrd, *Champagne Jam*, their 1978 album, held a pleasant surprise for them. "Imaginary Lover" and "I'm Not Gonna Let It

Bother Me Tonight" were released as singles from *Champagne Jam*. Both quickly entered the Top 20. The album quickly went gold and then platinum.

Lynyrd Skynyrd and the tragedy that had befallen the band wouldn't soon be forgotten. "Large Time," another cut on *Champagne Jam*, paid tribute to Lynyrd Skynyrd. The song was extremely popular with the audience when The Rhythm Section took it on the road.

The band's special outdoor concerts were a huge success. Dog Day Rockfest in 1977 and 1978's Champagne Jam brought in more than 50,000 fans. At last the general music-listening public was aware of The Atlanta Rhythm Section. The band had finally been recognized. The guys' delivery of sophisticated melodies, rousing boogie, and sometimes amusing and offbeat lyrics demonstrated that there was little The Atlanta Rhythm Section couldn't do. Offers to have the band appear at prestigious events started to pour in. The members were invited to Bill Graham's Day on the Green, and their appearance was requested at Knebworth. They opened for The Stones, The Eagles, and The Allman Brothers Band.

President Jimmy Carter asked The Atlanta Rhythm Section to play at a Georgia barbecue at the White House; the band was delighted to accept. "The band played, and the President sat in the first row," remembers Buddy Buie. "The next week it was in *Time* magazine. Had pictures of the band on stage. Everybody just had a good time. We brought all the people who were influential in helping to break the band, and Carter introduced them. The most memorable thing that day was when Carter introduced the band. He said, 'It's great to be here tonight. When I ran for President, everybody said that I didn't have a chance. When this band started, everybody thought they didn't have a chance. So we all proved them wrong.' So that was fun."

While The Atlanta Rhythm Section was gaining momentum, The Marshall Tucker Band was losing its. A photograph of the band was used as cover art for the first time on *Together Forever* when it was released in late spring of 1978. The band itself was beginning to think that being together forever wouldn't be the case, no matter how much they wanted it to be so. The band was starting to come unglued.

Marshall Tucker had been sent down to Criteria Studio to cut *Together Forever*. It had been a wise choice. The record was a good one, opening with a unique guitar-driven blues number, "I'll Be Loving You." "Love Is A Mystery" runs more than seven minutes and is followed by a short burst of soul in "Singing Rhymes." The album also contains the mellow "Dream Lover" and the country-blues of "Everybody Needs Somebody." The latter song addresses a subject the Tucker band knew only too well: the loneliness that accompanies life on the road.

Tommy Caldwell fans were treated to two special numbers. Tommy's jazzy "Change Is Gonna Come" is featured, as well as Tommy playing acoustic guitar on "Asking Too Much of You." Another song on the album is "Without You." "'Without You' . . . that was one of my favorite songs," says Doug Gray. "Still is today."

Together Forever was the band's final album of new material for Capricorn Records. The album rode on the continuing popularity of "Heard It In a Love Song," rose to #22 on the *Billboard* Album Chart, and was certified gold. A greatest hits album was released later in the year. There had been several hit records by this time. Although *Marshall Tucker: Greatest Hits* didn't reach the Top 40, it, too, went gold.

The Tucker boys had developed quite a bit professionally. They had started to receive recognition for their individual talents. Toy Caldwell, especially, was finally being noticed as an extraordinary guitar player outside his immediate circle. "I've stood beside Toy Caldwell with quite a few guitar players in this country, and he's always held his own or pushed them passed where they were," says George McCorkle.

Toy's songwriting, while appreciated by fans, was so natural that it was almost taken for granted. "'Can't You See,' that's all you gotta say," reflects McCorkle. "I mean, take three words and make such a song that's gonna last another hundred years."

"I saw something on VH-1 . . . a video of Tucker doing 'Can't You See,' which was one of the songs that Toy sang," remembers Jeff Carlisi. "He's really a powerful singer. Combined with his songwriting talents and his guitar playing, was just really something. But his vocal performance . . . every time I hear it now, I listen to the song a whole different way . . . in a whole different light."

Tommy's bass playing was also getting noticed. "People don't play like that anymore," claims McCorkle. "Tommy was an inventive bass player. I think he was a powerhouse bass player. Tommy and Berry Oakley were real close to the same style of playing. Just really 'kick your ass' playing style of things. Tommy also liked to play leads on bass."

The talent of the members of The Marshall Tucker Band had grown and developed, but the same couldn't be said about the group's label. Capricorn was in trouble and facing bankruptcy. The band thought it best to sever its ties with Capricorn and find label support elsewhere. In the meantime, the guys continued touring as a band without a recording contract.

Any feelings of apprehension the band might have felt about leaving Capricorn after so many years wasn't evident in the band's performance. *Rolling Stone* dubbed Marshall Tucker "the hottest free agents to come to Madison Square Garden" during the fall of 1978. The magazine was most impressed with that show and reported that "The crowd was wildly enthusiastic from the start. Even though the set was barely half over [when] 'Can't You See' [was performed, the crowd] lit thousands of matches and cried for more when the song ended."

Both Capitol Records and Capricorn's distributor, Warner Bros., wanted to sign Marshall Tucker. Since Warner Bros. was already quite familiar with marketing the band, the decision was made to sign with that label. "It was good for our pocketbook," recalls Doug Gray. "But it wasn't exactly the smartest thing for our career because we were the ole' small, Southern band that had done a minor amount of success at that point in time. To us, we had done a great deal, but to other people it wasn't that much, comparatively."

Charlie Daniels was in much the same place as the Tuckers. The Charlie Daniels Band was tremendously popular on the road. Nothing had changed there. With record sales slipping, however, it was obvious that the live sound wasn't transferring to the recorded music. Charlie had been more than happy with Paul Hornsby producing over the years, but sometimes new blood brings new energy, and that was what seemed to be needed.

Epic suggested that producer John Boyland be brought in. Boyland had produced Linda Ronstadt, The Little River Band, and Pure Prairie League. Those acts covered a variety of musical styles. Boyland recognized Charlie Daniels as an extraordinary performer with a variety of musical styles himself. Boyland felt Charlie would be dynamite if he could just get back on the charts with a strong single.

Boyland took The Charlie Daniels Band to Nashville's Woodland Sound Studios in 1978. They titled the record *Million Mile Reflections*. As the recording progressed, Charlie realized that he had yet to come up with a fiddle tune to place on the album.

Charlie had been thinking about a Stephen Vincent Benet poem regarding a fiddle contest titled "The Mountain Whippoorwill." Using the premise of the fiddle contest, the line "The devil went down to Georgia" came into Charlie's head. The band picked up on Charlie's initial melody, and the song came together very quickly. Boyland knew that the band had a hit on its hands as soon as the record was completed and cut. Boyland had Charlie record two different versions, substituting the words "son of a gun" for "son of a bitch" because he knew that some of the radio stations would have a problem with it. Daniels, Boyland, and the band sat back to see what would happen.

The Outlaws continued to be popular and was waiting to see what would happen, too. The group recorded *Playin To Win* in 1978. The album was produced by Robert John "Mutt" Lange, who had worked with pub rocker Graham Parker and country music diva Tanya Tucker and would work with the heavy metal bands AC/DC and Def Leppard in the future. Billy Jones collaborated with Lange on "If Dreams Came True." "Take It Any Way You Want It," penned by Billy Jones and Hughie Thomasson, is a solid album-opening cut. The album, however, was only moderately successful.

By all indications, .38 Special had a solid shot at succeeding as a band. The guys dealt with their loss of Ronnie Van Zant and other Lynyrd Skynyrd members by entering the studio to record *Special Delivery*, their second album.

When *Special Delivery* was released in 1978, it sold more copies than the first album. The band's live appeal while opening for others kept them in front of large audiences and helped them to establish a large following of their own. Mark Spector, then working for A&M, took a special interest in the band and decided to help guide it in a direction that would produce hit singles. It was time for .38 Special to get back to work.

The Allman Brothers Band was in the same place. They, too, needed to get back to work. On August 16, 1978, the large crowd that had gathered to hear Dickey Betts's Great Southern at The Wollman Skating Rink in New York City's Central Park was surprised and delighted when Dickey was joined on stage by Gregg, Butch, and Jaimoe. They performed four Allman Brothers Band songs for the ecstatic crowd. The four Brothers made another appearance together the following week at the annual Capricorn Picnic in Macon.

The reunion talks began in earnest. It was time to patch up any remaining differences and set The Allman Brothers Band back in motion. There were just a few hitches. Even though Jaimoe was still technically a part of Sea Level, he was anxious to return to his roots with the Brothers. Sea Level was doing pretty well, and Chuck

Leavell and Lamar Williams were enjoying the musical direction of the band. Neither of them minded the lack of tension among the band members. They'd added Randall Bramblett and Davis Causey and had moderate success with *On the Edge*, their second album. They were currently recording their third record. Leavell and Williams decided to stay with Sea Level.

Since Dan Toler and Rook Goldflies had been playing with Dickey Betts, they weren't unfamiliar with his musical history. It was decided that they would replace Leavell and Williams. A new contract was signed with Capricorn Records. This one clearly excluded Phil Walden from any management duties in regard to the band. The Brothers felt that this time, through their having been advised by a multitude of managers and lawyers, the contract with Capricorn was more to their liking.

The Allman Brothers Band returned to Criteria Studios with Tom Dowd producing. "Tom Dowd is an absolute, fuckin' genius," future Brother Allen Woody would later say. "He understands what makes things tick. He understands how to make you think of something yourself."[25] With Dowd at the helm and their renewed dedication to their incomparable music, the prospects looked good for the band to record something they could be proud of.

Enlightened Rogues was released in March, 1979, after the Brothers' three-year recording hiatus. The album reflected the fact that the band members were happy to be back together, with tensions eased and confrontations forgotten. Gregg's vocals were where they needed to be, and Dickey's lead guitar was rollicking and inspired.

The standout on the album might have been the instrumental "Pegasus," which was later nominated for a Grammy Award. "Crazy Love," "Try It One More Time," and "Sail Away" are all exhilarating. "Blind Love" and "Just Ain't Easy" are Allman Brothers blues at its finest. The soulful vocals of Bonnie Bramlett appeared on some of the tracks and were an exciting addition to the record.

The album quickly attained platinum status and entered the Top 10. It was a smash hit for the band, and fans were delighted to be entertained in the manner they'd grown accustomed to when the Brothers toured that spring. The Allman Brothers Band was back on track.

CHAPTER 17

Moving On

1979

In an attempt to get on with their lives, Lynyrd Skynyrd's Artimus Pyle and Billy Powell were the first to return to music. Billy made a guest appearance on .38 Special's *Special Delivery*. Both he and Pyle participated in a project of Texas songwriter/pianist Leon LeBront. The others in the band started to sign on to projects as their recuperation permitted. Leslie Hawkins became a Williette with Wet Willie, replacing Etta Avery. Billy Powell and Leon Wilkeson signed on as session musicians for some old friends of theirs who had formed a band called Alias. The musicians included former Honkette Jo Jo Billingsley, Dorman Cogburn, Jimmy Dougherty, Randall Hall, Barry Harwood, Derek Hess, and Billy Powell's brother Ricky. The group released *Contraband* in 1979. Gary Rossington and Allen Collins had initially agreed to participate in the project but dropped out after a dispute with the producer. Alias was featured in a nationally broadcast live radio show from The Agoura Ballroom in Atlanta on November 29, 1979. *Contraband* failed to rise to the expectations of those involved, however, and the band dissolved.

Even though there was some initial dissension within the ranks of MCA, that company released another Lynyrd Skynyrd compilation album titled *Gold and Platinum*. Some of the label executives argued that such a record would cut into the sales of the previously existing catalog, but it turned out not to be the case. The compilation reached the Top 15 and was certified platinum. The interest *Gold and Platinum* generated brought new life to the Skynyrd catalog.

Allen Collins and Gary Rossington realized that they were anxious to return to their music. Their physical injuries from the airplane crash had been extensive. Gary suffered from having had both legs, arms, wrists, and feet broken, in addition to a fractured pelvis and several broken ribs. Allen's arm injury required several grafts and extensive physical therapy to make it operational. Both men had worked hard to get back to being the guitar players they'd been.

Allen and Gary formed The Rossington-Collins Band in 1979. Billy Powell, Leon Wilkeson, and Artimus Pyle signed on to play music and attempt to mend their hellacious emotional wounds. The new band immediately rejected the thought of a male singer. Dale Krantz, one of the backup singers in .38 Special, was brought in to take the microphone. Barry Harwood rounded out the band on third guitar.

Artimus Pyle had to drop out before the band's first project got off the ground. He'd been severely injured in a motorcycle accident, and his badly broken leg wouldn't allow him to participate as he wanted. He attempted to play his drums with his left leg, but decided that he wasn't well enough to give it his best effort. Derek Hess was called in to tend to the drums. There were no ill feelings. Pyle later introduced the band for their concert debut in Orlando.

The shows weren't quite what Lynyrd Skynyrd fans expected, but then this band wasn't Lynyrd Skynyrd. "There were few guitar-dominated songs like in Skynyrd," recalls fan Stan Warren. "Almost all of the songs ended with Dale singing, instead of a guitar solo or duet, like the old band." Still, The Rossington-Collins band was well received.

The Southern Rock family was doing its best to survive the Skynyrd plane crash. Most likely because "Atlanta" was such an integral part of the band's name, The Atlanta Rhythm Section had been firmly pitched into the Southern Rock genre and the guys were members of that family. The group was proud of its heritage. Although the band members felt that they were probably more pop than other Southern Rock bands, they were happy to have the recognition and the Southern Rock family camaraderie. The truth was, the moniker sometimes helped them, as it did other bands of the genre, get airplay.

In 1979 The Atlanta Rhythm Section released the aptly titled album *Underdog*. There was still life in the band after all. "Do It Or Die" and a jaunty remake of "Spooky" were accepted by radio and did pretty well. *Underdog* eventually went platinum. Roy Yeager replaced Robert Nix on drums in 1979. The same year, a double live album was released. *Are You Ready!* also went gold.

The Marshall Tucker Band, ca. 1979. (Back, left to right) Toy Caldwell, Doug Gray, George McCorkle. (Front, left to right) Tommy Caldwell, Paul Riddle, Jerry Eubanks. Credit: Warner Reprise/Doug Gray/Michael B. Smith.

The Marshall Tucker Band would have liked another gold album, but the group continued to have problems. The first Marshall Tucker album to be released on Warner Brothers was 1979's *Running Like The Wind*. Ironically, the band seemed to be running like the wind away from itself.

With the exception of the title cut and "Last of the Singing Cowboys," another paean to the loneliness of the traveler and seeker, the songs are fairly uninspired. "Answer to Love," "Unto These Hills," "Melody Ann," "My Best Friend," and "Pass It On" are all nice enough tunes but don't really hold up well to earlier Tucker songs.

The Marshall Tucker Band bounced back a little with *Tenth*, its next album. Again produced by Stewart Levine, the album opens with Toy's high-energy 1980 tour opener, "It Takes Time." Tommy's heartfelt "Without You" comes next, followed by the strangely prophetic "See You One More Time." The Tuckers close out the first side with one of their trademark jams on "Disillusion," a song written by George McCorkle and Jerry Eubanks.

Toy and Tommy Caldwell teamed together to pen the second side opener, "Cattle Drive." The song is a unique blend of jazz, country, and funk. The tale of the "Gospel Singin' Man" is musically offered by George McCorkle and vocally delivered by Doug Gray. Toy belts out "Save My Soul"; Tommy and Toy's "Sing My Blues" comes next. The band's roots and influences are paid tribute in the Toy Caldwell/George McCorkle instrumental "Jimi." The album closes with "Foolish Dreaming," an easy tune written by George McCorkle and Doug Gray.

(Left to right) Tommy Caldwell, Charlie Daniels, Toy Caldwell, Paul Riddle, ca. 1979. Credit: Courtesy Abbie Caldwell Collection.

The Marshall Tucker Band was starting to hit or miss in regard to its albums. Although the guys hung in there, they needed another strong album to keep them in the game. *Tenth* wasn't really their deliverance.

Charlie Daniels, on the other hand, was about to hit paydirt. When the "The Devil Went Down to Georgia" was released in April, 1979, it charted in the Top 10 on all pop and country lists and almost immediately went gold. The album it comes from was also immensely successful. *Million Mile Reflections* eventually went double platinum.

"The Devil Went Down to Georgia" reaped other rewards for Charlie and his band. Not only did the tune's popularity result in the Country Music Association (CMA) awarding it "Top Single" the following year, CMA also recognized The Charlie Daniels Band as "Best Band" and Charlie as "Instrumentalist of the Year." The more mainstream music industry recognized "The Devil Went Down to Georgia" with a Grammy.

John Boyland had been called to work on the movie *Urban Cowboy* while he was finishing up *Million Mile Reflections*. He recommended that "The Devil Went Down to Georgia" be included on the film's musical soundtrack. The film's producers were impressed enough not only to include the song, but also to have Charlie perform in the movie. "The Devil Went Down to Georgia" hadn't been released while the film was in production, but by the time *Urban Cowboy* opened, the song was a mega-hit. And so was Charlie Daniels. In fact, he was now an international star.

Charlie had been looking for a career boost, and he'd certainly found one. His name was on everyone's lips, and his music tore up the airwaves. "Mississippi" was released as the second single off *Million Mile Reflections* and immediately became a Country Top 20 hit. All of the interest in Charlie's music inspired Epic to reissue four of Daniels's earlier albums: *Fire On the Mountain*, *Honey In the Rock* (retitled *Uneasy Rider*), *Way Down Yonder* (retitled *Whiskey*), and *Te John, Grease and Wolfman*. Charlie's music was hot.

Although Blackfoot hadn't had a hit song or album in awhile, the group continued to make every effort to stay in the game, too. The band members played as many dates as possible and expanded their horizons by taking a short gig as the backup band for Ruby Starr, being billed as "Ruby Starr and Blackfoot." At least the gig kept the Blackfoot name out there.

Blackfoot. Credit: Michael Ochs Archives/Venice, CA.

The band members played a show with Brownsville Station one night and were introduced to Al Nalli, Brownsville's manager. Nalli saw a huge potential in Blackfoot and expressed interest in managing the group. Blackfoot had been through eight managers by that time, so the guys weren't particularly interested in hearing what Nalli had to say. They continued to open for such acts as Mahogany Rush and Gary Wright and bide their time.

Nalli persevered, however, and Blackfoot eventually signed with him for management. Nalli's sister Reen was associated with the newly formed Atco Records, and Nalli made arrangements for Reen and her partner Doug Morris to hear the band. They liked what they heard. Soon former Brownsville Station drummer Henry Weck was engineering a new Blackfoot album. *Strikes* was released in March, 1979, on the Arco label. The first single off that album was "Left Turn On A Red Light." The record received considerable airplay on the FM radio stations. Other singles from *Strikes* provided the band's breakthrough. The long and autobiographical "Highway Song" reached #26 on the *Billboard* charts. "Train, Train," a song by Shorty Medlocke, also reached the Top 40. *Strikes* eventually went platinum.

Rickey Medlocke has done a lot of thinking about the appeal of Blackfoot. "Blackfoot was kind of a different Southern band, in the way that we were like the only Southern heavy metal band," Medlocke says. "Our roots were heavier, deeply embedded into heavy rock. We took our basic influence, Cream and Hendrix, Deep Purple and Zeppelin, the real heavy bands, and applied it to our own Southern roots." The fans appreciated that heavy Southern Rock, and they started to appreciate Blackfoot.

Hughie Thomasson, The Outlaws, 1979. Credit: W. Robert Johnson.

Billy Jones, Outlaws guitarist, and Alan Walden, manager and publisher, 1979. Credit: W. Robert Johnson.

The Outlaws continued to be appreciated, but the group's record sales had started to slip. The band members needed to bring some life to their recordings by 1979. It was likely that their Southern Rock compatriots recommended that they look to either record producer Paul Hornsby or Johnny Sandlin to help them accomplish that goal.

Sandlin came in to produce *In The Eye of the Storm*. While members of The Outlaws wrote most of the songs, as was their successful tradition, the album contains a couple of surprises. "Miracle Man," a tune written by Elvis Costello, appears, as well as two other non-band compositions: "The Lights Are On (But Nobody's Home)" and "Long Gone." The album was good, and it satisfied The Outlaws' hungry fans for the time being. The new material was welcomed in concert. The Outlaws were riding again.

.38 Special had started its ride two years earlier, but it was 1979's *Rockin' Into the Night* that propelled the band into something that they'd hoped for but hadn't really expected to come so soon: commercial success. In the months before *Rockin' Into the Night* was recorded, former Skynyrd bass player Larry Jungstrom replaced Ken Lyons in the band. Jungstrom's timing was perfect.

Rodney Mills, so instrumental in Skynyrd's *Street Survivors*, was called in to produce .38's new album. He was enthusiastic about the band's sound. "They wrote love songs with real good melodies," he recalls. "They were still perceived as a pretty hard edge rock and roll band, which I thought was just wonderful."

Survivor's Jim Peterik wrote the album's title cut. "Rockin' Into the Night" was a catchy tune, and the band loved it. "Next thing we know, we're hearing the song on the radio," recalls Jeff Carlisi. "We're going 'Whoa, this is pretty cool. We're on the radio.'" "Rockin' Into the Night" became .38 Special's first hit single.

Southern Rock had started a downward spiral in the wake of the Skynyrd tragedy and the interest in disco music, but .38 Special began to rise to the challenge of the legacy. "Before we became successful, we got reviews saying 'Oh, another Southern Rock band following on the coattails of the brother,'" recalls Carlisi. "All of a sudden, we started getting on the radio, and we had our own style of music and hit songs. Then all of a sudden people started saying, 'Hey, the new band that's carrying the banner for the South.'"

.38 returned to the road as an opening act with a hit record. The band members toured relentlessly. "It just seems that the Southern bands did a lot of traveling around," says guitarist Danny Chauncey. "Maybe a lot of soaking up of some influences and cultures and seeing some of the other bands at that time, playing out. That's definitely one of the differences that I've noticed as far as when we come down and compare backgrounds."

The Allman Brothers Band was now back on the road, but the guys' money problems didn't go away. Chuck Leavell and Lamar Williams both sued the band for money they felt they were owed. A settlement was made with Leavell, while Williams's case against his former employers was dismissed. The remaining Allman Brothers resumed questioning whether Capricorn had treated them fairly when it came to residuals and finances.

"We had not made it to this point by taking anybody's money from anybody," says Capricorn's Phil Walden. "I have *never* taken anybody's money. I've earned every dime I have. And I've earned it the hard way. The old-fashioned way. I think it's very, very unfortunate that certain members of The Allman Brothers have chosen to go forward with this story. If there are problems with personality and someone doesn't like me, that's fine; I can deal with that. But don't accuse me of being a thief because there's nothing further from the truth. Their problems were created by someone within that saw it necessary to further their case. It was necessary to break the unbelievable relationship that I had enjoyed with The Allman Brothers for over a decade. That is the person that The Allman Brothers should be saying these awful things about. Because I am simply not guilty of taking anybody's profits."

Dickey Betts's case against Capricorn reached arbitration. It was decreed that Dickey should be awarded more than $870,000. Capricorn appealed. The subject continues to rankle Walden today. "They ruled that we owed him some money," says Walden. "But it was not based on the Capricorn deal. That's why that thing was under appeal, and it was never settled. They ruled on something they weren't suppose to rule on. They ruled it was a conflict of interest, and that was not what they were supposed to rule on. They were suppose to rule on whether Capricorn had paid Dickey Betts fairly. It says in that arbitration that Capricorn paid on every unit. My partner at the time was Warner Bros. Records. Warner Bros. did the royalties. Their attorneys allowed Warner Bros. to be removed from the lawsuit. Now why would they do that if I had stolen money? Because if I stole money, Warner Bros. stole money. The idea was not to get money. The idea was to break up the relationship between Phil Walden and The Allman Brothers Band. That was the sole purpose of it. And they were successful, unfortunately."

The Allman Brothers Band members saw it differently. Whether or not they've changed their minds in regard to some of it or all of it, only they know. Regardless, the relationship between the band and Capricorn was now severely strained, if not permanently damaged.

Capricorn's finances were further damaged when PolyGram called for the repayment of more than $5 million in loans. The Marshall Tucker Band threatened to file suit against Capricorn, and The Allman Brothers Band asked to be released from its contract. The Brothers, Paul Hornsby, and Johnny Sandlin filed claims for money due. On October 21, 1979, Capricorn's attorney filed for bankruptcy on behalf of the company.

The resolution in regard to the Capricorn acts was a small financial monetary settlement and the contractual release of all Capricorn bands. The subject of Capricorn's finances continued to be a hot potato among those who were involved. It will likely always be a controversial sore spot between Phil Walden and some of the members of the bands he helped catapult to stardom.

CHAPTER 18

Even More Tragedy

1980

The Rossington-Collins Band's *Anytime, Anyplace, Anywhere* was released in 1980. Skynyrd fans appreciated the effort, and the first single, "Don't Misunderstand Me," went gold. The song "Getaway" was also well received.

Shortly after the album's release, Allen Collins was sent reeling. Kathy, his young wife and the mother of his two little girls, who was pregnant with the couple's third child, died suddenly of a massive hemorrhage. Allen was devastated. He withdrew from family and friends into the warm, oblivious comfort of the bottle.

The Rossington-Collins Band's 1980 tour was postponed, then canceled when Gary Rossington broke his foot. It was probably just as well. Allen wasn't much interested in the music.

This Is The Way, Rossington-Collins's next album, failed to do anywhere as well as the band's debut album. The initial attraction to the band dissipated. The surviving members of Lynyrd Skynyrd seemed unable to lift the maleficent cloud that had descended on them.

Although the members of The Atlanta Rhythm Section didn't suffer any tragedy, they didn't fare any better than Rossington-Collins. The band had moved to CBS Records. *The Boys From Doraville* was released on that label in 1980. For some reason, disco music being the predominant factor once again, the boys from Doraville had fallen out of favor. The CBS album sold well, but not nearly in the numbers of the previous four. The band was disheartened. The guys had been together some time now and had worked hard. The Atlanta Rhythm Section had enjoyed a good bit of success, but the fickle public seemed no longer interested in supporting its music.

Toy Caldwell, ca. 1980. Credit: The Collection of George McCorkle.

By 1980 Wet Willie had been together a little more than ten years. Jimmy Hall decided to become involved in some solo work. He recorded *Touch You*, with Norbert Putnam producing; his second album was titled *Cadallac Tracks*. Both albums were released by Epic. Jimmy also became quite popular as a session musician and moved to Nashville. He performed on Jeff Beck's album titled *Flash*. Jimmy came away from the project with a Grammy nomination for "Best Male Rock Vocalist."

Toy Caldwell wasn't much interested in accolades. He loved his music but valued his family life and his Carolina roots more. Toy acquired an interest in horses early in his life. After he started to realize some financial success with The Marshall Tucker Band, Toy purchased several Arabians. He hired his brother Tim to work with his horses and tend to his farm/ranch while he was on the road. Tim enjoyed his position and liked working with Toy. Horses were Tim's life. He was an expert, and both trained and showed the horses. Tim obtained quite a reputation as a horse handler.

On March 28, 1980, twenty-four-year-old Tim Caldwell was killed when a car he was driving was involved in an accident with a county maintenance truck in Spartanburg. His brothers were devastated. Toy; Abbie, his wife; and their two little girls had been down in Florida at Disney World enjoying some long-overdue family time. Doug Gray and Paul Riddle met them at the airport with the incredible news.

Tragedy struck again only a month later. On April 22, Tommy Caldwell was nearing the intersection of Caulder Avenue and South Church Street in downtown Spartanburg when his Toyota Land Cruiser collided with a stalled Chevrolet. The Land Cruiser flipped over after catching the right front wheel of the Chevy. Tommy remained strapped in his vehicle because of his seat belt, but his head struck the pavement. He suffered massive head trauma and underwent brain surgery. He lay in a coma at Spartanburg General Hospital for six days. On April 28, 1980, Tommy Caldwell died from his injuries. He was just thirty years old.

"Tommy Caldwell was the greatest bass player," remembers Artimus Pyle. "He was the spark and the fire underneath that band. It was so great to watch him on stage." There would be a hollow, empty spot where Tommy Caldwell had once stood.

"Tommy was kind of the businessman in the band," remembers Charlie Daniels. "He was the kind of guy that kept everything going on an even keel and kind of took care of the business side. When he got killed, it really knocked a hole in that band for a good little while because it affected everybody so personally. Especially Toy. But they went ahead and rose above it, and kept going."

"Tommy would talk to me privately about Toy," remembers Abbie Caldwell. "He was amazed at Toy's talent and would go on and on about 'Brother.' It was as if he was talking about a guitarist he did not personally know, but someone he was impressed by. I don't believe Tommy ever knew that Toy spoke about him in exactly the same manner. They both had a tremendous respect for each other and their accomplishments. An incredible sense of pride and love. It was evident in their faces, the way their eyes lit up and their smiles. I'll never forget those smiles. They loved each other deeply."

The Marshall Tucker Band continued, but it was never the same. "With Tommy's death, Toy's desire to perform in The Marshall Tucker Band also died," says Abbie. "Toy had not given himself time to begin healing when he went back on the road. I did not understand that at the time." Yet back to the road Marshall Tucker went.

In 1980 Epic released *Full Moon*; it became Charlie Daniels's second consecutive platinum album. The songs on this album were a little bit different for Charlie. He'd been thinking about the direction he wanted to go with his music while recording *Full Moon*. He really didn't care which genre's bin he was thrown into as long as the songs reflected his desire to entertain and his need to be himself.

"The Legend of Wooley Swamp" is a simple ghost story that oddly appealed more to pop audiences than country. "Carolina, I Remember You," on the other hand, was big on country radio. Charlie's song "In America," inspired by the Iranian hostage situation, was a hit on both the pop and the country charts. Through the versatility of the songs from *Full Moon*, Charlie Daniels was heard all over the radio dial.

Stillwater, 1979. (Left to right) Bobby Golden, Mike Causey, Rob Walker, Al Scarborough. Sebie Lacey on drums. Credit: W. Robert Johnson.

In 1978 Capricorn attempted to break an act by asking Charlie Daniels to allow the band Stillwater to open his tour. Although the band members had been together since 1973, it wasn't until 1976 that Stillwater had been signed to the label. *Stillwater* was released in 1977.

Stillwater consisted of Mike Causey, Rob Walker and Bobby Golden on lead guitar, Al Scarborough on bass, and Bob Spearman on keyboards. Sebie Lacey played drums as well as provided lead vocals; Jimmy Hall (no, another one) provided additional vocals. The band delivered good, melodic, guitar-oriented songs, not unlike those of The Atlanta Rhythm Section. Buddy Buie produced Stillwater's first album, so the comparisons weren't unfounded. "We were influenced by all the stuff that went on around us at the time, but also by the European groups," says Mike Causey.

"Mindbender" was released off *Stillwater* and quickly rose to #38 on the *Billboard* Singles chart. The band went on the road to promote the single and the album, working with Daniels, Wet Willie, The Allman Brothers Band, The Marshall Tucker Band, The Outlaws, The Atlanta Rhythm Section, Blackfoot, and Lynyrd Skynyrd.

The musicians in Stillwater were happy to be welcomed into the Southern Rock family, but the camaraderie wasn't new to them. "Talk about a community of musicians," says Causey. "We [the members of Stillwater] all grew up together in Warner Robbins, Georgia. We had always been friends, and we are still close friends."

The band branched out from the Southern Rock acts to work with Toto and Foreigner. The music was well received. Stillwater's future looked bright.

Stillwater was on a roll by the time it released *I Reserve The Right*, its second album. A song from the album titled *Woman* was suggested as a single, but by that time Capricorn had declared bankruptcy. Stillwater was without a label, and the momentum for the band died. The boys from Warner Robbins were left to wonder what might have been.

Stillwater has continued to play regionally with Causey, Walker, Golden, Scarborough, Lacey, and a drummer named David Heck. They've recently opened shows for The Atlanta Rhythm Section and Wet Willie. In 1997, the band returned to the studio with Rodney Mills to record *Running Free*. They hope to secure a label and enable people to once again have the opportunity to hear Stillwater.

The Outlaws had enjoyed the radio play that "There Goes Another Love Song" had afforded them. The band members continued to write, perform. and record. The only change occurred when Harvey Dalton Arnold left the band to join Henry Paul's band. Arnold was replaced on 1980's *Ghost Riders* by Rick Cua.

Gary Lyons produced *Ghost Riders*, assisted by Billy Jones and Hughie Thomasson. The Outlaws had worked with some stellar producers, and the talent was not lost on the band, Thomasson in particular. "I personally benefited by learning quite a bit about the process of recording," says Thomasson. "I wanted to produce later on. I wanted to know how they were doing all these things. Why they did this, why they did that. Right down to where you put the microphone and what kind of mike it is, silly things like that. But [it] really makes a difference, you know, in the way you come off on record. So I spent a lot of time hanging out with these producers and engineers. I just really wanted to learn. So it's helped me, and continues to help me to this day, all the things that I learned and picked up from working with all these great producers."

"White Horses" and "Devil's Road" supported the western flavor of *Ghost Riders*. The album is rounded out by Billy Nichols's "I Can't Stop Loving You," Hughie Thomasson's "Angels Hide," and Billy Jones's "Freedom Walk." Almost all of the cuts on the album are interesting choices.

The Outlaws' rendition of Stan Jones's "[Ghost] Riders in the Sky" is outstanding. It became a concert favorite from the first time it was heard. The single reached #31 on the pop chart. *Ghost Riders* eventually reached #25 on the *Billboard* Album chart and became The Outlaws' third gold album.

Blackfoot continued to enjoy its success. As the group established itself as a viable rock band, it started to slip away from its Southern Rock brethren into a more stalwart hard rock berth. With the success of *Strikes*, the band found itself opening for a variety of acts, such as Blue Oyster Cult, AC/DC, Whitesnake, Journey, Ted Nugent, and Foreigner.

Blackfoot had been on the road for twenty-two of the past twenty-four months. Even so, the group found time to record. *Tomcattin'* was released in September, 1980. "Every Man Should Know (Queenie)" and "Gimme, Gimme, Gimme," two songs on the new album, became radio hits. .38 Special's "Rockin' Into the Night" was nearly considered classic rock by 1981. By the time of the group's next album, audiences not only knew who .38 Special was, but also knew to expect something big. The band didn't disappoint those who supported them.

The band enjoyed its role as the legacy to Southern Rock, even while positioning itself as mainstream and contemporary. *Wild-Eyed Southern Boys*, released in 1981, clearly postured .38 Special as Southern Rockers, although there is a bit of controversy as to whether that stance was intentional or not.

"The cover for *Wild-Eyed Southern Boys* had the girl in the hot pants, we had the pickup truck, we had the front of the bar and the beer cans on the ground," muses Jeff Carlisi. "It was kind of like, 'All right, this is a spoof.' But people thought, 'Hey, this is a great record. What a cool album cover.' I don't know who did the survey or how they analyzed this, but they figured that that album cover alone probably sold a quarter of a million records. And we were just making fun of ourselves."

Regardless of whether the band was goofing on the cover or not, something definitely clicked with the radio audience. This might have been partly due to the bad boys depicted on the cover, but it was the music that caught everyone's attention. *Wild-Eyed Southern Boys* contained three hit singles and eventually went platinum.

The title cut was a rowdy celebration of rednecks and paid homage to the album's artwork, if not the band. "Wild-Eyed Southern Boys" appealed to both males and females. There was a little in the lyrics for everyone.

The big hit, however, was a catchy tune titled "Hang On Loosely." The song, written in collaboration with Jim Peterik, features interesting musicianship and a memorable chorus. The song had Top 40 written all over it, and that is exactly where it headed. "We didn't know that was going to be a hit song, a classic song, when we wrote it," says Carlisi. "Except we knew we liked it. It was one of those things where you write it, 'Hey, this is pretty cool. . . .' Hair standing up on your arms, you know?"

Another hit, which would also become a .38 Special classic, was "Fantasy Girl." Not only did the song have a story that the band's audience could easily place themselves within, but a catchy melody as well. "Sometimes you're sitting on the couch and you're watching TV," says Carlisi. "And you're just strumming away on the guitar, and all of a sudden you just hit a groove. "Fantasy Girl," the very opening of the song, that's exactly the way that happened."

The guys in .38 Special were now proving the appeal of their songs not only in concert, but also on their albums. "[Ronnie] wrote songs from his heart, living songs, and I think I learned an awful lot from him," said Donnie Van Zant. "You write from your heart. You can't make stuff up, or it's not going to be believable to begin with and people are not gonna believe it. You write songs that move you spiritually and emotionally. If you can't do that, you can't expect it to do it for someone else." .38 Special had capitalized on a winning formula. The members had worked hard and written "from the heart." The group was now, officially, a certified, gold-record-selling, rock and roll band.

The winning formula of The Allman Brothers Band enabled them to rebound from the Capricorn debacle and sign with Arista. *Reach For The Sky*, released in 1980, the first album for the group's new label, was unfortunately extremely ineffective. Evidently all of the problems with Capricorn affected the band members' musical concentration. The album was simply ho-hum. Whether a reflection of the musicians' personal trials or a representation of the current state of rock and roll, The Allman Brothers Band's album had fallen on partially deaf ears.

Disco continued to rise in popularity throughout the United States. Everybody, even those who appreciated exceptionally good music, seemed plugged in to it. The genre known as Southern Rock seemed at an impasse. And so, once again, did The Allman Brothers Band.

When Jaimoe and his wife, Candace Oakley, continued to question the band's accounting, Jaimoe was fired. Frank Toler was brought in to replace him on live dates. Toler stuck around when the band went back into the studio to record its next album, *Brothers Of The Road*.

The new album wasn't much better than the first, and the lack of Jaimoe's contribution was obvious. One song from the album, "Straight From The Heart," at least offered something to those who heard it, but the album reflected the lack of enthusiasm that had enveloped the band. The Brothers blamed their ennui on the pressure from Arista to come up with a Top 40 hit.

CHAPTER 19

Transition

1981-1983

By 1982 Gary Rossington and Allen Collins found it difficult to work together. Dale Krantz had become closely involved with both men and eventually married Gary in May, 1982. The couple temporarily gave up performing and took up residence near the National Elk Refuge in the Grand Tetons.

Allen turned once again to his music and formed a band called Horsepower. The name was soon changed to The Allen Collins Band. MCA released Collins's solo effort, titled *Here, There And Back*, in 1983. The musicians who appeared with Collins on the record were Leon Wilkeson, Billy Powell, Jimmy Dougherty, Randal Hall, Barry Harwood, and Derek Hess. The album was well received by Allen's fans, but low sales resulted in MCA's dropping the band.

Artimus Pyle put together a band that he called A.P.B. and released two albums, *A.P.B.* (in 1982) and *Nightcaller* (in 1983). Pyle was more than just a drummer; he was a consummate musician and did well on vocals, too. A.P.B. was a popular bar and opening band but was never really promoted to be much more.

Gary Rossington wasn't the only Southern Rocker to temporarily retire from fronting a band. After the release of *Quinella* in 1982, Ronnie Hammond decided that he would become involved in other music-related pursuits and quit The Atlanta Rhythm Section.

Without its signature vocalist, The Atlanta Rhythm Section was lost. The band toured with a succession of fill-in musicians, but the magic was no longer there. J.R. Cobb, Paul Goddard, and Roy Yeager left the band within the next few years. Without any new product being delivered, The Atlanta Rhythm Section floundered.

Paul Hornsby, Charlie Daniels, and Toy Caldwell, ca. 1983.
Credit: Paul Hornsby.

The Marshall Tucker Band, on the other hand, soldered on. It wasn't the same without Tommy Caldwell, even though old friend Franklin Wilkie had been brought in to replace him on bass. Tommy was missed both personally and professionally.

Pat Halverson, Charlie Daniels's longtime assistant, remembers seeing Toy perform not too long after Tommy's death. "He was out on point, making love to his guitar," remembers Pat. "You know the way he did it, all bent over and playing for sheer joy. He had the biggest smile on his face. He turned to Tommy . . . but Tommy wasn't there. Toy looked at Franklin and just caved in. I don't mean that he quit playing, though he probably did miss a lick or two. He finished both that song and the set. To me he was playing strictly on technique. The passion was gone."

In 1982 The Marshall Tucker Band released an album dedicated to Tim and Tommy Caldwell. Tom Dowd had been brought in to head the production team. The album's tracks were laid at The Sound Emporium in Nashville.

Dedicated opens to the sound of Charlie Daniels's fiddle and the bombastic beat of Paul Riddle's drums in a Riddle/Toy Caldwell song about gossip titled "Rumors Are Raging." In addition to Daniels, Norton Buffalo guested on harmonica for "Someone Special" and "The Time Has Come." The gentle McCorkle-penned love song "Tonight's the Night For Making Love" follows. "Love Some" is a rarity inasmuch as it is the only song on the album not written by a member of The Marshall Tucker Band. The Tuckers then return to the West with McCorkle's "Silverado," and Side 1 closes out with a moving, heartfelt tribute to Tommy titled "Something's Missing In My Life."

Side 2 features Jerry Eubanks on saxophone in "This Time I Believe"; this is followed by the bluesy "Tell the Blues To Take Off the Night." It is a good, solid Marshall Tucker album. All that is missing is Tommy Caldwell.

Doug Gray, Jerry Eubanks, and George McCorkle decided to invest in their own recording studio at this time. Creative Arts Studio was close to home in the city of

Moore, South Carolina. They were advocates of the music of other Carolinians and had been able to help Lynyrd Skynyrd's former drummer get a deal with MCA for A.P.B., Artimus Pyle's band.

Tuckerized was recorded in 1982 at Creative Arts with Gary Klein producing. While the members of Marshall Tucker recorded their own songs, they decided to branch out and use several songs from other writers as well. A Randy Newman composition titled "Mr. President," is featured, as is a song from old friend Ronnie Godfrey, the piano-pounding "Even A Fool Would Let Go." "Heartbroke," a song by the highly lauded Guy Clarke that became a Top 40 Country hit for Ricky Skaggs, is included on *Tuckerized*, as is Michael Smotherman's "If You Think You're Hurtin' Me (Girl You're Crazy)." Other songs on the album are David Bryant's "Anyway the Wind Blows Rider" and the John Bettis/Michael Clarke tune "Reachin' For A Little Bit More." A sweet piano number, "Unforgiven," written by Tim Hardin and Ken Lauber, is featured. The album contains only two original Marshall Tucker songs, Toy Caldwell's "Sea, Dreams and Fairy Tales," and George McCorkle's love song, "My Sweet Elaine." The album closes with "Ace High Love," written by Henry Gaffney and Andy Goldmark. *Tuckerized* was a moderate success.

The Marshall Tucker boys went back to recording their own material on their next album, *Just Us*, which was released in 1983. This album was recorded at Creative Arts Studio, utilizing Billy Sherrill as engineer. The opening track, "8:05," written by McCorkle and Wilkie, features solos by Toy Caldwell and Jerry Eubanks. The acoustic guitar of "Stay A Step Ahead" is notable, as is Ronnie Godfrey's turn on "Time Don't Pass By Here." Toy's "Testify" is a scorcher, and a Gray/Eubanks love song, "Long Island Lady," harkens to an earlier, more innocent time. The band returns to its country roots with Toy's "A Place I've Never Been" and "When Love Begins to Fade," which Jimmy Rumsey's guest fiddle highlights.

"From the jazz-inspired swing in 'Paradise' to the string arrangements in 'Wait For You,'" wrote reviewer Don Stevens, "*Just Us* displays a creative maturation of The Marshall Tucker Band and proves to be one of the most varied and unique albums ever released by the band." [26]

In 1982 The Charlie Daniels Band released *Windows*. Charlie was happy to see Dan Dailey's song "Still In Saigon" become a hit for the group and climb up the pop charts. Charlie was known for speaking his mind, and he wanted now to use his voice to draw attention to the Vietnam veterans. The second single, "Ragin' Cajun'," appeared on both the pop and country charts. It was back to the country charts with the gentle, poignant "We Had It All One Time." All three of the singles drew attention to *Windows*, and the album went gold.

As with The Charlie Daniels Band, The Marshall Tucker Band, and other Southern Rock bands, Blackfoot had established a solid pattern of recording and touring. The group came off the road to record its next album. *Marauder*, released in 1981, didn't disappoint. The album contains several album-cut hits, such as "Diary of A Workingman" and "Too Hard To Handle."

Rickey Medlocke had written a song with his father, Shorty, titled "Rattlesnake Rock 'N' Roller." The song was well received in concert as well as on radio. "Good Morning" shot to #1 on the newly initiated heavy metal chart in the United Kingdom. "Fly Away" reached #1 on the album-oriented rock charts in the United States and entered the Top 50 of the pop singles chart.

Blackfoot was thrilled to have broken through to reach some acknowledged success, but it wasn't the end all and be all for the band. "I can tell you for a fact," remembers Medlocke. "Our focus back then . . . we didn't give a damn about being a rock star. We loved playing music and wanted to make a living out of playing music. All of a sudden, as it happened, we were very blessed and very fortunate to write hit songs that became classic tunes, they were catapulted into that stardom thing."

The success of "Good Morning" resulted in Blackfoot's embarking on a five-month tour of Europe. The band members weren't home long from the road when Atco's European arm asked them to return to work with The Rolling Stones mobile unit to produce a live album. *Highway Song—Blackfoot Live* was released in 1982 to critical acclaim in the United Kingdom but wasn't released at all back on the band's home turf.

Although Atco appreciated the band's popularity in Europe, the label felt that Blackfoot really hadn't established itself as an important act in the United States. The label wanted a commercial single to draw attention to the band. The band went into the studio to record its next album, seeking to determine what a commercial Blackfoot single might sound like.

Blackfoot entered the studio in Ann Arbor, Michigan, to make *Siogo*, its next album. The band told the record label that "siogo" is an Indian word for "closeness," but according to Charlie Hargrett, the name of Blackfoot's new album was actually an acronym for a very crude message the band's roadies had posted in their tour bus.

The record label wasn't happy when they discovered the truth, but the record had shipped by that time and there was nothing it could do about it.

Rickey Medlocke says that the recording of *Siogo* was the beginning of the end. Uriah Heep's Ken Hensley had been brought in to beef up the sound on keyboards. Musically, the band was fine. That wasn't the problem. The personal strife, the months and months of nonstop touring, plus the pressure to create a hit single, didn't serve Blackfoot well. Charlie Hargrett decided to quit the band, and Ken Hensley left six months later. After recording *Vertical Smiles* and while on tour to promote *Siogo*, the band came completely undone. Everyone but Medlocke quit. Within months, he was forced to buy out the Blackfoot name and continue on by himself.

The Outlaws were starting to have problems as well. By the time *Los Hombres Malo* was released in 1982, some big changes had occurred involving the future of The Outlaws. The band's songs for the album had been carefully selected and included several interesting and strong choices. *Los Hombres Malo* contains Joe Russo's "Running," "Rebel Girl" by Jim Peterik and R. Gary Smith, and "All Roads," a song Peterik had written with Sammy Hagar. Gary Lyons had returned to the producer's console. But by the time it came time to record the album, the group was down to a four-piece band.

The Outlaws continued to draw large numbers in concert, but the band had started to come apart as a unit. Billy Jones had been struggling with an alcohol problem. He finally decided that it was time for him to retire not only from the band, but from music. He didn't appear on *Los Hombres Malo*. Perhaps Jones made the right decision for himself at that time. He enrolled in college and eventually earned a Bachelor's degree in Mathematics. His ambition didn't end there. Jones took a job substitute teaching as he worked toward becoming a registered nurse.

The band continued without Billy Jones, but his loss was felt. *Los Hombres Malo* not only marked the departure of Jones, but was The Outlaws' last original recording for Arista. The label released *Greatest Hits* in 1982, and then Arista and The Outlaws followed separate trails.

The members of .38 Special, on the other hand, considered themselves a tight unit. The band's popularity had continued with 1982's *Special Forces* album. .38 Special experienced its first Top 10 single with "Caught Up In You." The band continued to tour successfully, and turned out an album every eighteen months.

The guys had finally been recognized as players and were asked to contribute a song to Aaron Russo's motion picture *Teachers*. The resulting song, "Teacher, Teacher," was tremendously popular and earned another hit single for the band.

As .38 Special hung together for the ride, the members of The Allman Brothers Band decided it was time for another break from each other. The guys had lost interest in their collective music. The Allman Brothers Band performed "Leavin'" on "Saturday Night Live" on January 23, 1982; this was the group's last public appearance for four years.

Jaimoe, Dickey Betts, and Gregg Allman went years without speaking, and Butch Trucks was once again unhappy with Gregg. Chuck Leavell had been forgiven any impropriety associated with his lawsuit and was soon playing in clubs with Dickey and Butch. After a short period of time, Butch left his music to build a recording studio in Tallahassee. Jaimoe played locally with pickup bands. Lamar Williams never got to play in any carnation of The Allman Brothers Band or its offshoots again. He was diagnosed with lung cancer and died at the age of thirty-four on January 23, 1983. It looked like the run of The Allman Brothers Band was finally at end.

CHAPTER 20

Disco to Reformation

1984-1987

In 1984 disaster struck Lynyrd Skynyrd again. One night while driving drunk in his new Ford Thunderbird, Allen Collins drove his car into a Mandarin, Florida, ravine. Debra Jean Watts, his new girlfriend, was killed. The legendary guitarist was paralyzed from the waist down. Allen pleaded no contest to DUI (Driving Under the Influence) manslaughter.

"He was the crazy one of the band, you know?" says Billy Powell. "He was really funny, all the time. He was an honest man, and he'd do anything for you, anything he could. When his wife died of a massive hemorrhage, pregnant with his third child in a theater . . . that's what destroyed Allen. He dove into a bottle and never came out."

In December, 1983, Toy Caldwell decided that he no longer felt comfortable as a member of The Marshall Tucker Band. "Toy returned from playing at the Volunteer Jam with Charlie," remembers Abbie Caldwell, Toy's wife. "On his flight home he had decided to leave the band. When he told me what he had decided, it was only then that I realized being on stage without Tommy was tearing his heart apart."

By June, 1984, George McCorkle had decided that life on the road and all of its craziness were no longer for him. He had a young son and wanted to be around the boy while he was growing up. "When I left the band, I just did not even want to see a guitar," remembers McCorkle. "I didn't want to fool with it anymore." When McCorkle called Paul Riddle to explain his intentions, Riddle said that it was time for him to move on as well. He'd come into the band with McCorkle and didn't feel it would be the same without George and Toy involved.

Toy still had his music in his soul. Even though he felt he'd given The Marshall Tucker Band all he had to give, he still had the need to play that guitar. He formed a loose unit he called The Toy Caldwell Band, a group that would perform only a handful of dates.

Charlie Daniels's last hit record had been in 1982. But he hadn't, by any means, been idle and had no intentions of retiring. Along with hundreds, maybe thousands, of tour dates during 1982-1985, The Charlie Daniels Band contributed music to Burt Reynolds's film *Stroker Ace*, and Charlie performed at the 1984 Super Bowl. He also somehow managed to find the time to publish a book of short stories titled *The Devil Went Down To Georgia: Stories By Charlie Daniels*. Music was still very much a part of Charlie Daniels's life.

.38 Special, 1987. (Back row, left to right) Max Carl, Larry Jungstrom. (Front row, left to right) Danny Chauncey, Donnie Van Zant, Jack Grondin, Jeff Carlisi. Credit: A&M Records/Jeff Carlisi Collection.

Music was still the main focus of the lives of the members of .38 Special, too. *Tour de Force*, released in 1984, contained several hit singles. "If I'd Been the One," "Twentieth Century Fox," and "Back Where You Belong" provided .38 Special with chart success. *Tour de Force* was declared a platinum album. "Like No Other Night" was another hit and resulted in a gold record for 1986's *Strength In Numbers*. It seemed that every .38 Special record contained at least one hit single. The boys in the band couldn't have been happier.

Life held more ups and downs for the surviving members of Lynyrd Skynyrd. In 1986 Gary Rossington and Dale Krantz returned to the music scene with a new album titled *Returned To The Scene Of The Crime*. Leon Wilkeson joined a Christian band. Billy Powell was arrested for DUI and sent to jail for thirty days. While incarcerated, Powell also saw "the light" and eventually formed his own Christian band named Vision. "That's when I finally just realized to learn to forgive and forget the past and just try to move on," he says.

Surviving Honkettes Leslie Hawkins and Jo Billingsley also continued to get on with their lives. Hawkins signed on to sing backup with Molly Hatchet. Billingsley traveled throughout the South witnessing through a personal ministry.

The individual members of the defunct Lynyrd Skynyrd struggled on as they attempted to play their music and live their emotionally ravaged lives. MCA had temporarily stopped releasing Lynyrd Skynyrd product. *Best Of The Rest*, which had been released in 1982, is a compilation of rare tracks and outtakes. It seemed possible the record company had finally run out of enthusiasm for the band.

Charlie Daniels's excitement for his music was as high as ever, and his audience continued to be supportive of his efforts. In 1986 Epic released *Me and the Boys*. Taking on significant American issues continued to be important to Charlie as a songwriter. He sang this time about the "American Farmer," another song that touched the hearts of all who heard it. "American Farmer" quickly became a country staple when it was released as a single. Charlie followed "American Farmer" with the rocking, honkytonk tune "Drinkin' My Baby Good-bye." He soon found his record on the Country Top 10. Charlie Daniels was having a good time.

In 1986 Henry Paul returned to The Outlaws for *Soldiers of Fortune*, which was released on Pasha Records. Hughie Thomasson held on to his rein as the band's leader, and David Dix remained as drummer. Chuck Glass was brought in on bass and Steve Grisham on guitar. A slew of additional guest musicians came aboard to help the effort, such as Randy Bishop, Jimmy Glenn, Buster McNeil, and Dwight Marcus. Randy Bishop produced the album in conjunction with Spencer Proffer. The album contains several good songs, but one stands out. Not knowing whether or not this carnation of the band would work, the album's first cut was ironic. The song was a Bishop/Glass tune titled "One Last Ride."

The Allman Brothers Band decided to take at least one more last ride. The band performed for the first time in several years at Charlie Daniels's Volunteer Jam in 1986. Dan Toler continued his association with the Brothers, and Chuck Leavell returned to play with the band. Three months later, the Brothers appeared at a Bill Graham-produced benefit at New York City's Madison Square Garden. Any immediate plans for recording or continuing as a unit, however, were put on hold. A reunion of The Allman Brothers Band on a permanent basis was a bit premature.

Gregg Allman and Dickey Betts decided to continue their solo careers yet toured "together" for a short time. Gregg had his band, and Dickey had his. They would play their individual music and then come together for an extended encore. When the Allman/Betts tour reached Macon, Butch Trucks, Jaimoe, and Chuck Leavell joined Gregg and Dickey onstage for a ninety-minute jam.

Gregg knew he had to play music or he might retreat into the dark world he sometimes seemed unable to escape. He put together a band with Dan and Frankie Toler and played a variety of clubs and small venues. Gregg wanted to stay in the game. He landed a recording contract with Epic and released another solo album, 1987's *I'm No Angel*. The title cut not only reflected Gregg's personal history, but touched a nerve with his long-suffering fans. The song also received a lot of airplay. People were appreciative of Gregg's candor and his talent.

Epic Records also signed Dickey Betts. His solo effort, *Pattern Disruptive*, was released in 1988. There was nothing wrong with either Gregg or Dickey's albums, but it became increasingly obvious that their best bet for financial and artistic success would be through their association with The Allman Brothers Band.

"There was a couple of years there when Disco came, in the '80s," says Gregg. "We just had to break up. It was like no place for us. Then that Disco rolled down, all that electronic music. People went to see live music again. They got all that *Urban Cowboy* crap out of their heads. And, you know, we got back to work."

Billy Powell had gone back to work with Vision, his Christian band. The reception to the few Skynyrd songs the band performed was overwhelming. "We were playing more bars than we were churches," recalls Powell. "We were on the road with [former Grand Funk Railroad frontman] Mark Farner the fourth year. Every single time, every night, in between songs, people would start yelling 'Skynyrd!' It was the people yelling Skynyrd is when a light bulb finally went off in my head."

Powell came to feel that the only way he and his former bandmates were likely to mend their emotional trauma and obtain any kind of musical and commercial success was by regrouping and giving Lynyrd Skynyrd a second birth. "We were bitter, into heavy drug use and felt guilty," reflects Powell. "We needed to learn how to be blessed. Be blessed that I'm still alive and have all ten of my fingers and can carry on this music that Ronnie, Gary, and Allen started."

Gary Rossington was initially hesitant about reforming the band. After all, after the crash the surviving members of the band had signed a legal document with Judy Van Zant stating that they would *not* re-form Lynyrd Skynyrd or use the name. Besides, how could they possibly replace their beloved frontman, Ronnie Van Zant? Also, when Billy Powell talked to Gary about his idea, Gary was concerned about the future of his band and his wife's role in it. Powell had an idea how to solve the problem.

A short, six-week Lynyrd Skynyrd tribute tour could commence with a performance during their friend Charlie Daniels's XIII Annual Volunteer Jam in September, 1987. If the event were successful, the band would take it from there. If the band members were so inclined, they could attempt to work out any legal issues with Ronnie's widow and address how they would posture the band without Van Zant.

Charlie Brusco, Gary Rossington's manager, thought it was a great idea. He talked to Gary, who finally agreed to give it a shot. Ronnie Van Zant's brother Johnny, a Ronnie sound-alike, was recruited for the mini-tour.

Johnny Van Zant was at first reluctant to try to fill his brother's shoes. He discussed the matter with his family and came to a conclusion. "Hell, I was a Skynyrd fan, too, so I figured Skynyrd was over with, you know?" remembers Johnny. "These guys were asking me to be a part of something that was, God, their lives. The last thing my brother ever did with Lynyrd Skynyrd was have an airplane crash and die. He deserved a little more than this and to make what he started carry on. It'd be a chance to kind of set things a little bit straight, too. Instead of Lynyrd Skynyrd ending on a bad note, you know?"

Johnny Van Zant, the third Van Zant brother, was born on February 27, 1960. Johnny listened to The Beatles, Elvis, Free, Ray Charles, Marvin Gaye, and Merle Haggard, and others while growing up in Jacksonville, Florida. He remembers watching his brothers Ronnie and Donnie get involved with music and thinking, "Wow, you know, that looks very cool."

Johnny liked playing the drums at first, but the family music business was singing. He was encouraged to give vocals a try. He briefly was associated with a garage-type band called The Austin Nichols Band, but soon formed The Johnny Van Zant Band. Eric Lundgren, Robbie Gay, Robbie Morris, Jim Glover, and Danny Esposito rounded out the group. PolyGram offered The Johnny Van Zant Band a contract; the group recorded three albums for the label before signing with Geffen Records.

Johnny's career eventually drew interest from Ahmet Ertegen of Atlantic Records. Johnny remembered how his involvement with Ertegen came to be. Joe Boyland, Johnny's manager, had made the arrangement for Van Zant and Ertegen to meet. "We made a date at 2 in the afternoon; we'd be out at the airport and meet this guy Ahmet Ertegen, who I knew very little about," chuckles Johnny. "We go to this hotel. . . . It was a Holiday Inn right at 95 there. So we go in the restaurant and we're talking, you know, and [Ertegen] says, 'Well, Joe tells me this is what you want, blah, blah, blah. . . . Who's your lawyer?' The deal was done."

Although Johnny Van Zant had agreed to record for Atlantic, his solo project was put on hold. For the time being, he was the vocalist for Lynyrd Skynyrd. Johnny had the full support of the rest of the band. "I know Ronnie, Steve, Dean, and all of them are very proud of us," claims Billy Powell. "And I know Ronnie's going, 'Go for it, little brother! I'm very proud of you. Keep it up. Keep the music going. Don't let the legend die.'"

The new Skynyrd band consisted of Gary Rossington, Billy Powell, Leon Wilkeson, and Ed King. Randal Hall, the guitarist who had worked with Allen Collins in The Allen Collins Band, was brought in on guitar. Allen had hand-picked Hall to play his guitar parts.

Artimus Pyle had been living in Jerusalem, where he and some friends had initiated plans to create The World Peace Center. A massive concert was being planned to promote the new organization. Still, Pyle wanted to support his friends and returned to join them in their new venture. He would commute back and forth between the United States and Israel. Pyle was in.

The band rehearsed at a makeshift studio on Jacobs Avenue and prepared for the emotionally charged gig. Offering Johnny-sung Skynyrd classics and an instrumental "Freebird" tribute, the band was well received at that Volunteer Jam. Fans of the original group were anxious to rekindle the magic. It was an emotional night for the band. "I was scared shitless," laughs Johnny Van Zant. "I didn't know what the fans were going to think or do. I screwed up on 'Three Steps.' I actually came in on the third verse, halfway through the guitar leads. It's all kind of a blur."

Re-forming the group was emotionally difficult, and an outstanding legal obligation hung over the reestablishment of one of rock and roll's legendary entities. Lynyrd Skynyrd widows Judy Van Zant and Theresa Gaines sued the band, demanding that Rossington, Powell, et. al., either follow the early dictate of no Skynyrd name or cut them in for their husbands' share of the profits. The suit was settled out of court with Van Zant and Gaines emerging triumphant.

The initial dates of the Lynyrd Skynyrd mini-tour were an overwhelming success. "We didn't realize the magnitude of the success until it happened," recalls Billy Powell. "Then that's when we decided, 'Wow, this is a good thing. . . . Let's keep it going.'"

A thirty-two-city reunion tour eventually was booked. The first concert would be held in Baton Rouge, picking up where the 1977 tour had so painfully ended.

Allen Collins was brought on board as musical director. Collins selected the set lists, supervised the stage, and arranged the songs. Part of Collins's DUI manslaughter sentence had dictated that he use his fame to raise public awareness of drunk driving issues. He used the reunion tour as an opportunity to fulfill his legal obligations, taking the stage in his wheelchair to painfully tell Skynyrd's fans why he could no longer play with the band he loved. The fans, although mixed in their emotions to see the band without Ronnie Van Zant, Allen Collins, and Steve Gaines, decided that this Skynyrd was preferable to no Skynyrd at all. The tour was quite successful. Lynyrd Skynyrd was back on the boards.

In an effort to capitalize on .38 Special's success, A&M released *Flashback*, a "Best of" compilation, in 1987. The album demonstrated the band's appeal and complemented the path .38 Special had chosen to walk. "We don't put what we call fillers on a .38 Special record," said Donnie Van Zant. "We really feel that the songs that we put on a CD are the very best that we can do at that particular time. If we don't feel that, they don't make it. All of us gotta like it to begin with. If one person in the group don't like a particular song, it don't make the .38 Special record. You gotta please a lot of people. We work real hard at that, and we go through a lot of songs to get eleven songs."

In 1987 Don Barnes decided to leave .38 Special for a life independent of the road. Danny Chauncey came into the group on guitar, and Max Carl joined the band to handle drums and percussion. Chauncey and Carl were outside of the Southern family but were welcomed into the fold.

"Max came out from L.A., and I came out from San Francisco," recalls Chauncey. "One of the first things that the band did to kind of initiate us into the Southern thing, the culture at least, was to take us to a restaurant on the St. John's River called Whitey's Fish Camp. There was a whole section of the menu called "Swamp Vittles." An entire page. We're like, 'Is this a part of the deal?' There's gator tail and frog legs and turtle bits that are fried. But we enjoyed ourselves. Before we played with a Southern Rock band, we have to eat some gator tail. After that it was like, 'All right, you guys are cool. You didn't puke.'"

Danny Chauncey brought a lot of experience to .38 Special. Even if his history wasn't completely steeped in that of Southern Rock, he did have ties to the genre. One of his first professional associations was in the 1970s when, as a member of The Stu Blank Band, he backed up Al Kooper.

While Chauncey was involved with a band he'd formed called Billy Satellite, he wrote a song called "I Want To Go Back." The single became a Top 10 hit for San Francisco rocker Eddie Money. Chauncey also played occasionally with The Alameda All Stars, a band that had attracted the attention of Gregg Allman and that currently backs him on his solo outings.

When Don Barnes left .38 Special, former Skynyrd soundman and .38 producer Kevin Elson recommended that Chauncey replace him. Chauncey was delighted to be with the band. "I was struck by the commitment," he remembers. "And the work ethic. Man, these guys are serious. You practice hard; the show has gotta go off like clockwork. Constantly revising and updating and trying to assess what works good with the audience. .38 is all about driving people crazy."

CHAPTER 21

The Family Business

1988-1989

MCA decided to release more vintage Lynyrd Skynyrd product via an album titled *Legend*. Produced by Tom Dowd, the album contained B sides and uncompleted and unreleased songs from the original band. *Legend* was an interesting mix and not all together a rehash of previously recorded material. Its release was soon followed by an album of new material by the re-formed Skynyrd. *Southern By The Grace Of God*, a double live recording from the tour, was released in 1988. Lynyrd Skynyrd was rising from the ashes at last.

Gary Rossington didn't abandon his solo career. His *Love Your Man* album was also released that year. He'd probably learned the hard lesson that nothing lasts forever and was hedging his bets in regard to the future of Lynyrd Skynyrd.

Johnny Van Zant was having a hard time with everyone wanting him to be a Ronnie clone. Johnny was talented in his own right and wanted to put his own stamp on Lynyrd Skynyrd. He also realized that the fans still wanted the Skynyrd that they loved and were used to hearing. Johnny was becoming increasingly frustrated as the comparisons to his brother Ronnie rolled in nonstop. "They were some big shoes to fill," says Donnie Van Zant. "I don't think I could have done it. [Johnny's] done a great job."

Johnny was doing all that was asked of him, but the toll of conjuring the specter of a fallen hero every night was frustrating and fatiguing. He started to have mood swings and sometimes behaved as Ronnie might have under the worst of circumstances. "He was filling Ronnie's footsteps there for awhile," remembers Billy Powell.

"You know, the Dr. Jekyll and Mr. Hyde syndrome." Johnny Van Zant's job wasn't an easy one.

While Lynyrd Skynyrd rose from the ashes, those who were left in The Marshall Tucker Band simply chose to keep on keeping on. Five years had passed since the Tucker band had issued any new material. Even though Doug Gray and Jerry Eubanks were the only original members left in the group, they felt that the music was worth pursuing and that the Marshall Tucker name should endure.

Toy Caldwell wanted The Marshall Tucker Band name to be retired, but he'd previously been outvoted on that issue in a band meeting. With the breakup of the original band, Tucker's contract with Warner Brothers was now invalid. Gray and Eubanks bought the Marshall Tucker name and signed a new contract with PolyGram.

In 1988 producer Larry Butler was called in to work with Gray, Eubanks, and a group of Nashville studio musicians that included Rusty Milner, Bobby Ogdin, and James Stroud. These musicians were familiar with the Marshall Tucker sound because they'd been touring with Gray and Eubanks. Spartanburg musicians Stuart Swanlund, Tim Lawler, and Ace Allen were asked to join the band in an attempt to recapture some of the Marshall Tucker magic.

The effort didn't quite work as traditional Marshall Tucker. None of the material had been written by the band, and there were no Toy Caldwell compositions to send the music soaring. The record seemed empty without Caldwell and McCorkle's guitars, but Gray's vocals remained a familiar reminder of what had once been. *Still Holdin' On* did, however, produce two Top 40 Country songs: "Once You Get the Feel of It" and "Hangin' Out In Smoky Places." The only other standout on the album is Bob McDill's "Why Didn't I Think of That," which was given excellent vocal treatment by Doug Gray and was later recorded by Doug Stone.

Despite the two country hits, PolyGram didn't see much future in the revamped Marshall Tucker Band, and the group was dropped from the label. Doug Gray and Jerry Eubanks were determined to prove PolyGram wrong.

Rusty Milner and Tim Lawler were now full-time members of The Marshall Tucker Band. Milner was another Spartanburg boy, a guitar player who was influenced by Jeff Beck and Larry Carlton. Milner had been with a group called Jasmine and had played with Artimus Pyle in his band. Milner was welcomed also as a songwriter.

He would go on to co-write several Marshall Tucker songs, including "Tan Yard Road" and "Carolina Party."

Tim Lawler was also born in Spartanburg. He played his first gig at the age of thirteen at a neighborhood tavern. Lawler joined Professional Arms Entertainment after graduating from high school and toured throughout Puerto Rico, Cuba, and the Caribbean. He played on a variety of gospel and country albums and contributed to Marshall Tucker by writing "Stay in the Country" and "Drivin' You Out of my Mind."

The influx of new musicians didn't faze Charlie Daniels. He wasn't overly concerned when *Powder Keg* failed to produce a single upon its release in 1987. The album kept The Charlie Daniels Band in the game and, it was hoped, would pave the way for another hit album. The opportunity to release quality product was really all that mattered to Charlie.

Because of Charlie's ever-present desire to remain current and vital, he decided to change producers for his next album. *Homesick Heroes* was produced by James Stroud in 1988. "Boogie Woogie Fiddle Country Blues," the single released off the album, was reminiscent of "Devil Went Down to Georgia" and quickly became another Country Top 10 hit for The Charlie Daniels Band.

Although Charlie Daniels had been raised a Southern Democrat, he thought that the hippie mores he'd embraced when he was younger had, perhaps, paved the way for the permissive, amoral society in which he now found himself involved. He'd always been outspoken and his music in the past certainly hadn't shied away from revealing his point of view on issues he felt important. By 1988 Charlie felt the need to not only readdress the state of society, but also to make his stand in songs that would clearly reflect his own morals and beliefs. He re-cut "Uneasy Rider" for *Homesick Heroes*. The rednecks who harassed the long-haired hippie in the original version of the song had been replaced by gay men in a gay bar in Houston.

Lynyrd Skynyrd wasn't afforded the opportunity to move away from its past and produce wholly contemporary music. In 1989 MCA, wringing every last piece of music out of the band's prerecorded catalogue, released *Skynyrd's Innyrds*, a greatest hits package. It seemed that there was a bottomless pit of repackagable Skynyrd material.

Allen Collins was taken to a Jacksonville hospital suffering from pneumonia in September, 1989. He died there on January 23, 1990. He was thirty-eight years old. "Allen just really burned as far as the way he felt about music, the way his personal life was, the way his professional career was . . . he just burned . . . wide open all the time," says Rodney Mills. "I think sometimes it got him in trouble, sometimes it didn't, but he just had that passion and fire in him." Skynyrd carried on without Allen and his guitar, but like his brothers before him, he was missed.

Times had changed for all of the bands involved in the Southern Rock movement. There had been changes in music, changes in performances, and changes in personnel through death and departure. But the core appeal of the music remained. Now if only the band members who had survived these upheavals could simply get the music out to the people who appreciated it.

In 1989, ten years after The Atlanta Rhythm Section's last hit record, Buddy Buie decided to revitalize the band and see if the musical climate had changed enough to allow a resurgence of the group's music. Ronnie Hammond returned to the band to see if his vocal appeal might make a difference. The Atlanta Rhythm Section briefly become officially known as The ARS.

CBS released *Truth In A Structured Form* in 1989. The record didn't have much of an impact, but it did reestablish the band with its diehard fan base. The ARS reverted to its original name and continued to play as many dates as the fans demanded.

All that Charlie Daniels's fans demanded was that Charlie remain true to his roots. When you listen to 1989's *Simple Man*, you can't feign ignorance of what Charlie is talking about in "(What This World Needs Is) A Few More Rednecks" or Charlie's comment on the current state of law and order in "Simple Man."

Charlie was criticized for his right-wing tendencies and direct approach to the problems he identified, but the "simple man" didn't back down. He just kept singing. Evidently not everybody disapproved of his stance: *Simple Man* went gold. A large portion of the public wasn't tired of The Charlie Daniels Band or put off by Charlie's politics and beliefs. Epic released *A Decade of Hits* in 1989, and it became Charlie's third platinum album.

.38 Special continued to make records and please audiences. In 1989 the band released *Rock and Roll Strategy*. The album contains "Second Chance," a ballad written by Jeff Carlisi and sung by Max Carl. "Second Chance" quickly rose up the Adult Contemporary charts into the Top 10. It became *Billboard* magazine's "Adult Contemporary Song of the Year."

"I wrote ["Second Chance"] with a friend of mine, and actually wrote it five years before we ever recorded it," recalls Carlisi. "Then when Max Carl joined the band, he really brought it home and had such a marvelous voice. I mean, the guy could sing 'Mary Had A Little Lamb' and you'd go buy it, he was so good. He really sold that song. I was really proud of that, especially at the time when we had the split with Don and people were saying, 'Oh, what are you gonna do now? You've lost a singer. You can't do that. Not a good thing.' I've always had the attitude that you can do anything. I mean, just because you eliminate one part of an equation doesn't mean you can't have something equal up to, or something greater, or as good, or whatever. It was a challenge. It was just like, 'Hey, we're still songwriters.' Then to have a song that was almost #1. It wasn't the trademark song that 'Hang On Loosely' was, but it was a huge song."

For some reason, A&M Records lost interest in .38 Special and didn't renew the group's contract. *Bone Against Steel*, the band's next album, was released on the Charisma label. The album doesn't contain any blockbuster songs and was only a moderate success.

But .38 Special continued to be a strong concert attraction. The band members' approach to their performances bolstered their appeal. ".38 Special will continue to give every other band that we do a show with a scare . . . a big time run for their money," says Danny Chauncey. "Cause we don't mess around when we get on stage. We're out there, and we're going to fight for that audience. We're going to do everything we can to get them in our back pockets, and God help the band that's not prepared to do that. We'll give them hell."

Although The Allman Brothers Band was ready to get back to work, their plans remained on hold until PolyGram released a box set of their material. The release was successful as a tool to reintroduce the band to old fans and initiate new listeners into the special musical world of The Allman Brothers. *Dreams* remained a constant seller over the years, although its primary achievements were to serve as an incentive to radio to play The Brothers' music and to make a very strong statement that The Allman Brothers continued to be a viable musical force. The Brothers were relieved to see that their music was once again in vogue.

Dreams was so successful it drew the attention of the media in a big way. There were many reviews. *The New York Times* carried an in-depth review on the June 25th, 1989 cover of its *Sunday Magazine* section, and addressed the issue of why the band hadn't been recognized as a major force in rock and roll after so many years of critical and audience acclaim.

In 1989 The Allman Brothers Band hammered out an agreement with Epic Records whereby the group would deliver an album if it were given complete artistic control to record it. The label agreed, and The Brothers returned to the studio.

Chuck Leavell had been asked to rejoin the band but decided instead to cast his lot with The Rolling Stones. The Brothers decided that they would erase the disappointment of their previous incarnation by not inviting the Toler brothers back into the fold. Dickey Betts had become acquainted with a funky blues player from North Carolina named Warren Haynes. Haynes had been working with David Allan Coe and had added his tasty licks to Dickey's solo effort on the road. Haynes was asked to join Dickey when it came time to record for Epic, and the two guitarists found a remarkable compatibility.

"I was a fan before I ever knew any of those guys," Haynes says, referring to The Allman Brothers Band. "My oldest brother had the first record as soon as it came out in '69. I was nine years old. I didn't start playing guitar for a few more years, but I'd already started singing. I was very influenced by all the soul music: Otis Redding, and The Four Tops, and The Temptations, and James Brown, all that kind of stuff. Then I started hearing rock music. It really made me want to play guitar, so I was exposed to the music right from the beginning. When I joined David Allen Coe's Band in 1980, he was friends with the guys in The Allman Brothers and knew I was a big fan, so he made the introductions."

Haynes was asked to take over the "Duane" spot. He was that good. But Haynes wasn't replacing or copying Duane; he was playing his own unique lead and complementing Dickey. "They allowed me to kind of interject my own personality into the music," says Haynes. "They didn't want me to just sound like Duane. They wanted me to sound like me, but pay homage to Duane, which is a natural thing to do in The Allman Brothers Band. He was one of my favorite players growing up. He's a great guitar influence over all, but especially when it comes to slide guitar. There are very few people that made that kind of an impact on slide guitar. He's somebody that I always listened to. I must've listened to the *Fillmore East* album a thousand times."

Standing in Duane's position was certainly something Haynes was happy to do. "I'd studied The Allman Brothers music as a fan for so many years that it just felt very natural. A lot of the songs I'd played for years with other people, not quite as well. By the time I got the opportunity to play 'Statesboro Blues' and 'Dreams' and 'One Way Out' and all these songs with The Allman Brothers . . . I had played them in garage bands and cover bands and bar bands and stuff, so it's just a thrill to play 'em with those guys and to feel how they really played them, you know?"

Johnny Neel was called in to provide piano for The Brothers. Auditions were held to find the ever-important bass player the band needed to complete the new ensemble. Butch Trucks suggested that the band listen to a player named Allen Woody. Ironically, Woody had been born in the same Nashville hospital as Duane and Gregg Allman.

Woody had been working with Artimus Pyle. "We were working on some demos down at Butch's studio in Tallahassee," remembers Woody. "Butch heard me play bass and started like, 'You know something, man? We're fixing to put The Brothers back together.' I was about halfway kidding him, and I said, 'Really? Well, I guess you'll be needing a bass player, huh?' He goes, 'Well, yeah. That's what I wanted to talk to you about. Look, we're looking for this and this and this, and you fit the bill.' I'm still a guitar player. I'm not a frustrated guitar player; I'm way more frustrated by my bass playing. It was like [Berry] Oakley had that going. There's no lead-bass-type players, and a lot of them are guitar players, too, and quite good ones for that matter. He knew what they were looking for, and he knew what he was looking for, and he was like, 'Look, I maybe can get you to come down and play for Dickey and Gregg and Jaimoe. I know when they hear you play, they're gonna want you in the band.' And thank God, they did."

Woody was very happy to take over Berry Oakley's bass position. "I was very influenced by him," Woody says. "I stole a great deal from him. I think actually Warren and I thought together that we could bring back the spirit of what Duane and Berry did. I think we managed to do that. I knew that I played enough like Oakley and Warren obviously played enough like Duane, but we both are single-minded enough in our own playing. We play like ourselves, but obviously there is going to be a lot that sounds similar between Warren and Duane because Warren was very influenced by Duane. It's very similar with me and Oakley. There's obviously going to be a lot of things. When I'm playing in The Allman Brothers, I couldn't help but play even more like it because I'd heard Oakley do it for twenty years up to that point. All the records for years and years and years." Haynes and Woody were welcome additions to the band as The Brothers attempted to get back on their feet and recapture their glory.

The Allman Brothers Band embarked on a soldout tour. The band was in high gear. Everything had come together as if the complex disagreements and the long musical interval had never taken place. The band members had some personal surprises along the way, but this time they weren't always negative. A son had been born to Berry Oakley and Julia Densmore the year Berry had died. Berry never had the opportunity to see his son, Berry Duane Oakley. "Berry Jr." had been raised knowing who his father was, but he hadn't been a part of The Allman Brothers Band family.

"The first encounter was in L.A.," remembers Berry Jr. "[The Brothers] played at the Greek Theater, and I was there. I was sitting out in the crowd cause I didn't know anybody yet. I was real nervous about trying to get backstage and, 'Well, I'll just sit here and watch the show. No big deal.' Til somebody went and ran and told somebody that I was there. Red Dog, one of the old roadies, came out to the stage and was looking around. He got on the mike and rather than saying 'Berry Oakley' . . . he didn't want the crowd to freak out. My middle name is Duane so he . . . . 'Duane Oakley, please come to. . . .' 'Oh, shit . . . Ohhhh.' It was kinda neat, though. I walked up there, and Red Dog just took a look at me, grabbed me, pulled me right up on the stage, walked me over to Jaimoe. . . . He almost crushed me. Then Red Dog walked me all around, and I met everybody and from that moment on just kinda hung out."

The band members were delighted to learn that Berry Jr. had inherited his father's gift for playing the bass guitar. During the tour, the sixteen year old was asked to come on stage and play. Berry Jr. was happy to oblige.

Another Allman Brothers Band son became involved in the tour. Gregg's boy Devon had started to develop musically. Devon was asked to sing "Midnight Rider" with his father during one of the last dates of the tour. Elijah Blue, Gregg's son with Cher, performed whenever he had the opportunity as well.

Dickey Betts's son Duane made an appearance on the tour, too. Even though he was only a teenager, Duane was already playing guitar with the same vengeance as his father. It was evident that Duane Betts had an abundance of raw talent.

The younger versions of The Brothers were having the time of their lives. "It was like a big family event," says Berry Oakley, Jr. "It was a lot of fun just hanging out with everybody. All the guys in the band were great. Elj, Devon, Duane, everybody else was out there. It was cool. It was just like a big traveling entourage."

The tour was incredibly successful. Now it was time for The Allman Brothers Band to go back into the studio to see what would happen there. If they were to continue as a vital rock and roll entity, The Allman Brothers Band needed another hit record.

CHAPTER 22

Tributes

1990-1994

Lynyrd Skynyrd experienced another emotional moment in December, 1990. Johnny Van Zant hadn't been willing to sing his brother's words to "Freebird." Instead, a lone spotlight that emphasized where Ronnie would have stood if he were performing the song had been employed while the rest of the band played the song instrumentally. Finally, during a Skynyrd show at the Arco Arena in Sacramento, Johnny soulfully sang "Freebird."

"I tell you, that was the most moving experience of my life," recalls fan David Halliburton. "When Johnny sang the song the first time, you just knew that everyone was there—Ronnie, Steve, Cassie, Dean, Allen. I think all of us shed a tear that night for we had seen the before and now the after of a big part of our lives. When Johnny sang the last note then walked off the stage and was hugging people on the side of the stage while the band ripped through the second half of the song, I know I for one just wanted to be there with them on stage to be a part of the moment."

While the band members were experiencing a transitional moment, Doug Gray was struggling to keep Marshall Tucker a popular band. It was important to Gray to continue to make the music that had been the fabric of his life. The fans had given every indication that they wanted Marshall Tucker to continue.

On August 16, 1989, Gray was hospitalized with peritonitis and diverticulitis. The hospitalization caused him to reflect on his lifestyle. He decided then and there to give up drugs, hard liquor, and cigarettes. Unlike many of his friends, Gray would be a survivor.

Gray was feeling well enough by 1990 to co-produce a new Marshall Tucker Band album with Jerry Eubanks. Once again Billy Sherrill engineered the album. This time, however, the releasing label was Sisaspa Records out of Ohio. *Southern Spirit* showcases the band's new recruits at the time: Tim Lawler on bass, Rusty Milner on guitar, Don Cameron on organ, Ace Allen on drums, and Stuart Swanlund on slide. "Stay In the Country" opens the album. The song has all the marks of a traditional Marshall Tucker tune; the only difference is that it features some nontraditional Tucker harmonies. Another Tuckeresque tune is "Ballad of MTB," a song about the band itself that Tim Lawler wrote. Swanlund proved himself worthy of entering the Tucker sweepstakes with "Why Can't You Love Me," a song he not only wrote but on which he performs lead vocals. Another tip of the Tucker hat went out to the West with "Modern Day Man."

Several love songs are featured on the album, including "Chase the Memory" and "Special Lady." The carefree spirit of the old Marshall Tucker Band is evidenced through "And the Hills" and "Country Road." "No Mercy" and "Love Will" are reflective tunes that round out the album nicely. Although the album didn't bring the band quite the level of recognition Doug Gray longed for, it was an extremely enjoyable piece of work.

The Allman Brothers Band was looking for its own recognition. The guys recorded *Seven Turns* at Criteria with Tom Dowd in 1990. The band members knew that the material had to be top-notch and their delivery of it as good, if not better, than anything they'd done before. Critics recognized *Seven Turns* as a contemporary application of the formula that secured The Brothers' unrivaled reputation, rather than as just another reunion attempt to stay in the game. Warren Haynes and Allen Woody were fabulous additions to the band and spurred the founding members to recapture all of what made them dynamic and extraordinary in the first place.

The album's title track, which Dickey Betts wrote, not only reflects The Brothers' state of mind at the time, but is an uplifting testimonial to life's uncertainties, which can be applied to anyone listening. Haynes demonstrates why he was worthy to be in the band on such numbers as "Low Down, Dirty Mean" and "True Gravity." His slide envelopes Gregg Allman's sensuous vocals and serves as a springboard for the musical exertion of everyone else. "Gamblers' Roll" is exceptional blues, demonstrated by Dickey's sweltering guitar execution and Gregg's stellar vocal dramatization.

Dickey's guitar is exquisite throughout *Seven Turns*. Jaimoe and Butch Trucks punch up the record. Their performances prove that their instruments are as vital a part of the band as any other.

"True Gravity" is an instrumental composition that Dickey Betts and Warren Haynes co-wrote. The song is proof of the band's flexibility. It was nominated for a Grammy in the category of Best Rock Instrumental.

Seven Turns is an excellent album. It showed that The Brothers were a *band* once again. The Brotherhood had somehow survived.

Although Wet Willie didn't survive as a recording unit, the band continued to be popular on the radio. In 1990 a hometown contingent asked Jimmy and Jack Hall if they might resurrect Wet Willie for a few special performances. The first reunion concert was held at the Macon City Auditorium, back where it all had started for Wet Willie. Toy Caldwell had flown in to perform with the band, ever grateful to Jimmy and Jack Hall for putting a bug in Capricorn president Phil Walden's ear about The Marshall Tucker Band all those years ago.

The members of Wet Willie enjoyed their special performance. They decided that even though their individual careers might take them all over the world, they would definitely put on a Wet Willie performance if they ever found themselves in the same place at the same time. Although not on any permanent basis, Wet Willie would live.

Charlie Daniel's career remained very much alive. In 1990 he returned to his nonpolitical roots by releasing *Christmas Time Down South*, his first self-produced album. In April, 1991, *Renegade*, The Charlie Daniels Band's last Epic recording, appeared in the stores. The sentimental "Little Folks" returned Charlie's music to the country charts. Charlie once again paid tribute to Duane Allman by including a moving version of "Layla" on *Renegade*. Charlie Daniels had neither forgotten nor abandoned his rock and roll roots.

Rickey Medlocke attempted to return to Blackfoot's roots, even though he was the only member of the original band left performing under that name. He owed one last Blackfoot album to Atlantic/Atco. Medlocke hired a group of competent musicians, including Wizard, Mother's Finest bass player. *Rickey Medlocke and Blackfoot* was released in 1990.

The "new" Blackfoot went back on the road with Medlocke, drummer Gunner Ross, bass player Rikki Mayr, and guitarist Neal Casal. Medlocke was reluctant to give up the music of Blackfoot. "I really enjoyed those years with that band," he says. "You don't ever think about the bad part of it; you only think about the good part of it as it goes along. I enjoyed it, and that's what I remember. I'll always have fond memories and all that and savor those moments and you know? No regrets at all."

After the tour Medlocke signed a one-album contract with Music For Nations. It was agreed that he would produce a Blackfoot album to be released in Europe. *Medicine Man* enjoyed some success and was eventually released in the United States on Nalli Records.

"Doin' My Job," one of the songs on the album, drew radio attention, and Medlocke continued his presence on rock radio with "Guitar Slingers Song and Dance." He felt that "Guitar Slingers" represented his place in the rock and roll world. "It's so to the point and so right on," Medlocke says. "I guess on my headstone they could write, 'Here lies the Guitar Slinger Song and Dance.'"

Lynyrd Skynyrd returned to the studio to record *Lynyrd Skynyrd 1991*. Tom Dowd again produced the band. The songs "Pure and Simple," "Smokestack Lightning," and "Keeping the Faith" all stand out on the album, as well as sum up the state of Skynyrd 1991. "[The album] to me was kind of a different Skynyrd," says Billy Powell. "I don't know if it's more technical or more to it or something. Even though all the songs to me were real good."

A dissatisfied Artimus Pyle left Lynyrd Skynyrd in 1991. He claimed that his personal goals weren't compatible with the band's alleged drug use. A drummer named Custer replaced Pyle.

Pyle was soon facing an additional trauma. After he left Skynyrd and lost his "rock star status," as he puts it, Angela, his girlfriend of several years, had him arrested on capital sexual battery. She claimed Pyle had sexually abused their three-year-old daughter while giving her a bath. Those who know Pyle found the charges suspect from the beginning.

"Three days after I was thrown in jail, not one, but two of her boyfriends moved into my house," claims Pyle. "She gave them all of my cars. I had four beautiful automobiles. She gave them ten sets of drums that I had collected all over the world. And my home. Brand new television set, brand new vacuum cleaner, cause I had gotten a settlement from Skynyrd, and I bought everything for my family. I bought Angela a new car. I bought a new refrigerator, new washer, dryer, all stuff for the family. As soon as that money was spent, that's when she did this."

After spending nearly $500,000 on his legal defense, Pyle ran out of money and was forced to plead guilty to "touching his children." He claims he innocently touched his children "as a father should. To care for them." He was placed on eight years probation with two years of counseling.

Pyle felt that even though he'd been an integral member of the Lynyrd Skynyrd family, the other members of the band did nothing to support him, physically, financially, or emotionally. He was extremely hurt by their seeming lack of compassion for what he went through. "I've been a hard working, loyal member of Lynyrd Skynyrd for twenty-five years," Pyle says.

The members of .38 Special remained a hard-working ensemble themselves. Their loyalty to the music continued, but the band members' relationships had become problematic. By 1991 Don Barnes had returned to the .38 Special family, ready to give life on the road and in the studio another try. At this point, Max Carl had left the band and was replaced by Scott Hoffman. Keyboard player Bobby Capps had been drafted to round out the sound.

Another change soon followed. Jeff Carlisi left the band this time, whether by his own design or at the request of the other band members. "There may have been a part of me that was showing a bit of apathy," Carlisi concedes. "Where the band was going, career-wise, wanting to do some other things or just face some other challenges. Maybe they felt that the cause celebre was no longer there with me. But still I believed in the music and worked very hard to try to be a part of what made the band great."

Donnie Van Zant probably wasn't pleased to see his old friend go, but he was resigned to the fact. Carlisi and Barnes had experienced a somewhat tempestuous relationship from the beginning, and they obviously both felt it was time for a separation. "A band is like a marriage," muses Donnie. "Sometimes you just have to get away from each other."

Now that members of The Allman Brothers Band had patched things up in their musical marriage, they experienced a renewed interest in the group. Their successful tours resulted in feature magazine articles in premier rock publications and a special tribute to the band on VH-1. A taping of MTV's "Unplugged" show was very well received.

The band members continued to have intermittent squabbles among themselves, but for the most part their work progressed smoothly. The guys dealt with issues immediately so that they didn't get out of hand. The Brothers enjoyed their reemergence into the rock and roll arena.

The band's next album, 1991's *Shades of Two Worlds*, was recorded with The Brothers' original six pieces. Johnny Neel had left the group to pursue other work. *Shades of Two Worlds* contains some interesting material. Warren Haynes and Dickey Betts enfold Gregg Allman's poignant vocals on "End of the Line" with assurance and sensitivity. "Nobody Knows" is another of Dickey's masterworks; it is a fabulous exhibition of his skill as one of the premier rock guitarists. Every song on the album is a keeper.

The members of The Marshall Tucker Band had been looking for keepers themselves to put on their next album. *Still Smokin'* was released in 1992 on the Cabin Fever Music label. The lineup appearing on the preceding album was employed, with Doug Gray continuing to provide most of the vocals.

Still Smokin' showcases the traditional Marshall Tucker song variety. The album contains blues: "Full Moon Rising," "Can't Take It Anymore," and "Let Me Come Home"; country: "Drivin' You Out Of My Mind," a tune whose video received significant play on Country Music Television; and dance tunes: "Frontline" and "Carolina Party." Listeners are treated to a soulful ballad in "I Love You," which Doug Gray, Rusty Milner, and Tommy Caldwell co-wrote, and to a salute to all things Tucker in "Southern Spirit."

Toy Caldwell remained friends with his old band, but he felt the time had finally come for him to try something on his own. In 1992 Cabin Fever Records released *Toy Caldwell*, Toy's first solo album. Although he'd recorded some tracks for a solo album while he was still under contract to Capricorn, the time didn't seem right to release an individual effort. But Toy was now ready.

Toy's new band featured Toy on guitar, Tony Heatherly on bass, Pick Pickens on second guitar, and Mark Burrell on drums. Toy's old friends Charlie Daniels, Paul Hornsby, Gregg Allman, and Willie Nelson joined in to lend their musical support.

Toy had been long appreciated as an extraordinary songwriter and remarkable guitarist, and now everyone stood back to see what he could do as a solo performer.

The album abounds with original Toy material, yet he chose to open with "I Hear the South Callin' Me," a song that R.C. Bannon and John Bettis co-wrote. "Midnight Promises" is a pensive song highlighted by Gregg Allman's participation on the final verse. Toy also decided to update two Marshall Tucker tunes. On *Toy Caldwell* "Fly Like An Eagle" features electric guitar instead of acoustic, and "This Ol' Cowboy" includes guitar riffs and a horn section rather than Jerry Eubanks's familiar flute. Willie Nelson, who joins Toy on "Night Life," is said to have been very pleased with Toy's cover of his song. Toy returns to the West in "Shadow Rider" and "Mexico" and examines his love of the blues in "Why Am I Crying." He took a break from vocals to feature bassist Heatherly in Toy's country-paced "Wrong Right." All in all, *Toy Caldwell* is a reflective, inspired first solo effort.

In 1992 Jimmy Hall joined Hank Williams, Jr.'s touring band. Although a contemporary of Hall's, Hank represented another musical generation of Southern Rock influence. "He's singing songs up there about The Allman Brothers and Lynyrd Skynyrd and is doin' some of their songs on his set," says Hall. "Travis Tritt, same thing. He'd be going on and on about how they were fans of what we did. A lot of those bands influenced some of the more rocking country players." Hall worked with several different Southern Rock bands, including The Prisoners of Love and The Nighthawks. Hall was a musician who wanted to make music. Although Wet Willie made only infrequent appearances, Hall continued to play as much as he was able.

The other members of Wet Willie continued to work as well. Jack Hall participated in his brother Jimmy's first solo record, then joined country singer Terri Gibbs's band for a worldwide tour. Mike Duke moved to San Francisco to write songs. His tune "Doin' It All For My Baby" was a big hit for San Francisco's pop-rock band Huey Lewis and The News. Duke missed performing, however, and returned to the road with country/folk songwriter Delbert McClinton and his band.

Toy Caldwell continued to enjoy his music. He played at one of Charlie Daniels's Volunteer Jams as a solo act and also at Willie Nelson's Farm Aid show in Dallas. Life wasn't the same for him, however, without the company of his two beloved brothers. "His heart was broken," remembers Artimus Pyle.

In late February, 1993, Toy Caldwell fell ill. He'd been anxious to really hit the road in promotion of his first solo release, and he'd already played a few dates. Toy had suffered with a chronic cough for some time, and it was thought that he now had an extreme case of the bronchial flu. On February 25, Toy got up from his bed at 4 A.M. coughing. He said he was going to go to the couch so that Abbie, his wife, could get some sleep. Abbie told her husband to stay where he was, that he needed his sleep, and that she would go sleep with one of their daughters. Then Abbie kissed Toy, told him that she loved him and that she would see him in the morning.

Abbie and daughter Geneal entered the bedroom in the morning. Abbie called her husband's name, but she knew. Toy was dead in his bed. The county coroner later revealed that Toy had died of viral myocarditis, a deadly disease that attacks the heart muscle. He was forty-five years old.

The Southern Rock world was devastated by the news. Representatives of each band of the genre came forward to offer praise for Toy Caldwell's musical contributions and personal character. Dickey Betts was present at Toy's funeral to pay tribute to his friend. "He is such a gentleman, and Toy thought the world of him," remembers Abbie Caldwell. "I asked Dickey if he would come play. He did not hesitate in saying he would be there."

"Can't You See" was a moving tribute, sung by the family and friends of the song's writer. In the company of Toy's father and Toy's daughters Cassady and Geneal, Abbie Caldwell laid her husband to rest at a cemetery in Spartanburg. The Charlie Daniels Band dedicated its Radio City Music Hall concert the following week to Toy Caldwell.

Toy and Tommy Caldwell were not only exceptional musicians, but also very special individuals. Now they were both gone. Their absence left a huge hole in the hearts of all who knew them.

Toy was missed, but the music of Marshall Tucker continued. The current incarnation of the band was quick to follow up the last album with 1993's *Walk Outside The Lines*. The album, released on the Cabin Fever Music label, was produced by Doug Gray and Jerry Eubanks, engineered by Billy Sherrill, and recorded in Nashville.

Walk Outside The Lines contains some nice surprises. Country superstar Garth Brooks and Charley Stefl, his writing partner, co-wrote the title track.

The accompanying video continues to receive play on country video channels. Tim Lawler contributed to the songwriting duties with "Daddy's Eyes" and, co-writing with Gray, "If That Isn't Love." Rusty Milner's writing talent is evident in "Alright Without You," "The First One to Say Goodbye," and, also with Gray, "Lost In Time."

This album made it clear that although the face of Marshall Tucker had changed, the vocal and instrumental talent within continued to have a vital voice. Toy Caldwell, after all, had written the majority of the group's music. Although the band members would continue to draw upon Toy's catalog, it was time for other writers to step forward.

The Outlaws were about in the same situation as Marshall Tucker. Hughie Thomasson remained, but the rest of The Outlaws were new to the fold. Chris Hicks had come in on guitar and vocals, Timothy Cabe supplied additional guitar, Jeff Howell appeared on bass, and B.B. Borden was now the drummer.

Blues Bureau released The Outlaws' *Hittin the Road - Live!* in 1993. The album had been recorded at various gigs in Rochester, New York, Dallas, and Seattle. Thomasson produced the album with Mickey Mulcahy.

With the exception of Timothy Cabe, The Outlaws remained intact for one final original recording. Lynyrd Skynyrd friends Gary Rossington and Billy Powell, along with several other musical collaborators, made guest appearances on 1994's *Diablo Canyon*. While Arista would release yet another compilation, 1996's *Best of the Outlaws*, *Diablo Canyon* was The Outlaws' last ride.

Although The Allman Brothers Band had continued to produce new projects, two records were released to emphasize the fact that the band had been around playing its peerless brand of music for quite some time. *A Decade of Hits* was just that, and *An Evening With the Allman Brothers Band* had been recorded live at Boston's Orpheum Theater in March, 1992. After a frenzied resurrection, the band members needed a short break from one another. These two albums, while not nearly as exciting as the last two, provided an opportunity to keep The Brothers' legacy alive.

The band members did come together for President Bill Clinton's inauguration in January, 1993, but even that appearance failed to excite them enough to eliminate the burnout. Gregg Allman's recollection of the performances and Washington parties is succinct: "They were real long, and I was glad to get home."

Warren Haynes and Allen Woody, on the other hand, hadn't been previously exposed to Washington, DC, and its varied personalities. The musicians had a great time. "It was an honor, but was very strange," Haynes remembers. "There were all these people that were there just to see Clinton talk or see him wave and shake hands and stuff. So there were a lot of older people that didn't know or care who The Allman Brothers were that were right down in the front row where it's really loud. They didn't know how loud it was going to be, you know? This one old woman in particular was right in front of Dickey's amp, which is where you don't want to be. It's very loud in that zone. I remember seeing this tiara in her hair, and then about twenty minutes into the show her whole hairdo had taken a different slant. It was like leaning off to the side. She was just determined to keep her spot next to the President, but she was hating life while we were up there playing."

"I remember looking down at her a couple of times and she was just grimacing, but bless her heart she hung right there," recalls Allen Woody. "She wouldn't give up that seat for nothing."

Both musicians found the incident amusing, but they enjoyed the event in spite of its peculiarities. "It wasn't the easiest gig we ever had," muses Haynes. "It wasn't like playing to tons of adoring fans." But the President seemed to enjoy it. "I think he liked it a lot," Haynes notes. "He gave us the thumbs up."

In the spring of 1993, The Allman Brothers band began another tour, but they still hadn't worked out the problems that they'd been having. Dickey Betts left the band to get his health in order. He was temporarily replaced in concert by first Zack Wylde, then David Grissom, and finally Jack Pearson. By the fall, Dickey was back. The Brothers rolled on.

The Last Rebel was released during the twenty-year anniversary of Lynyrd Skynyrd's first album in 1973. Skynyrd signed with Phil Walden's newly reformed Capricorn Records in 1994 and released an entirely acoustic album titled *Endangered Species*. The new songs were good, but the magic of Ronnie Van Zant's writing was obviously missing. "[Ronnie was] the most unbelievable storyteller and poet that I've ever seen come from the South," says Rickey Medlocke.

In 1995 the documentary film *Freebird . . . The Movie* premiered at The Fox Theater in Atlanta. The film chronicles the lives, times, and tragedy of Lynyrd Skynyrd. "Freebird Fest" marked the occasion, and a sizable number of the musicians who had participated in Skynyrd's career jammed with the band. Lynyrd Skynyrd still had a lot of friends in the music industry, and the guys still knew how to rock.

Although *After the Reign* was released in 1994, it became time for Blackfoot to lay down the mantle as the South's hardest rockers. The group's songs had been instrumental in the musical lives of such heavy metal bands as Ratt and Metallica, but it was now time to move on. Rickey Medlocke decided to throw his lot in with his old friends, Lynyrd Skynyrd.

Blackfoot's original members probably weren't unhappy to see the band finally die. By this time, Gregg Walker had temporarily retired from music to live on a Montana ranch. Jakson Spires was playing sessions, and Charlie Hargrett was working in a band called The Dixie All Stars, often with Spires. Blackfoot was no more. The band, throughout its several incarnations, had enjoyed a long and successful ride.

The successful reformation of The Allman Brothers Band resulted in another studio album. *Where It All Begins* was released in the spring of 1994. Like the songs on the albums' recent predecessors, the tunes on this latest effort address the songwriters' inner turmoil, questions, and revelations. For example, Warren Haynes and Dickey Betts bring the longing for harmony and brotherhood to a musical crescendo on "Back Where It All Begins."

"Sailin' 'Cross the Devil's Sea," which was co-written by Gregg Allman and Jack Pearson, remains one of Gregg's favorite songs. As well as substituting for Dickey on the last tour, Pearson had played with Gregg's solo band. Pearson had also enjoyed stints with Memphis soul man Bobby "Blue" Bland and Delbert McClinton.

The Allman Brothers Band had decided not to play at the original Woodstock in 1969, but when Woodstock '94 was announced, the guys thought it might be fun. The Brothers were extremely well received. The opportunity to bring the second generation of Allman Brothers musicians and their talent to the more than 300,000 audience members was realized when Duane Betts stepped up to do a solo. "That was surreal," remembers Duane. "I had never been around that many people before. Visually I kinda knew what to expect, but I didn't know how I was going to feel when I got there. A fantastic opportunity."

Warren Haynes remembers Woodstock '94 as being an important event as well. "I gave a lot of thought to what the original version must've been like when I was nine years old," muses Haynes. "It was a surprise to us that we got to do [the 1994 show] because we had been booked in Boston for several months and couldn't cancel it. It was a soldout show. We got offered Woodstock, and the only way we could do it was if we played early in the day and then flew to Boston and played the same night. So, we went on at like noon, which was the only way we could really feasibly make it happen. By the time we did our show and did all of our meeting the press and interviews and posing for pictures and made it to our private plane to fly to Boston, we just barely made the gig. We all thought the Boston gig was going to suck because of how tired we would be, but it turned out to be one of the best shows of the tour cause the weight was lifted, you know? We'd already done Woodstock."

Although popular at previous festivals, .38 Special wasn't invited to play at Woodstock '94. The band hadn't enjoyed a hit record in some time. While the guys continued to tour, the personality problems in the band and other unknown problems had somehow affected their ability to keep their finger on the pulse of the music industry. The musicians did, however, keep very current with the lives of their friends and families and with society in general. The band members were now ready to express their views on the state of life in the 1990s.

.38 Special bounced back hard with 1997's *Resolution*. The album, which was produced by ZZ Top/Steve Earle producer Joe Hardy, offers a variety of musical genres. "I think there's a song on this record for everybody," said Donnie Van Zant. The band enjoyed working with Hardy. "[Hardy] let you be yourself and let you have the freedom *to* be yourself and not try to hold you back," claims Donnie. "That shows when you record on a record."

What showed on the record was that the members of .38 Special had matured as a band. They were capable of a lot more than the pop music label the rock press had sometimes saddled them with. "I think lyrically, as we grow older, we have more things to talk about," muses Danny Chauncey. "I think that deepens the lyric content as opposed to everything being about girl issues, you know? There were more diverse life issues to talk about."

"Fade To Blue" was a Top 20 single for the band, its first hit in years. "When we were making the record, Don and I would get in the van and drive from the studio back to the hotel, and we'd play back whatever we did," recalls Chauncey. "Toward the end of the record, we had an early mix of 'Fade To Blue.' You put that on, you find your foot would go down on the gas pedal. You'd find yourself passing the hotel, and we'd be on the freeway somewhere like, 'Where the hell are we going?'"

Another standout on the album is "Shatter the Silence," a strong statement about the effects of child abuse. Not only is the message resolute, the music is intricate, powerful, and effective. "I'm very much into how the music alone paints a picture," says Chauncey. "At the very beginning of the song there's that instrumental piece, and that's kind of symbolic of the child. At the end, it's the same chord structure but with very angry undercurrents in it, from the guitar playing, to the voluminous strength. That was to paint the picture of the adult 'child,' so the story is told in between those two pieces of music."

Donnie Van Zant contributed several songs to the album; one of the most compelling is a poignant ballad called "Lonesome Guitar." "Donnie just sings the hell out of that, doesn't he?" says Chauncey. Donnie's "After the Fire Is Gone" is another dominant piece of *Resolution*. .38 Special was back, rocking as hard as ever.

Two members of The Allman Brothers Band continued to rock hard, but with a twist. Warren Haynes had been working on his own solo album and, with Allen Woody and drummer Matt Abts, sometimes opened for The Brothers. The trio called themselves Gov't Mule, and it was hot. As the group worked out some exciting new music and sharpened its onstage presentation, it became apparent that something special had been born.

Haynes and Woody worked two shows a night, first as Gov't Mule and then with The Brothers. "It was a lot of work," remembers Haynes. "But you know, that's what you're there for. We were able to turn a lot of people on to what Gov't Mule was about."

Eventually, Haynes and Woody decided that they'd taken their association with The Allman Brothers Band about as far as was appropriate. They were ready to try their own wings. It wasn't an easy decision. They considered a lot of factors, including the continual personality conflicts between the founding members of The Allman Brothers Band. "They're one of the greatest bands in the world," says Woody. "[But] I really hate the dysfunction that swims around among the partners in that band. I think what can happen to you is that if you get too successful too young, I think you're afforded all this money and fame and free time. I guess everybody handles it the best way they can. If I had made it as young as those guys did, I'd be dead right now."

Woody and Haynes decided to quit The Allman Brothers Band and cast their lot with Gov't Mule. The Brothers weren't happy about the decision, and some hard feelings resulted. "It's still very sad to Warren and me that it went the way it did," says Woody.

Jack Pearson was brought in to replace Haynes on lead/slide guitar, and Oteil Burbridge, a founding member of Aquarium Rescue Unit, was asked to join The Allman Brothers Band on bass. "Oteil Burbridge and Jackie Pearson add a whole lot to the band, they really do," says Gregg Allman. "They're young blood, you know, and they keep us old guys going. You gotta keep up with them, a couple of jumps in front of them."

The Brothers brought in Marc Quinones on percussion. Quinones was a child prodigy who played drums in a Latin production at Carnegie Hall at the age of nine. He was playing with the jazz group Spiro Gyra when Butch Trucks heard him play. A couple of months later, Butch asked Quinones to participate in the recording of *Where It All Begins*.

The music was still enjoyable, and the band played on. The Allman Brothers Band was inducted into the Rock and Roll Hall of Fame on January 13, 1995. The music of The Allman Brothers Band, past and present, continued to be important to the world of rock and roll.

CHAPTER 23

The Legacy

1992-THE PRESENT

In 1997 Lynyrd Skynyrd released *Twenty*, new product in the form of an album dedicated to the twentieth anniversary of the tragic plane crash that took the lives of several band members. Artimus Pyle claims that Gary Rossington had asked him to return to the band at that time. Pyle says he agreed, but the call never came. Owen Hale was named drummer. Hale himself would be replaced in May, 1998, by Bill McCallister.

Twenty was important to the current members of Lynyrd Skynyrd. Not only did the album keep the band in the ball game, they felt it reflected their past. "*Twenty*, I think, was one of the closest to our original roots, as far as musically, since the new band formed in 1987," says Billy Powell.

Twenty also provided Johnny Van Zant with an opportunity to sing with his brother Ronnie. Rickey Medlocke had mentioned the Hank Williams Sr./Hank Williams Jr. digitally blended recording and thought it would be interesting to do one of Ronnie and Johnny. At first Johnny resisted the idea of "singing" with his oldest brother on "Travellin' Man."

"I thought it might be a little cheesy," Johnny remembers. "So I ended up talking to the producer and the engineer, Josh Leo and Ben Fowler. They kind of reassured me that we could do it pretty cool. Then the band actually started playing it in the studio, man, and I was singing along, and I thought about where Ronnie could sing and stuff. The more I thought about it, the more I got into it. In the end, I'm really proud that we did it, you know? Especially live, man, just to hear the audience go crazy when Ronnie's picture come up on stage."

Fans embraced "Travellin' Man" immediately. The album also contains several other songs that became identified with the new band. "Bring It On," "Home Is Where the Heart Is," and "Talked Myself Right Into It" were popular with the fans.

Although Ed King had rejoined Skynyrd, he soon found his playing hampered by a persistent health problem. Once again King had to leave the band when he learned that he had an enlarged heart and would eventually require a transplant. He asked his friends in Skynyrd for financial assistance based on his long-term involvement with the band. King says his request was denied. "They promised to take care of me, and I had agreed to work on the anniversary album," says King. "Next thing I knew, the management is telling me I won't be needed and Gary isn't returning my calls." King felt betrayed by his friends and filed suit. "They'll say it's sour grapes," believes King. "I don't know why the whole thing had to happen that way."

Guitarist Randal Hall toured with the band from 1988 to 1994 using Allen Collins's Fender Stratocaster. After Hall was fired from Skynyrd, he sued the band for $500,000. Hall claimed that he was entitled to a share of Skynyrd's earnings through tickets, merchandise, albums, and videos. Skynyrd's management claimed Hall was an employee, not an owner, of the band and as such was entitled to nothing more than his salary.

One night new guitarist Rickey Medlocke rather roughly showed a former "associate" of the band's the door and told him his "services" were no longer required. The associate filed suit against Medlocke and the band, claiming he'd been assaulted. Lawsuits seemed to be getting filed against Lynyrd Skynyrd left and right. Skynyrd was no longer one big happy family.

Public attention was focused on the "new" band with the twentieth anniversary of the plane crash in 1997. Rickey Medlocke of Blackfoot and Hughie Thomasson of The Outlaws had been added to the band to revitalize the Skynyrd sound. "Rickey is the new electricity of the band," claims Billy Powell. "He brings a whole new feeling of energy to everybody. He reminds me of Allen. Allen was the one who did all the high jumping and dancing around and going nuts on stage a lot, where everybody else just kind of did their own thing. Ricky's a showman like that, too."

Medlocke has no problem admitting that on a lot of the songs he is paying tribute to Allen Collins's playing. "I gave [Gary Rossington] my word that if I got the job, I would play Allen's stuff note for note," says Medlocke. "Mine and Allen's styles was very similar, technique and stuff. Actually we played the same guitars as each other, ironically."

"We're there to play for our audience, for a crowd, for fans," says Thomasson. "We feed off of that, believe it or not. I mean, they give it back to you, they get it back ten times over. They're part of the show."

Like Steve Gaines before them, the new recruits provided a formula that worked well. "I'll tell you what, boy," says Leon Wilkeson. "Good call for Gary Rossington, recruiting Ricky Medlocke and Hughie Thomasson."

Dale Krantz Rossington and Carol Chase now provide backup vocals. "They both look real good, and they both work together real good, and they both have beautiful voices," says Billy Powell of the new Honkettes.

Artimus Pyle continues to attempt to overcome the complicated and devastating events of the past twenty years of his life. He reestablished A.P.B. (All Points Bulletin) with Tim Lindsey, Mike Estes, and Greg Baril. Estes toured with Lynyrd Skynyrd playing guitar for two years; he also appeared on two of the group's albums. Lindsey toured with Skynyrd on bass for the Last Rebel tour and the Tribute tour. He was also a member of The Rossington Band. Baril has played guitar with B.B. King and Stevie Ray Vaughn. A.P.B. is a very popular band that continues to play ceaselessly to sellout club crowds. Pyle found personal happiness in 1999 when he married Kerri Hampton on Valentine's Day.

In a desire to perpetuate the legacy of Ronnie Van Zant and the original Lynyrd Skynyrd band, Ronnie's widow, Judy Van Zant Jenness, and daughter Melody established The Freebird Foundation. The Foundation funds financial-need, four-year college scholarships in the names of Ronnie, Allen Collins, Dean Kilpatrick, and Steve and Cassie Gaines (the scholarships were established initially through The Foundation by Steve's daughter Corrinna). In addition the Foundation sponsors both an internet website that dispenses information about the band past and present, and a food drive for Jacksonville's homeless.

Judy, Melody, and Tammy, Ronnie's eldest daughter, also donated money to Clay County, Florida, to buy land and build Ronnie Van Zant Park. The park is a ninety-acre recreation area with a fishing pond, softball fields, tennis courts, and a large children's playground. The expansion of the park has become a project of The Freebird Foundation.

Leon Wilkeson continues to enjoy being a player in Lynyrd Skynyrd. "He pulls some crazy stunts sometimes, but we call him basses extraordinaire," says Billy Powell. "He is a bass player's bass player."

Powell continues to feel grateful for the opportunity to make music through his association with Lynyrd Skynyrd. "I'm real proud of the music the band has produced in the last twenty-twenty-five years," he says. "Still being a part of it and still carrying on the music is just a real good feeling."

Gary Rossington's contribution to the Skynyrd sound hasn't gone unnoticed. "People don't give Gary a lot of credit for his guitar playing," says Rickey Medlocke. "But I'm telling you, being a guitar player and being around him, sometimes he really amazes me, he really does."

After years of internal struggle, Johnny Van Zant, at last, feels that he is being afforded the opportunity to come into his own rather than merely appearing as a clone of his oldest brother. "He's doing great," says Powell. "And he's a hard worker."

"I'm at peace with myself with it," says Johnny. "A few years there I didn't know for sure. There was so many lawsuits. Sometimes you just start doubting yourself, whether it's the right thing to do. Then I'd go out and I'd sing, and the fans would be just going nuts, you know, cause they'd love that music. I always say Lynyrd Skynyrd's bigger than the people that's in it. The name and the music of Lynyrd Skynyrd will live on long after the people in the whole band's gone, you know? I believe that."

Skynyrd fans abound, and record sales are on the rise for this legendary rock and roll band. Although *Lyve At Steeltown* received mixed reviews and MCA continues to release product from the original band, Skynyrd looks forward to the records they'll produce in the future. In the meantime, they are happy to be appearing before sellout audiences. "It's Christmas, our birthday, all wrapped in one when we go on the stage," says Leon Wilkeson.

"Our gimmick has always been our music," says Powell. "Not our lights, not our sound system. Not really necessarily that much of a visual thing as a musical thing." There is one old standby that irks Powell, however. "We've been using that dadgum mirror ball for God knows how long," Powell laments. "I'm gonna shoot it down the next time I see it."

As Charlie Daniels has sung, "The South's gonna do it again." So, apparently, is Lynyrd Skynyrd. "Nothing's going to break this band up, unless there's another tragedy," says Powell. "God forbid."

The Atlanta Rhythm Section, 1998. (Left to right) Justin Senker, Barry Bailey, R.J. Vealey, Ronnie Hammond, Dean Daughtry, Steve Stone. Credit: Buddy Buie/Atlanta Rhythm Section.

"Lynyrd Skynyrd is timeless," says Rickey Medlocke. "I believe that there'll never be a time that you won't hear it on the radio. I don't think there's ever going to be a time that somebody won't want to listen to it on CDs and hear it in their car. Even today, with the younger audiences. They can remember where they were the first time they ever heard "Sweet Home Alabama," or "Gimme Three Steps," or "What's Your Name," or "Freebird." It brings back memories. It is beautiful to me because that to me means that the music is timeless."

Lynyrd Skynyrd has sold more than thirty million records. Who would have thought that the opening act for The Quadrophenia Tour would eventually outsell even The Who? "Freebird" has been played on the radio more than two million times according to BMI. In 1999 Skynyrd will be touring nationally with Hank Williams Jr. Fans will once again flock to hear the sounds and enjoy the experience that was, and is, Lynyrd Skynyrd.

The Atlanta Rhythm Section has been a popular live band for more than twenty-five years. In 1996 the band was inducted into The Georgia Music Hall of Fame. The group's performance during that event marked the first time in sixteen years that all of the original band members performed together.

In 1997 The Atlanta Rhythm Section celebrated its twenty-fifth anniversary with the release of *Partly Plugged*, an excellent contemporary offering. Part of the album is devoted to a reworking of the group's hits, such as "So Into You" and "Imaginary Lover." The album also offers some topical songs that are worth listening to and thinking about.

"I Don't Want to Grow Old Alone" is one of those songs. Buddy Buie and Ronnie Hammond co-wrote the tune during Hammond's breakup with his wife. "I had a 'Father Knows Best' childhood," says Buie. "My mother and daddy were so happy. I just couldn't picture myself growing old alone and not having what they did. But I'm happily married. I think today that so many people are out there that have a troubled relationship. That pretty much is bottom line. It might be your fondness or your love for another person, but the bottom line, you think about yourself. When you get too old to rock and roll, where you gonna go?"

The Atlanta Rhythm Section, rejuvenated with a lineup that currently includes Hammond, Bailey, Daughtry, Steve Stone, Justin Senker, and R.J. Vealey, clearly isn't too old yet to rock and roll. Such diverse artists as country rocker Travis Tritt and jazzman David Sanborn have recently recorded the band members' songs. In 1998 the band members returned to the studio with new material and a new, age-induced edge that promises to not only appease their fans, but also entice new ones. *Eufala* was released by Platinum Records in February, 1999.

The Atlanta Rhythm Section plans to be around a lot longer. "I don't think history has judged us yet," says Ronnie Hammond.[27]

Wet Willie's Jimmy Hall continues to perform both as a solo act and as a member of Gregg Allman's band. Hall released *Rendezvous With the Blues*, his first-ever totally blues record, in 1997. The album contains many Hall-penned songs, as well as blues staples from Sam Cooke, Willie Dixon, and Muddy Waters. Former Hour Glass drummer and Capricorn producer Johnny Sandlin produced the album. The Allman Brothers Band's Jack Pearson provided some inspired co-writing, as well as titillating guitar. Hall's band consisted of members of the Muscle Shoals Rhythm Section. The album has a live feel to it that is right on the money, providing some stellar roots music.

Currently Jimmy and Jack Hall, with their sister Donna on backup vocals, musicians John Anthony and T.K. Lively, and guitarist Ric Seymour have kept their promise to keep Wet Willie alive. The band members appear whenever they are all able, much to the delight of their fans. The Black Crowes, as well as many other bands, have often said that Wet Willie has influenced them. The music of Wet Willie and the group's hit "Keep On Smilin'" will forever remain a staple of American rock and roll.

In 1993 Cabin Fever Music Video released "Then & Now," a video history of The Marshall Tucker Band. In 1994 Marshall Tucker signed with AJK Records and released a double-CD compilation from the Capricorn albums titled *The Capricorn Years*. Other compilations include *Country Tucker* in 1996 and *Marshall Tucker Blues* in 1997. Audiences both old and new continue to be hear Toy Caldwell's tremendous musical contributions.

In 1997 Jerry Eubanks decided that his days on the road were over. He wanted to spend time with his six children. Doug Gray made the decision to continue to deliver Marshall Tucker music to the people who continued to love it. Gray was now the only original member in the band. In various incarnations, along with Milner and Lawler, Gray has played on the road with Chris Hicks, David Muse, Gary Gazardo, and B.B. Borden. Hicks toured with The Outlaws before joining The Marshall Tucker Band in 1997. David

Doug Gray, 1995. Credit: Doug Gray/Michael B. Smith.

Muse came to the group after a stint with Firefall. Borden had experienced success as a drummer with Mother's Finest, Molly Hatchet, and The Outlaws. Gray continued to surround himself with excellent musicians.

The former Tuckers had chosen to devote their time to other endeavors. Paul Riddle owns a drum stick company called "The Carolina Stick Company." George McCorkle is a songwriter in Nashville. "I'm not doing it to try and be a major success," he says. "I mean, I'm an artist, and I've got something to say. And I need to say it. That's sort of the way I look at it."

On September 19, 1995, The Marshall Tucker Band was inducted into The South Carolina Hall of Fame in the company of such entertainers as James Brown, Chubby Checker, Aaron Tippin, and Joanne Woodward. Charlie Daniels, a Carolina boy himself, set the tone for the evening with poems he'd written for Toy and Tommy Caldwell. The Marshall Tucker Band and its members might be continually changing, but Toy and Tommy's names will forever be associated with the unique and substantial mark the original band made on the face of contemporary music. The Caldwell brothers' peerless instrumentation and Toy's exceptional songwriting talent continue to be admired and appreciated by their musical contemporaries and virtually all who hear their music. Their musical legacy is one of the most important of Southern Rock. Toy and Tommy Caldwell won't be forgotten.

After the Hall of Fame ceremony, the audience was treated to a reunion of all of the members of The Marshall Tucker Band. This was the first time the original members of the band had played together since their 1983 breakup. The audience was treated to nearly a dozen songs, including "Heard It In A Love Song," "Desert Skies," "Long Hard Ride," and "Fire On The Mountain." The evening concluded with "Can't You See."

Years after the high of The Marshall Tucker Band being inducted into the South Carolina Hall of Fame, it was with sadness that Abbie Caldwell felt the need to hire an attorney to reclaim money she felt Toy's family was owed for songwriting royalties. "I would never want or expect to share in royalties received for songs written by others, just as I do not want or expect to share the royalties for Toy's compositions," says Abbie. It is hoped that the matter will be ironed out.

On a more positive note, Abbie Caldwell was delighted to learn that Charlie Daniels and his manager David Corlew bought the rights to Toy's solo album with plans to rerelease it on their Blue Hat Records label. Abbie was happy to hear that the album would have new life. "It was truly like a pot of gold at the end of a rainbow!" Abbie says. "A wonderful, great, big, happy surprise for me." Toy Caldwell's music would live on.

Toy Caldwell and the other Tuckers continue their international appeal. It seems they'll always be popular in Europe and Great Britain. English fan Craig Eason reflects on their allure when he states, "They are one of the top five acts in the appreciation stakes [in England]."

Does it bother the surviving members of The Marshall Tucker Band that they've never enjoyed huge commercial success? "To this day it doesn't bother me," says George McCorkle. "Cause most bands that have had major hits have not sold ten million records, or eleven million, whatever. . . ."

The Marshall Tucker Band, in whatever incarnation it happens to be, will go on. "It'd be kind of a drag to think that we took all this money and all this stuff from all these people, and all these accolades, and how good we were, and all the memories and everything, and give up on it," says Doug Gray. "I'm having a good time. That's all I want people to know. That I didn't get up there and pull their leg around the block, you know, and make them think I'm just having a good time just to keep on being out here. I'll never do that. I'll probably die singing anyway, so it'll be all right."

Charlie Daniels has no thought of retiring either. Since 1992 he has continued to release records that run the gamut of musical styles: gospel, country, patriotic, blues. He was involved with his own cable television series, "Charlie Daniels' Talent Roundup" for TNN, and his reworked "The Devil Came Back to Georgia" was nominated for a 1994 Country Music Association award. *The Door*, an album of gospel and religious songs that Sparrow released in 1994, was honored with a Dove Award from the Gospel Music Association. Charlie's participation in the multi-artist *Amazing Grace: A Country Salute to Gospel* won a Grammy in 1995.

Charlie Daniels, 1997. Credit: Jim McGuire/Charlie Daniels.

In 1996 Sony Music released *The Roots Remain*, a boxed set featuring songs from Charlie Daniels's decades-long musical career. Through this collection Charlie pays homage to not only his musical roots, but also a key element of the development of Southern Rock: The Charlie Daniels Band. Charlie continues to be an advocate of the Southern Rock family. "I don't think you can overstate the importance of Toy Caldwell and Tommy Caldwell, Ronnie Van Zant and Duane Allman," says Charlie when reflecting on the genre. "I think that this whole thing hinged to a big extent on those four guys. If you trace the roots, you're gonna find the start of the root right there."

The roots of Southern Rock would wither and die without the continued involvement of Charlie Daniels. There isn't a musician involved who doesn't believe that Charlie is the heart and soul of the genre. In 1999 he released *Tailgate Party*, on which he pays tribute to his Southern Rock friends and some of the songs that define the genre: Toy Caldwell's "Can't You See" and Lynyrd Skynyrd's "Freebird" and "Statesboro Blues" are included. *Tailgate Party* is dedicated to Duane Allman, "The Bottleneck Bandit." For the first time, Charlie's Volunteer Jam will tour the

United States. Scheduled as of this writing to appear in 1999 are The Marshall Tucker Band, Jimmy Hall, and Dickey Betts. Charlie will continue to entertain as long as he is able to take the stage. His current project is a fiddle album on which he'll showcase some of his previous fiddle tunes, updated and reworked. The roots remain, but Charlie Daniels's musical legacy continues to grow.

Although Grinderswitch is no longer a working band, its existence has also contributed to the legacy of Southern Rock. The group recorded *Macon Tracks* and *Pullin' Together* before leaving the Capricorn label. Grinderswitch was never really commercially successful, but the musicians were well respected within the Southern Rock community and gave one hell of an exciting live show. "Grinderswitch was a great little boogying band," says Paul Hornsby. "I say 'little' only from the standpoint that they never had the push some of the bigger groups got. They were the Capricorn trench soldiers, so to speak. Hardly any promotion was ever done regarding them. We recorded the albums with all our heart and soul, then they just sort of came out, not released with any fanfare. I hate to call Grinderswitch a 'boogie' band, but they could play a shuffle better than anyone I know. The title of their first album was appropriately titled *Honest to Goodness*. That's the music they played."

The members of Grinderswitch continue to be involved in music. Joe Dan Petty stays musically active and has returned to The Allman Brothers Band. Dru Lombar eventually became involved with session work, recording with such artists as keyboard player Bobby Whitlock, Molly Hatchet, and folk/rock singer Alex Taylor. Lombar now fronts a blues band called Dr. Hector and The Groove Injectors, a popular act that has produced several albums.

Even without a continued presence as an active band, Grinderswitch would remain one of Southern Rock's unsung heroes. When you listen to their albums, you realize that their music is as entertaining and vital today as it was back when they recorded it. The band might have been short-lived, but the music is still a formidable legacy.

There have been rumbles that the original members of Blackfoot might reunite, at least for a tour. None of the former members of the group rules out that possibility. Jakson Spires and Greg Walker, in the meantime, have plans to release an album by their group, The Southern Rock All-Stars, titled *NDN*.

Although Blackfoot is no more, Rickey Medlocke has, of course, become an integral member of the revived Lynyrd Skynyrd. He plans to stay on the road, making his music as long as he can. "I just love to tour," he says. "If I had my choice, I'd probably be on the road eleven months out of the year. I think it has to do with the Native American blood in me because Native Americans were so nomadic. I just love the freedom, the openness, of being able to be on the highway and travel. Johnny [Van Zant] and I were talking one day, and Johnny goes, 'What's gonna happen one day when we are no longer touring? When we're older people and we're off the road?' I got to really seriously thinking about that. I said, 'You know, as much as I love to travel and be on the highway and stuff, what in the heck am I going to do?'" Then Medlocke laughs. "I think I got it figured out. What I'm going to end up doing is, I'm just going to take all my money and just buy a bus myself."

Medlocke might love the road, but what he loves more is performing. "There's no place I'd rather be than on that stage," he says. "If I died on stage, if I fell over from exhaustion, keeled over and died right then, hey, guess what? I went out doing exactly what I love to do."

"I think we had a unique style," reflects The Outlaws' Hughie Thomasson. "A combination of playing and singing that we put together that was really, totally unique. Had a Southern flair to it, if you will. I think that the songs spoke for themselves. They had a message. They said something. That's one of the strong points of The Outlaws." While The Outlaws of old perhaps can never return, there is hope for their fans. Although Billy Jones, for reasons known only to himself, took his life several years ago and Hughie Thomasson went on to become an integral part of Lynyrd Skynyrd, the prospect of an Outlaws reunion seems likely. Thomasson thinks so anyway. "The Outlaws," he asserts, "will ride again."

.38 Special is enjoying the success of *Resolution* and continuing to tour most of the year. The group members welcome the continued opportunity to work with Lynyrd Skynyrd and look forward to recording more albums and introducing their music to a new generation of fans. .38 Special, like the Southern Rock bands before it, is not only part of the history of the genre, but an integral part of the legacy.

Gregg Allman decided at the onset of 1997, a year before he would turn fifty, that he wanted to make some changes in his legacy. He says he'd stopped using drugs prior to that date, but decided to completely give up alcohol, drink only healthy drinks, and start lifting weights and making his body stronger. He was influenced by other rockers who had traveled the same wild road and found it dangerous to their own lives. "Bonnie Raitt . . .," reflects Gregg. "God, she's an influence to us all. She influenced me into getting sober because I figured if she could do it, by God, anybody could."

Gregg became engaged to marry Stacy Fountain and returned to the studio for another solo album. Gregg was ready when it came time to lay down the tracks for *Searchin' For Simplicity*. Blues musicians Mickey Buskins, Roger Hawkins, David Hood, and Clayton Ivey join Gregg on the album, which also contains appearances by Jack Pearson and Oteil Burbridge. The record is Gregg Allman at his best.

Gregg knew what he was looking for in an independent effort. "I was just thinking, my kind of favorite one is the first one, *Laid Back*," he says. "That was my first solo record, and I was trying to get back to that, just regular lay it down, smack 'em, whack 'em, rock and roll blues. Just good old simple music cause that's what my life has kinda gotten back to, and I really enjoy it."

Gregg's reworking of "Whippin' Post," on a dare from Red Dog, updates the classic and evokes a regenerated emotional response. Gregg reaches far back to his roots on the poignant "Dark End of the Street," one of his brother Duane's favorite songs. The album also includes strong blues numbers and even a country music send-up.

Gregg is happy with his new sobriety, his life, and his music. "It is really good," he says. "It gets better every day." Gregg seems sure about what he hopes his rock and roll legacy will be. "That I played good music, and I didn't let anybody talk me into playing something that I didn't want to play," reveals Gregg. "And that I always played each gig like it was going to be my last one." Then Gregg laughs. "And that I wasn't some big-headed rock and roll star asshole. That's what I hope my legacy's not."

The Allman Brothers undertook a massive summer tour in 1998, which included a homecoming to The Fox Theater in Atlanta. After *Mycology: An Anthology* was released in June, 1998, the Brothers planned a return to the studio. The next Allman Brothers Band album promises to be important. The band continues to evolve. Jack Pearson left the Brothers in March, 1999, to be replaced by young slide guitar wiz Derek Trucks.

The Brothers might be a bit uncomfortable with the term Southern Rock, preferring to call their music progressive rock, but their contribution to the genre is still foremost and critical. As has been sung, the road seems to go on forever. The music of The Allman Brothers Band will remain a rock and roll staple at least that long.

AFTERWORD

T he music of the original Southern Rockers continues to be a vital voice in the contemporary world of rock and roll. The historical recordings enjoy airplay on a variety of current radio stations, as well as those stations devoted to classic rock. The current trend in film scoring—the use of classic rock standards in such films as Forrest Gump and Con Air—not only gives the archetypal fan the opportunity to return to the music but introduces an entirely new generation of younger people to the music of "The Masters."

Most of the bands I've examined continue to tour. It is the norm, rather than the exception, that at least 50 percent of their current audiences are multi-generational, a result of the original fans introducing the groups to their sons and daughters. Rock masterpieces, such as "Layla," "Freebird," "Whippin' Post," "In Memory of Elizabeth Reed," and "Can't You See," coupled with standards, such as "Heard It In A Love Song," "Keep On Smilin'," "Imaginary Lover," "The Devil Went Down To Georgia," "There Goes Another Love Song," "Ramblin' Man," and "Sweet Home Alabama," ensure airplay, concert attendance, and artist awareness for years to come.

It stands to reason that these artists and these songs, would influence a younger generation of songwriters and hit makers, from contemporaries like Hank Williams Jr., whose music is a bold presentation of standard country and western, contemporary country, and Southern Rock, to Travis Tritt, who claims to have written his hit "Put Some Drive In Your Country" at the graveside of Duane Allman and Berry Oakley. The influence is said to extend to the new wave of rock heroes and contenders, including Widespread Panic, Derek Trucks, Screamin' Cheetah Wheelies, and The Dave Matthews Band. Many of the bands who have ventured to fan the flame and who have picked up the baton are direct offshoots of the original Southern Rockers. Gov't Mule, OKB, Van Zant, Dr. Hector and The Groove Injectors, The Jimmy Van Zant Band,

Phil Walden, 1998. Credit: Rick Diamond/Capricorn Records.

Devon Allman and Elijah Blue, A.P.B., and the yet-to-be-named King-Carlisi band not only keep the music alive but dramatically propel it to new heights.

Capricorn's Phil Walden believes that not only is there a definite place in today's music for classic Southern Rock, but that there is room to invite in those who have been influenced by and who perpetuate the music of those who came before them. "I think [bands such as Gov't Mule, Widespread Panic, et. al., are] part of the evolution of this music," he says. "This music has been changing since it was created. I think they're the latest flag bearers of this wonderful music. There is no denying The Allman Brothers' influence is primary over all of these folks. Their influence is pretty awesome. But I don't think any of these contemporary bands attempt to copy anything from The Allman Brothers. It's [just] that wonderful influence of guys playing very well and of talented people getting together and expressing themselves through their music."

Walden was with Capricorn Records in the beginning to help give voice to the musicians who offered a new, unique, and compelling sound. Although Capricorn was forced to declare bankruptcy, Walden renewed his friendship with Warner Bros. Records chairman Mo Ostin in the 1990s. Ostin offered distribution and funding should Walden care to reestablish Capricorn Records as a Warner Bros. boutique label. Walden took Ostin up on his offer. Capricorn seemed to be back in the game.

The first act that Walden signed was Widespread Panic from Athens, Georgia. Like The Allman Brothers, Widespread Panic's music is a combination of several different genres. "It's blues, it's rock 'n' roll, and it's definitely improvisational within the framework of the songs," according to J.B. Bell. *Light Fuse Get Away*, the band's latest album, is an example of Widespread Panic's Southern rock influences.

In 1994 Capricorn's deal with Warner Bros. expired, and Warner, allegedly due to financial constraints, chose not to renew. That same year, Capricorn signed with Sony's RED for distribution. It released a variety of albums by such acts as CAKE, Junior Kimbrough, and Shoejerk. Lynyrd Skynyrd came onboard for *Endangered Species*, its first acoustic album.

Jimmy Hall released *Rendezvous With The Blues* on Capricorn and Gov't Mule weighed in with *Dose*. While the members of Gov't Mule hesitate to call themselves Southern Rock, their roots and music indicate otherwise. "The only way the torch can really be carried in a true fashion is for somebody to sound different, to make it today's version, you know what I mean?" says Gov't Mule's Warren Haynes. Although the musicians of Gov't Mule have a strong history with the classic act of the genre, they believe they take that basis to augment their compositions in order to make the music something fresh and exciting. "I'm a little more open with this, actually, than I was with The Allman Brothers because with The Allman Brothers [it was] a case of 'When in Rome . . .,' " says bassist Allen Woody.

Gov't Mule isn't ashamed of the fact that its rock and roll roots are very evident in the music the band creates today. "People say it's a power trio, and I guess it is, but I don't think we sound like anybody else that would be considered a power trio," says Haynes. "And I'm not saying that's a good or bad thing. We're just aspiring to be something different, but all of our influences, for the most part, are old influences. We're not influenced or inspired by a lot of new music, although we are inspired by a lot of the open-mindedness that some of the new music has."

The musicians of Gov't Mule thrive on introducing new audiences to their music and the influences of their peers. "No matter what age group you bring in, young kids, the kids a little older in their twenties and thirties, and then the old kids like me in their forties and fifties, I think if you can get them under one tent with us, we can convert most of them because we don't play to just one age group," believes Woody. "That's something The Brothers had, that's something The Dead had. Hot Tuna has it. I think it's a real blessing if you got it, where you're not just locked into one age group."

"I think young people today feel that they have to look to the past in some cases for genuine, real, timeless music," says Haynes. "There are certain generations of young people today that the music that represented their generation was not something they're extremely proud of. It was all about drum machines and computers and sequencers and synthesizers. Nobody really cared about blues or rock and roll or emotional guitar playing, or any of that stuff."

Gov't Mule believes in very emotional guitar playing and music. The trio consists of Warren Haynes on guitar and vocals, Allen Woody on bass, and Matt Abts on drums. Abts complements the former Allmans nicely. "I just haven't seen anybody that has that finesse and the power and all those things rolled into one," says Woody. "This cat's hittin' on all eight cylinders, all the time."

The band released *Gov't Mule* in 1995. That record was followed by 1996's *Live At Roseland Ballroom*. 1998 brought the band's strongest entry yet when *Dose* was released on Capricorn.

Several standout songs on the album garnered a lot of attention, both when played in concert and when heard on the radio. One song in particular was a very successful reworking of The Beatles' "She Said, She Said." "We released 'Blind Man' as a first single, kind of holding 'She Said' back as kind of a one-two punch, like 'Here you go, here's one coming right behind. This one's gonna tear you up," says Woody. "Basically, 'Blind Man' is going to be less accessible to a lot of people than 'She Said' because, let's face it, 'She Said is a Beatles song. . . .'"

Gov't Mule plans to be around for a long time to come, contributing and growing. "We're exploring a lot of directions that are unique to us," says Haynes. "We're at least trying to combine influences in a way that hopefully nobody's done."

Another offshoot of The Allman Brothers Band is OKB. OKB consists of Berry Oakley on bass and vocals; Duane Betts on guitar; Waylon Krieger, son of The Doors' Robbie Krieger, on guitar; and Alec Puro, who has recorded with Elijah Blue, on drums. They have been together as a band for only a couple of years.

OKB started as a group called Bloodline, which included Oakley and Krieger. Bloodline released a self-titled album on EMI, and the band's single "Stone Cold Hearted" rose to #32 on *Billboard*'s Rock chart. The band toured with Lynyrd Skynyrd, among other top acts, and made several television appearances. Bloodline eventually broke up due to creative differences.

OKB's music, like that of any band that has traditionally been associated with the term Southern Rock, has roots in the blues and includes blues, rock and roll, and a little jazz. "It is bluesy, and there is some heavier stuff with some very '90s sounding chord progressions," says Duane Betts. OKB's influences include Stevie Ray Vaughn, Eric Johnson, B.B. King, Smashing Pumpkins, Soundgarden, James Brown, and, of course, Berry Oakley, Duane Allman, and Dickey Betts.

Berry Oakley and Duane Betts have toured with The Allman Brothers Band as part of The Allmans' extended family. Duane Betts toured with his father, Dickey, and the band for more than five years. The young musician relished the experience. "Every tour was different," Duane Betts recalls. "Meet different people, jam with different people, learn a lot, just get a lot better."

Berry Oakley played with The Brothers' Dreams tour for three months. "I was really impressed that everybody invited me along cause I had just met the band recently," he remembers. "It was actually Duane's father who said, 'Yeah, why don't you just come along and hang with us?' So I did."

Betts, Oakley, and Krieger have all been influenced by their fathers. Sometimes the influence has been helpful. "[Robbie] took us out when The Doors movie came out," remembers Waylon Krieger. "He booked a tour and just basically hired me and Berry to back him up and give us some road experience, show us the ropes and all that. It was a great experience."

Sometimes that influence hasn't come easy. Duane Betts remembers the early years as a guitar-playing son of a international guitar-playing hero. "I used to be really hard-headed," remembers Duane. "[My father would] be telling me stuff, but I'd think I'd know more than him. Then I grew up a little bit and figured out that I didn't really give him enough credit. I always gave him credit for being a great, great, great, great guitar player, but I didn't really know how hard it was to do what they do. And now I do. So now when he gives me advice, I'm like, 'Okay.'"

Sometimes the influence is bittersweet. "As far as my dad's concerned, I know that he left a great legacy of playing, for a lot of bass players," says Berry Oakley. "The records he recorded on I think are great. All bass players who are serious, not just because he's my dad, they should listen."

Alec Puro met members of OKB through his association with Elijah Blue's musical endeavors. "We did a record," says Puro. "Totally different music. Almost like a new sound. Like really good somber chorus mixed with early '80s synth. Way farther than any alternative is classed. It's freaked out, I tell ya."

The young men of OKB have already demonstrated that they have a natural musical talent, but they have their heads on straight and know that a successful career will come from hard work and continued growth. They don't feel any need to attempt to ride on their fathers' coattails. "As far as my father's legacy, I always thought he was great," says Berry Oakley. "Fortunately for me, I have it in my blood, and I'm pretty sure I can make him proud. I just want to keep going."

"Chances are I probably will not write a 'Light My Fire,' or 'Touch Me,' or 'Love Me Two Times,' or some things like [my dad] did, but that's not what it's about, you know?" says Krieger. "He's left these steps at the foundation, and then he moves on. Now it's our turn to continue that and build the bridge."

OKB is hard at work playing a lot of dates and touring. The young musicians continue to draw attention and acclaim. "Those guys are great," says Warren Haynes. "What they're doing I guess could be considered Southern Rock. They definitely had that heritage, but they're adding other elements, and you know they're influenced by other things as well, so they're making a mixture of all their influences, which is what any good band does."

Derek Trucks isn't one of The Allman Brothers' sons, but he is one of the family. Derek is the nephew of Brother Butch Trucks. Derek's slide guitar playing has drawn kudos from other musicians and the media alike. The teenager is already opening for major acts and sells out nearly wherever he appears. "He's a slide man. He's going to scare everybody from a slide guitar perspective," says Warren Haynes. "Derek is pretty incredible, and slide guitar is such a specialized instrument. It's one thing for a seventeen- or eighteen-year-old kid to be a really good guitar player, but it's yet another thing for a seventeen- or eighteen-year-old kid to be a great slide player. It's a dying art, and there are very few people that are that good, and none of them are as young as him."

Another Southern Rock family act is Van Zant. Donnie and Johnny Van Zant don't tour as a band, both being busy with their duties in .38 Special and Lynyrd Skynyrd, respectively. But the surviving brothers of Ronnie Van Zant took time in 1998 to do something that they've wanted to do for a very long time: record an album together.

"Over the years we've just wrote tons of songs together," says Johnny. "And we've had so many people go, 'Man, why don't y'all do something together?' We were always like, 'Well, I got my own thing, he's got his own thing,' you know? It just never evolved or was the right time. [And then] last year on the *Twenty* album, me and Ronnie sang a song together, 'Travellin' Man.' I started thinking, 'Now's the time for me to do something with me and Donnie.' And we had a great time doing it."

"It was great to have the opportunity, and we're proud of it," says Donnie. "No matter what. Johnny said the other day, 'Well, I don't care if it sells but one or it can sell a million. It don't make no difference to me.' And I told him he was crazy, but when it comes down to it, that's about the truth. We had the freedom to do it [the album, *Brother to Brother*], and we had the opportunity to do it. And we got to spend time together, which is something we haven't been able to do in the last ten years. It was worth it just to be able to do that."

While the Van Zant brothers enjoyed doing the album, they're both committed to their bands and don't have any immediate plans to record together again. "It's just a once in a lifetime thing here," claims Donnie. Perhaps so, but even with only *Brother To Brother*, the Van Zants have continued the music and perpetuated the legacy.

Screamin' Cheetah Wheelies is a band based in Nashville, but since Capricorn Records has perpetuated the music of the Wheelies, this band has sometimes been mentioned as part of the Southern Rock legacy. It is true that those elements of jazz, blues, and rock and roll are present, and the band did record its *Big Wheel* album at Memphis's Ardent Studios, where many of the Stax artists recorded their albums. It is a little too early to tell the influences of the Wheelies music and how closely the band's music will parallel that of earlier Southern Rockers. Whether the band truly fits the mold and will carry the Southern Rock torch remains to be seen.

The blues, having been born of circumstance and emotion, will continue to move listeners and evoke impassioned responses. Country music, ever popular and ever changing, continues to regale us with hard luck stories and reflect the American experience. And, as that Canadian guy sang, rock and roll is here to stay. Combining these popular musical genres, Southern Rock was born, exploded into our consciousness, lived large, and faltered. Although the genre might have stumbled, the music of those who made it popular and who continue the legacy still excites us and offers a outlet and shelter from the storm of everyday life. Southern Rock is, indeed, relevant and timeless. Rock on.

NOTES

1. "Memories of a Brother by Candace Oakley." October 19, 1992.

2. *Rolling Stone*. Record review by Lester Bangs, June, 1970.

3. "Memories of a Brother by Candace Oakley."

4. *Hittin' the Note*. Dickey Betts in "The Elusive Mr. Betts" by Kirsten West. Issue 10.

5. "Memories of a Brother by Candace Oakley." October 19, 1992.

6. *Sounds*. "A Tale of Two Skynyrds" by Pete Makowski. November 16, 1974.

7. Ibid.

8. *Sounds*. "Ronnie Van Zant Kicked His Scotch Habit: It's Wine Now..." by Andy McConnell. May 21, 1975.

9. *Sounds*. "A Tale of Two Skynyrds." November 16, 1974.

10. *Rolling Stone*. "Lynyrd Skynyrd In Sweet Home Alabama" by Tom Dupree. October 24, 1974.

11. *People*. November 7, 1977.

12. *Variety*. August 21, 1974.

13. Freebird Foundation Website. FAQ.

14. *Creem*. "Lynyrd Skynyrd: Not Even A Boogie Band Is As Simple As It Seems" by Robert Christgau. August, 1975.

15. Ibid.

16. *The Washington Post*. "Southern Boogie." June 21, 1975.

17. *Sounds*. "Ronnie Van Zant Kicked His Scotch Habit: It's Wine Now..." by Andy McConnell. May 21, 1975.

18. *Pop Top*. "Lynyrd Skynyrd: No Flash or Frills" by Doug Collette. August/September, 1975.

19. Stroud, Kandy. *How Jimmy Won,* p. 148.

20. Freebird Foundation Website. Steve Gaines bio.

21. *The Roots Remain.* Charlie Daniels. Liner notes.

22. Freebird Foundation Website, Steve Gaines bio.

23. Smith, Michael B., *Carolina Dreams,* p. 90.

24. Ellison, Bill. Radio interview with Kenny Peden for WZZQ. October, 1977.

25. *Hittin' the Note.* "Special Interviews." The Allman Brothers Band Web Page.

26. Stevens, Don. The Marshall Tucker Band Web Page.

27. *The Atlanta Journal-Constitution.* "Recalling the Rhythm" by Miriam Longino. January 12, 1997.

SELECTED ALBUM DISCOGRAPHY

ALIAS
1979   *Contraband* (Mercury)

THE ALLEN COLLINS BAND
1983   *Here, There and Back* (MCA)

THE ALLMAN BROTHERS BAND
1969   *The Allman Brothers Band* (Capricorn)
1970   *Idlewild South* (Capricorn)
1971   *At Fillmore East* (Capricorn)
1972   *Eat A Peach* (Capricorn)
1973   *Brothers & Sisters* (Capricorn)
1973   *Beginnings* (Capricorn)
1975   *Win, Lose, Or Draw* (Capricorn)
1975   *The Road Goes On Forever* (Capricorn)
1976   *Wipe the Windows, Check the Oil, Dollar Gas* (Capricorn)
1979   *Enlightened Rogues* (Capricorn)
1980   *Reach for the Sky* (Arista)
1981   *Brothers of the Road* (Arista)
1989   *Dreams* (Polydor)
1990   *Seven Turns* (Epic)
1990   *Live at Ludlow Garage, 1970* (Polydor)
1991   *Shades of Two Worlds* (Epic)
1991   *A Decade of Hits 1969-1979* (PolyGram)
1992   *An Evening With The Allman Brothers Band* (Epic)
1992   *The Fillmore Concerts* (Polydor)
1994   *Where It All Begins* (Epic)
1995   *2nd Set* (Sony)
1998   *Mycology: An Anthology* (Sony)

DUANE ALLMAN
1972   *Duane Allman: An Anthology* (Capricorn)
1974   *Duane Allman: An Anthology, Volume II* (Capricorn)

GREGG ALLMAN
1973   *Laid Back* (Capricorn)
1974   *The Gregg Allman Tour* (Capricorn)
1977   *Playin' Up A Storm* (Capricorn)
1978   *I'm No Angel* (Epic)
1988   *Just Before The Bullets Fly* (Epic)
1998   *Searchin' For Simplicity* (Sony)

A.P.B.
1982   *A.P.B.* (MCA)
1983   *Nightcrawler* (MCA)

THE ATLANTA RHYTHM SECTION
1972   *The Atlanta Rhythm Section* (MCA)
1973   *Back Up Against the Wall* (MCA)
1974   *Third Annual Pipe Dream* (Polydor)
1975   *Dog Days* (Polydor)
1976   *Red Tape* (Polydor)
1977   *A Rock and Roll Alternative* (Polydor)
1978   *Champagne Jam* (Polydor)
1979   *Underdog* (Polydor)
1979   *Are You Ready!* (Polydor)
1980   *The Boys From Doraville* (CBS)
1982   *Quinella* (CBS)
1989   *Truth In A Structured Form* (CBS/Imagine)
1997   *Partly Plugged* (River North)
1999   *Eufala* (Platinum)

DICKEY BETTS
1974   *Highway Call* (Capricorn)
1977   *Dickey Betts and Great Southern* (Arista)
1978   *Atlanta's Burning Down* (Arista)
1988   *Pattern Disruptive* (Epic)

BLACKFOOT
1975   *No Reservations* (Island)
1975   *Flyin' High* (Epic)
1979   *Strikes* (Atco)

1980	*Tomcattin'* (Atco)
1981	*Marauder* (Atco)
1982	*Blackfoot Live* (Atco)
1983	*Siogo* (Atco)
1984	*Vertical Smiles* (Atco)
1985	*Rickey Medlocke and Blackfoot* (Atco)
1990	*Medicine Man* (MFN)
1994	*Rattlesnake Rock 'N' Roll: Best of Blackfoot* (Rhino)
1994	*After the Reign* (Wildcat Records)

BLOODLINE
1994	*Bloodline* (EMI)

TOY CALDWELL
1992	*Toy Caldwell* (Cabin Fever)
1998	*Toy Caldwell: Can't You See* (Coda)

COWBOY
1970	*Reach For the Sky* (Capricorn)

THE CHARLIE DANIELS BAND
1970	*Charlie Daniels* (Capitol)
1970	*Te John, Grease and Wolfman* (Kama Sutra)
1972	*Uneasy Rider* (Kama Sutra)
1974	*Fire On the Mountain* (Kama Sutra)
1975	*Nightrider* (Kama Sutra)
1976	*Volunteer Jam* (Capricorn)
1976	*Saddle Tramp* (Epic)
1977	*Whiskey* (Epic)
1977	*High Lonesome* (Epic)
1977	*Midnight Wind* (Epic)
1978	*Volunteer Jam III and IV* (Epic)
1979	*Million Mile Reflections* (Epic)
1980	*Volunteer Jam VI* (Epic)
1980	*Full Moon* (Epic)
1981	*Volunteer Jam VII* (Epic)
1982	*Windows* (Epic)
1983	*A Decade of Hits* (Epic)
1985	*Me and the Boys* (Epic)

1987	*Powder-Keg* (Epic)
1988	*Homesick Heroes* (Epic)
1989	*Simple Man* (Epic)1990 *Christmas Time Down South* (Epic)
1991	*Renegade* (Epic)
1993	*All-Time Greatest Hits* (Epic)
1993	*America, I Believe In You* (Liberty)
1994	*The Door* (Sparrow)
1994	*Super Hits* (Epic)
1995	*Same Ol' Me* (Capitol Nashville)
1996	*Steel Witness* (Sparrow)
1996	*The Roots Remain* (Sony Music)
1997	*By The Light of the Moon* (Sony Music)
1997	*Blues Hat* (Blue Hat Records)
1999	*Tailgate Party* (Blue Hat Records)

STEVE GAINES
1988	*One In the Sun* (MCA)

GOV'T MULE
1995	*Gov't Mule* (Relativity)
1996	*Live At Roseland Ballroom* (Foundation)
1998	*Dose* (Capricorn)

GRINDERSWITCH
1974	*Honest To Goodness* (Capricorn)
1975	*Macon Tracks* (Capricorn)
1976	*Pullin' Together* (Capricorn)
1977	*Redwing* (Atco)
1979	*Right On Time* (Auric)
1981	*Have Band Will Travel* (Robox)
1995	*Live Tracks* (One Way)

JIMMY HALL
1996	*Rendezvous With the Blues* (Capricorn)

WARREN HAYNES
1993	*Tales of Ordinary Madness* (Megaforce)

DR. HECTOR & THE GROOVE INJECTORS

1988	*Prescription* (Kingsnake)
1990	*House Calls* (Kingsnake)
1992	*Emergency* (Kingsnake)
1995	*Bad Connection* (Kingsnake)

HOUR GLASS

1968	*Hour Glass* (Liberty)
1969	*Power of Love* (Liberty)

LYNYRD SKYNYRD

1973	*Pronounced LEH-NERD SKIN-ERD* (MCA)
1974	*Second Helping* (MCA)
1975	*Nuthin' Fancy* (MCA)
1976	*Gimme Back My Bullets* (MCA)
1976	*One More From the Road* (MCA)
1977	*Street Survivors* (MCA)
1978	*Skynyrd's First and ... Last* (MCA)
1979	*Gold and Platinum* (MCA)
1982	*Best of the Rest* (MCA)
1987	*Legend* (MCA)
1988	*Southern By the Grace of God* (MCA)
1989	*Skynyrd's Innyrds* (MCA)
1991	*Lynyrd Skynyrd [Box Set]* (MCA)
1991	*Lynyrd Skynyrd 1991* (Atlantic)
1993	*The Last Rebel* (Atlantic)
1994	*Endangered Species* (Capricorn)
1995	*Southern Knights* (Phantom)
1996	*Freebird ... The Movie* (MCA)
1997	*Twenty* (CMC)
1998	*Lyve From Steeltown* (CMC)
1998	*The Essential Lynyrd Skynyrd* (MCA)
1998	*Skynyrd's First: The Complete Muscle Shoals Album* (MCA)
1999	*Skynyrd Collectibles* (MCA)

THE MARSHALL TUCKER BAND

1973	*The Marshall Tucker Band* (Capricorn)
1973	*A New Life* (Capricorn)
1974	*Where We All Belong* (Capricorn)
1975	*Searchin' For A Rainbow* (Capricorn)
1976	*Long Hard Ride* (Capricorn)
1977	*Carolina Dreams* (Capricorn)
1978	*Together Forever* (Capricorn)
1979	*Greatest Hits* (Capricorn)
1979	*Running Like the Wind* (Warner Brothers)
1980	*Tenth* (Warner Brothers)
1981	*Dedicated* (Warner Brothers)
1982	*Tuckerized* (Warner Brothers)
1983	*Just Us* (Warner Brothers)
1984	*Greetings From South Carolina* (Warner Brothers)
1988	*Still Holdin' On* (Mercury/Polygram)
1990	*Southern Spirit* (Cabin Fever)
1992	*Still Smokin'* (Cabin Fever)
1993	*Walk Outside the Lines* (Cabin Fever)
1994	*The Marshall Tucker Band: The Capricorn Years* (ERA)
1996	*Country Tucker* (ERA)
1997	*M.T. Blues* (ERA)

THE OUTLAWS

1975	*The Outlaws* (Arista)
1976	*Lady In Waiting* (Arista)
1977	*Hurry Sundown* (Arista)
1978	*Bring It Back Alive* (Arista)
1978	*Playin' To Win* (Arista)
1979	*In the Eye of the Storm* (Arista)
1980	*Ghost Riders* (Arista)
1982	*Los Hombres Malo* (Arista)
1982	*Greatest Hits* (Arista)
1986	*Soldiers of Fortune* (Pasha)
1993	*Hittin' the Road - Live!* (Blues Bureau)
1994	*Diablo Canyon* (Blues Bureau)
1996	*Best of the Outlaws* (Arista)

ROSSINGTON

1986	*Returned to the Scene of the Crime* (MCA)
1988	*Love Your Man* (MCA)

THE ROSSINGTON COLLINS BAND

1980	*Anytime, Anyplace, Anywhere* (MCA)
1981	*This Is The Way* (MCA)

SEA LEVEL

1977	*Sea Level* (Capricorn)
1977	*Cats On The Coast* (Capricorn)
1978	*On The Edge* (Capricorn)
1979	*Long Walk On A Short Pier* (Polydor)
1980	*Ball Room* (Arista)

STILLWATER

1977	*Stillwater* (Capricorn)
1978	*I Reserve the Right* (Capricorn)

.38 SPECIAL

1977	*.38 Special* (A&M)
1978	*Special Delivery* (A&M)
1978	*Rockin' Into the Night* (A&M)
1981	*Wild-Eyed Southern Boys* (A&M)
1982	*Special Forces* (A&M)
1984	*Tour De Force* (A&M)
1986	*Strength in Numbers* (A&M)
1987	*Flashback* (A&M)
1989	*Rock and Roll Strategy* (A&M)
1991	*Bone Against Steel* (Charisma)
1997	*Resolution* (Razor & Tie)

VAN ZANT

1998	*Brother to Brother* (CMC)

JOHNNY VAN ZANT

1980	*No More Dirty Deals* (Polygram)
1981	*Round Two* (Polygram)
1982	*Last of the Wild Ones* (Polygram)
1990	*Brickyard Road* (Atlantic)
1994	*The Johnny Van Zant Collection* (Polygram)

WET WILLIE

1971	*Wet Willie* (Capricorn)
1972	*Wet Willie II* (Capricorn)
1973	*Drippin' Wet* (Capricorn)
1973	*Keep On Smilin'* (Capricorn)
1974	*Dixie Rock* (Capricorn)
1975	*The Wetter The Better* (Capricorn)
1976	*Left Coast Live* (Capricorn) *Wet Willie's Greatest Hits* (Capricorn)
1994	*The Best of Wet Willie* (Polydor)

BIBLIOGRAPHY

BOOKS

All Music Guide to Rock. Miller Freeman Books, San Francisco, 1997.

Freeman, Scott. *Midnight Riders: The Story of the Allman Brothers Band*. Little, Brown and Company, Inc., Boston, 1995.

The Harmony Illustrated Encyclopedia of Rock. Harmony Books, New York, 1992.

Odom, Gene. *Lynyrd Skynyrd: I'll Never Forget You*. A S C Publishing, 1983.

Smith, Michael B. *Carolina Dreams: The Musical Legacy of Upstate South Carolina*. Marshall Tucker Entertainment, Inc., Beverly Hills, CA, 1997.

Stroud, Kandy. *How Jimmy Won*. William Morrow & Co., Inc., New York, 1977.

Van Zant, Lacey. *The Van Zant Family: Southern Music Scrap Book*, 1995.

Wheeler, Leslie. *Jimmy Who?* Barron's Educational Series, Woodbury, NY, 1976.

MAGAZINES AND ARTICLES

Best of the ARS. Liner notes by John Swenson. Polydor Records, 1991.

Circus. "Lynyrd Skynyrd Fight Rock 'n Roll Civil Wars With Nuthin' Fancy." June, 1975.

Circus. Bashe, Phillip. "Marshall Tucker At Home." June 30, 1981.

Circus Raves. "'We Want This Hit Bad,' Say Skynyrd." April, 1975.

Concert News. "Lynyrd Skynyrd" by Bob Moore. November, 1974.

Creative Loafing, Vibes. "Midnight Rider" by Todd A. Prusin. March 19, 1994.

Creem. "Lynyrd Skynyrd: Not Even A Boogie Band Is As Simple As It Seems" by Robert Christgau. August, 1975.

Good Times. "Grinderswitch, Honest To Goodness" by Ellen Mandell. September 11-24, 1974.

Hittin' the Note: The Quarterly Allmanac for Allman Brothers Band Fans. "The Elusive Mr. Betts" by Kristen West. Issue 10.

Hittin' the Note: The Quarterly Allmanac for Allman Brothers Band Fans. Issue 17, Spring, 1998.

Hittin' The Web with The Allman Brothers Band. "Dickey Betts at the Hall of Fame" by Lana Mazarelli.

Melody Maker. "Caught In The Act. Skynyrd: Southern Fried Boogie" by Chris Charlesworth. December 21, 1974.

"Memories of a Brother: Raymond Berry Oakley III" by Candace Oakley. October 29, 1992.

New Musical Express. "Skynyrd's Own Rainbow Show." December, 1974.

"Notes from the Capricorn Years," Marshall Tucker Band, by Rick Clark. Performance. "Hard Rock Nation, Land of Contrasts" by Michael Point. April 25, 1975.

People. "The Rock Road Claims Another Tragic Victim: Ronnie Van Zant of the Lynryd Skynyrd Band." November 7, 1977.

Pop Top. "Lynyrd Skynyrd: No Flash or Frills" by Doug Collette. August/September, 1975

Record World. 1975. Review of *Carolina Dreams* by Don Stevens. The Marshall Tucker Band Official Web Page. 1997.

Review of *Dedicated* by Don Stevens. The Marshall Tucker Band Official Web Page. 1997.

Review of *Just Us* by Don Stevens. The Marshall Tucker Band Official Web Page. 1997.

Review of *Long Hard Drive* by Don Stevens. The Marshall Tucker Band Official Web Page. 1997.

Review of *M.T. Blues* by Michael B. Smith. The Marshall Tucker Band Official Web Page. 1997.

Review of *Southern Spirit* by Craig Cumberland. The Marshall Tucker Band Official Web Page. 1997.

Review of *Still Holdin' On* by Craig Cumberland, Marshall Tucker Band Official Web Page. 1997.

Review of *Still Smokin'* by Craig Cumberland. The Marshall Tucker Band Official Web Page. 1997.

Review of *Tenth* by Michael B. Smith. The Marshall Tucker Band Official Web Page. 1997.

Review of *The Marshall Tucker Band* by Craig Cumberland. The Marshall Tucker Band Official Web Page. 1997.

Review of *Together Forever* by Don Stevens. The Marshall Tucker Band Official Web Page. 1997.

Review of *Toy Caldwell* by Craig Cumberland. The Marshall Tucker Band Official Web Page. 1997.

Review of *Tuckerized* by Michael B. Smith. The Marshall Tucker Band Official Web Page. 1997.

Review of *Walk Outside The Lines* by Craig Cumberland. The Marshall Tucker Band Official Web Page. 1997.

Rolling Stone. "Lynyrd Skynyrd In Sweet Home Alabama" by Tom Dupree. October 24, 1974.

Rolling Stone. "Second Helping - Lynyrd Skynyrd." November 7, 1974.

Rolling Stone. Southern Sounding Column. May 20, 1975.

Rolling Stone. "Marshall Tucker Plays Dead" by John Swenson. January 25, 1979.

Sounds. "A Tale of Two Skynyrds" by Pete Makowski. November 16, 1974.

Sounds. "Southern Fried to Roasting" by Billy Walker and Pete Makowski. November 23, 1974.

Sounds. November 27, 1974.

Sounds. "Nuthin' Special" by Billy Walker. April 12, 1975.

Sounds. "Ronnie Van Zant Kicked His Scotch Habit: It's Wine Now ..." by Andy McConnell. May 21, 1975.

"Toy Caldwell Remembered" by Jim Brown. The Marshall Tucker Band & Other Carolina Dreamers Web Page. 1997.

NEWSPAPERS

The Atlanta Journal - Constitution. "Recalling the Rhythm" by Miriam Longino. January 12, 1997.

Associated Press. "Allman at 50 takes stock of life" by Mary Campbell. 1998.

Jacksonville Times-Union. "Guitarist: Lynyrd Skynyrd Pushed Me Out" by June D. Bell. 1997.

Jacksonville Times-Union. "Airplane 'Just Flat Ran Out of Gas'" by John Carter. October 19, 1997.

Macon Telegraph and News. "Sounds Amid Peach Trees" by Madeline Hirsiger. April 21, 1974.

Macon Telegraph and News. "Wet Willie." September 21, 1990.

Macon Telegraph. "Randall Hall Lawsuit." January 8, 1997.

Pensacola Journal. "Lynyrd Skynyrd To Play." March 29, 1975.

Providence Journal-Bulletin. "Gregg Allman Straightens up and flies solo" by Andy Smith. December 26, 1997.

Richmond Times-Dispatch. "Music" by C. A. Bustard. July 26, 1974.

Spartanburg Herald Journal. "Piano Tuners' Name Worked to His Advantage." February 26, 1995.

Spartanburg Herald Journal. March 16, 1995.

Variety. August 21, 1974.

The Washington Post. "Southern Boogie." June 21, 1975.

WEBSITES

"Atlanta Rhythm Section" Official Web Page.

Freebird Foundation. Hittin' the Web, The Allman Brothers Band. Lynyrd Skynyrd Official Web Page.

"Where We All Belong" Marshall Tucker Band Official Web Page.

MEMORIES FROM THE FANS AND FRIENDS

Steve Avery. The Marshall Tucker Band. August 3, 1997.

Mark Baird. The Allman Brothers Band. January 19, 1998.

Troy Berryman. Lynyrd Skynyrd. November 2, 1997.

Andy Blake. Lynyrd Skynyrd. October 21, 1997.

Randy Davis. The Marshall Tucker Band. February 13, 1998.

Craig Eason. The Marshall Tucker Band. March 9, 1998.

Nils-Petter Eriksson. The Allman Brothers Band. January 1, 1998.

Nancy G. The Marshall Tucker Band. February 22, 1998.

David Halliburton. Lynyrd Skynyrd. April 16, 1998.

Pat Matthews. Lynyrd Skynyrd. December 12, 1997.

Doug P. The Marshall Tucker Band. March 16, 1998.

Steve Powell. Lynyrd Skynyrd. October 10, 1997.

Todd Remsburg. The Outlaws. November 7, 1998.

Angelo Ruiz. The Marshall Tucker Band. January 13, 1998.

Rob Scherini. Lynyrd Skynyrd. October 13, 1997.

John Stucchi. Lynyrd Skynyrd. January 13, 1998.

Stan Warren. Lynyrd Skynyrd. April 29, 1998.

CORRESPONDENCE

Abbie Caldwell to author. August, 1998.

Terry Collins to author. January 18, 1998.

INTERVIEWS

Gregg Allman. The Allman Brothers Band.
May 26, 1998; June 3, 1998.

Duane Betts. OKB; The Allman Brothers Band.
September 13, 1997.

Buddy Buie. The Atlanta Rhythm Section.
November 4, 1997.

Jeff Carlisi. .38 Special. March 30, 1998.

Mike Causey. Stillwater. August 19, 1998.

Danny Chauncey. .38 Special; Gregg Allman Band.
February 6, 1998.

Charlie Daniels. The Charlie Daniels Band.
March 17, 1998.

Charlie Faubion. January 6, 1998.

Doug Gray. The Marshall Tucker Band.
February 10, 1998.

Warren Haynes. Gov't Mule; The Allman
Brothers Band. November 18, 1997.

Jimmy Hall. Wet Willie; Gregg Allman Band.
April 7, 1998.

Paul Hornsby. Hour Glass; The Marshall Tucker Band;
Grinderswitch; Wet Willie. January 7, 1998.

Judy Van Zant Jenness. Lynyrd Skynyrd.
February 5, 1998.

Harriet Kllpatrick. Lynyrd Skynyrd. March 26, 1998.

Ed King. Lynyrd Skynyrd. November 7, 1997.

Al Kooper. Lynyrd Skynyrd. November 25, 1997.

Waylon Kreiger. OKB. September 13, 1997.

George McCorkle. The Marshall Tucker Band.
November 11, 1997.

Jim Dandy Mangrum. Black Oak Arkansas.
April 1, 1998.

Rickey Medlocke. Blackfoot; Lynyrd Skynyrd.
March 10, 1998.

Rodney Mills. Lynyrd Skynyrd; .38 Special;
The Atlanta Rhythm Section. April 10, 1998.

Wayne Moss. Barefoot Jerry. August 14, 1998.

Berry Oakley Jr. OKB; The Allman Brothers Band.
September 13, 1997.

Artimus Pyle. Lynyrd Skynyrd. March 20, 1998;
May 8, 1998.

Billy Powell. Lynyrd Skynyrd. March 10, 1998.

Alec Puro. OKB. September 13, 1997.

Hughie Thomasson. The Outlaws; Lynyrd Skynyrd.
April 8, 1998.

Donnie Van Zant. .38 Special. January 22, 1998.

Johnny Van Zant. Lynyrd Skynyrd. March 11, 1998.

Phil Walden. July 16, 1998.

Jerry Wexler. July 16, 1998.

Leon Wilkeson. Lynyrd Skynyrd. April 7, 1998.

Allen Woody. Gov't Mule; The Allman Brothers Band.
February 13, 1998.

RADIO INTERVIEWS

Ellison, Bill. Interview with Kenny Peden
for station WZZQ, Jackson, Mississippi.
October, 1977.

Ladd, Jim. Interviews with Ronnie Van Zant
and Gary Rossington. Syndicated INNER VISIONS.
1977.

INDEX